SOVEREIGNTY AT THE
CROSSROADS?

EX
LIBRIS

SAINT
JOSEPH'S
COLLEGE
RENSSELAER
INDIANA

SOVEREIGNTY AT THE CROSSROADS?

Morality and International Politics in the Post–Cold War Era

edited by
Luis E. Lugo

ROWMAN & LITTLEFIELD PUBLISHERS, INC.
Lanham • Boulder • New York • London

ROWMAN & LITTLEFIELD PUBLISHERS, INC.

Published in the United States of America
by Rowman & Littlefield Publishers, Inc.
4720 Boston Way, Lanham, Maryland 20706

3 Henrietta Street
London WC2E 8LU, England

British Cataloging in Publication Information Available

Library of Congress Cataloging-in-Publication Data

Sovereignty at the crossroads? : morality and international politics in the
post–Cold War era / Luis E. Lugo, ed.
p. cm.
Includes bibliographical references and index.
1. Sovereignty.   2. Sovereignty—Moral and ethical aspects.   3. International
relations—Philosophy.   I. Lugo, Luis E.
JX4041.S63 1996   320.1'5'09049—dc20   96-3835 CIP

ISBN 0-8476-8214-5 (cloth : alk. paper)
ISBN 0-8476-8215-3 (pbk. : alk. paper)

Printed in the United States of America

♾ ™ The paper used in this publication meets the minimum requirements of
American National Standard for Information Sciences—Permanance of Paper for
Printed Library Materials, ANSI Z39.48—1984.

Contents

Part 2: Cases

Conclusion

Foreword

This book is a product of the Calvin Center for Christian Scholarship (CCCS), which was established at Calvin College in 1976. The purpose of the CCCS is to promote creative, articulate, and rigorous scholarship that addresses important, theoretical, and practical issues. Such scholarship focuses on areas of life in which it may be expected that a Christian position could be worked out and for which previous Christian scholarship has been too parochially expressed, too superficially developed, or too little in accord with Christianity itself.

Professor Luis Lugo's efforts have resulted in the present volume. Though he was aided by his colleagues in the Department of Political Science at Calvin College and by the staff of CCCS, the inspiration was his, and the book exists because of his creativity. Professor Lugo was awarded a grant from the CCCS to host a conference that would produce a worthwhile book. The conference was held at Calvin College in October 1994.

The research questions addressed at the conference included the following:

- In view of the dynamically altered world situation since the collapse of communism, how useful are existing theoretical models of international relations?
- Is there an emerging consensus on the limits of nation-states to deal with the new dynamic?
- How can we—academics and citizens alike—make moral sense out of the current situation of flux?

The authors have dealt with these and other questions in their wide-ranging analyses.

Since the time of the conference, Professor Lugo, CCCS staff member, Donna Romanowski, and I have worked with the authors on revisions of the conference papers. We now believe that—taken together—the papers present a perspective on the putative "new world order" that will interest academics, policymakers, and citizens.

Ronald A. Wells, Director, CCCS
Grand Rapids, Michigan

Introduction
State Sovereignty and International Morality in the Post-Cold War Era

Luis Lugo

It should be clear by now to all but the most Pollyannaish among us that the end of the protracted Cold War struggle between the United States and the Soviet Union has not, and is not likely anytime soon, to lead to a new world order of justice and peace under the effective rule of international law. Renewed ethnic and nationalist strife, the proliferation of nuclear and other means of mass destruction, rogue states that disregard the most elementary norms of international conduct, repressive regimes that violate all standards of human decency in their treatment of their own citizens, massive flows of people within and across national borders, and the widespread use of terrorism, among other worrisome trends, underscore the dangerous and rather unpredictable nature of international politics in this post-Cold War period. It is equally clear that to contend with these problems, not to mention with such broader global challenges as safeguarding the ecological integrity of the planet and promoting economic development for the vast majority of the world's population, we shall have to move beyond the familiar ways of thinking to which we have become accustomed during the last half-century. It would seem that a thorough rethinking of the established verities is much in order if we are to forge new, forward-looking approaches that engage these pressing concerns in a meaningful fashion.

We can begin the much-needed reassessment with a consideration of the assumptions that have shaped our understanding of world politics not merely during the Cold War, but indeed, since the Peace of Westphalia in the mid-seventeenth century. The end of the Cold War has served to bring many of these assumptions, especially as they touch on matters relating to the nature and limits of state sovereignty, much closer to the surface. This provides an important window of opportunity for scholars and policymakers alike to tackle and bring into clearer focus some very important questions. How relevant are existing models of world order in light of recent changes in the international political system? Are we witnessing a historic transformation in our understanding of the proper limits of state sovereignty, and are there historical precedents that can inform our thinking concerning these changes? What are we to make of such disparate challenges to the present system as the new nationalism, the more frequent practice of humanitarian intervention, and calls for the universal enforcement of human rights? What moral and political resources shall we draw on to help us make sense of all this?

To encourage serious reflection on these matters, the Calvin Center for Christian Scholarship sponsored a conference in the fall of 1994 on the theme "Sovereignty at the Crossroads? International Morality and the Search for a New World Order." The aim was to explore these issues not with an eye on the technical details but rather with a serious concern for their underlying moral-philosophical dimension. The conference papers, which are gathered in this volume, draw on a long and rich tradition of Christian political reflection—Catholic, Protestant, and Orthodox—to cast a moral light on the issues and thus hopefully enrich the broader public conversation on these important matters.

The first part of the volume situates the contemporary debates within a broad political, historical, and ethical context. Locating the issues within this large framework should put us in a better position to appreciate the nature of the problems and of the underlying assumptions that shape our thinking and discourse on them. The second part of the volume takes up specific cases that serve to highlight in very poignant ways some of the moral dilemmas and choices that we face in this post-Cold War period. In their own way, nationalism, humanitarian intervention, and the universality of human rights each draws our attention to the requirements of a more just international order, as well as to the capacity of the modern state to secure those requirements. Given the unique, high standing of the United States in world affairs, all this surely is of great significance for American diplomacy. Accordingly, the concluding section examines the moral implications of these sea changes in world politics for the future course of United States foreign policy in this post-Cold War era.

The first topic we take up in this volume is the various ways in which we think about the question of world order in modern international politics, including the sorts of normative assumptions that undergird our thinking. Justin Cooper's chapter, "The State, Transnational Relations, and Justice: A Critical Assessment of Competing Paradigms of World Order," helpfully surveys the various paradigms (realist, pluralist, and globalist), offers an informed judgment on their relative merits, and points us toward an alternative model. His argument is that existing models of world order operate on the basis of an inadequate understanding of the nature of political authority and with insufficient acknowledgment of the social diversity that characterizes human life at the international level. He suggests that if we are to move toward a more just world order, we will need to pay more careful attention to how new forms of transnational political authority (accountable and appropriately limited in their functions) might complement the established authority of the nation-state.

In his response Alberto Coll expresses considerable agreement with Cooper's critique of existing paradigms and commends him for incorporating into his proposed alternative elements that are often missing from similar proposals for sweeping institutional change, but he points to two major problems with Cooper's argument. The first involves what he believes to be Cooper's failure to sufficiently clarify his alternative approach. This, according to Coll, leaves Cooper suspended between existing models and unable to resolve the tension between them. Coll's second and more serious criticism is that Cooper moves much too quickly to a consideration of the requirements of justice to the neglect of questions regarding power and security. Coll invokes St. Augustine to make the point that any notion of even a modestly limited framework of international justice must necessarily presuppose the existence of some minimal level of world order, one that is firmly anchored on military power and on which we can rely for our basic security.

The second chapter looks at the contemporary debate from the vantage point of a broader historical perspective. In "On the Cusp of Sovereignty: Lessons from the Sixteenth Century," Daniel Philpott contends that remarkable similarities exist between international politics in the post-Cold War era and those of early modern Europe leading up to the settlement of Westphalia in 1648. Most importantly, he argues, in both periods we witness a serious wrestling with moral dilemmas that are central to the notion of state sovereignty, with those who accept a morally and politically fragmented system of sovereign states pitted against those who hold out for an international order based on some

overarching political authority and a common morality. Philpott believes
that by examining closely early Christian responses to the evolving norms
of sovereign statehood, we might be able to glean useful moral insights
that will help us assess the significance of recent challenges to the norm
of sovereignty, more specifically, humanitarian intervention and the
integration efforts of the European Union. He points to the tradition of
natural law as providing a viable basis for building a strong moral
consensus on delimiting the exercise of the presumed sovereign prerogative of states.

James Skillen concurs that we certainly need to question absolute
notions of state sovereignty and that, moreover, we should support the
formulation of norms that can guide the actions of states and help sustain
an international order of justice. He is deeply skeptical, however, of
whether it is either feasible or desirable to recover a natural law framework as the basis for universal moral and legal standards. Instead, in
terms that recall Cooper's line of argument, Skillen calls for a deeper
appreciation of the institutional differentiation that has come to characterize the post-Westphalian world of international politics, as well as for
greater normative clarity on the specifically political obligations of states
in this increasingly interdependent world.

The third chapter picks up on this normative angle and examines a
central moral theory that has profoundly influenced all discussions on
the role of ethics in international politics during the last two hundred
years. In "Kantian Ethics, International Politics, and the Enlargement of
the *Foedus Pacificum*," John Hare examines Kant's universalist vision of
a just world order and the strong links that it posits between the advance
of liberal democracy and the quest for world peace. Cutting through the
debate between realists and idealists, Hare relates Kant's ethical theory
to his optimistic predictions concerning a future pacific union and
discusses at length a recent objection to Kantian ethical theory advanced
by communitarian and feminist critics alike: the objection from particularity. It is Hare's contention that a form of this objection succeeds, and,
furthermore, that it undermines Kant's cosmopolitanism in significant
ways. He suggests that the pursuit of the Kantian cosmopolitan agenda
might paradoxically undermine liberal regimes even as it makes conflicts
between liberal and nonliberal regimes not only more frequent but also
more violent.

David Lumsdaine professes an admiration for Kant's normative international theory and sees it as the best starting point for thinking about
world peace, though he acknowledges that Hare's critique is basically on
target. His main concern is to advance the discussion by laying out three

challenges that he believes Kantian ethics must face squarely if it is to mount a successful defense against its critics. First, Kantian ethics must show how Kant's overall argument relates to various levels of analysis in international theory and, in particular, how his concept of rationality differs from that now prevalent in the literature. Second, it must incorporate elements of particularity into Kant's excessively rigorist universalism—but without losing a sound basis for common standards of human rights and international law. Third, it must revisit the Christian philosophical roots of Kant's ethics and work to recover a more satisfying union between the universal and the particular in moral thought and action.

Part two of the volume moves from contextual questions to specific cases that highlight the difficulties that surround the post-Westphalian conception of state sovereignty. Arguably, nationalism represents the greatest contemporary challenge to the establishment of a more just order in international relations. In "Identity, Sovereignty, and Self-Determination," Jean Bethke Elshtain parses this great political passion of our time—nationalism—in terms of the three interwoven themes suggested by her title. Her purpose is to delineate more carefully the differences between an uncivil nationalism, on the one hand, and a robust form of patriotism, on the other. She draws on Catholic social thought to show how religion can be conducive to a healthy sense of civic identity, one that avoids the pitfalls of nationalism and that nurtures the kind of genuine universalism that recognizes the diversity of social forms. Picking up a theme from Hannah Arendt, Elshtain underscores the importance of the virtue of forgiveness in situations where it is not possible to right every wrong and reverse every injustice.

Vigen Guroian is very appreciative of Elshtain's attempts to chart a middle course between a bloodless liberal rationalism and a reactionary cultural nationalism. He is not convinced, however, that this proposed third way would be very effective in many of the actual situations we face today. Guroian argues that if we hope to gain a better handle on this phenomenon, then we must learn to bracket completely (at least initially) our deep-seated liberal democratic biases. He points to the misunderstandings that have surrounded the person of Alexander Solzhenitsyn as illustrative of the inability of Western thinkers to grasp the need of peoples in Eastern Europe to look beyond an advanced secular liberalism and its unbounded faith in democracy and tap the Christian roots of their own rich cultural heritage. Only in this way, Guroian contends, will they be able to counter effectively the ethnic pride and extreme nationalism that lead invariably to violence against neighbor.

One of the most hotly debated issues in the aftermath of the Cold War, and one that bears most directly on the question of state sovereignty, is the issue of humanitarian intervention. In "Humanitarian Intervention, Christian Ethical Reasoning, and the Just War Idea," James Turner Johnson considers the moral case for the interventionary use of military force to alleviate massive humanitarian needs resulting from domestic armed conflicts. Drawing heavily on the thinking of St. Augustine and Paul Ramsey, Johnson argues that the idea of just cause within the Christian just-war tradition can indeed be understood to encompass actions of this kind. He acknowledges that there are important considerations that point in the opposite direction but concludes that these should be used to temper and balance the obligation to intervene, rather than merely to negate it.

Alexander Webster strongly resists Johnson's suggestion that we ought to enlarge the doctrine of just war to encompass several of the humanitarian interventions of the last few years. In Webster's view such a radical expansion of the just-cause criteria does not adequately appreciate the potential for extensive abuse that is inherent in these undertakings, leaps too quickly from what is permissible to what is imperative, and fails to reckon with the fact that in the actual debate many of these interventions often are urged for the sake of promoting democracy. Webster finds these democratic grounds for intervention significantly less compelling from a moral standpoint than the protection of human rights.

The question of the universality of human rights is another highly contentious issue in many discussions of morality and international politics. In "Universal Human Rights and the Role of the State," Paul Marshall argues that a defense of human rights based on the notion of innate rights is very susceptible to the charge that these rights are but a species of secular individualism flowing out of a parochial, Western liberal agenda. He puts forth a conception of rights that is tied less closely to Western individualist ideas and that is rooted more firmly in the actual nature of rights in law. Marshall suggests that we might yet rescue the notion of the universality of human rights if we base our claims on a theory of the just state rather than on inherent individual rights, and if we carefully limit these claims to negative rights that place limits on the power of the state and whose guarantee is a necessary feature of any just government.

Joseph Boyle, though generally sympathetic to Marshall's attempts to defend universal human rights independently of the framework within which they are normally justified, is of the view that Marshall makes this defense more difficult by rejecting altogether the notion of inherent or

natural rights. Boyle argues for the truth, as well as the political useful-
ness, of a certain notion of natural rights that also makes possible a
strong commitment to the universal nature of positive economic rights,
such as the right to health care and to education. He finds a solid basis
for this approach in Catholic social thought, which takes as its point of
departure the requirements of human well-being and the specific duties
deriving from them.

In the concluding chapter, "Idealism Without Illusions: Christian
Morality and International Politics in the Post-Cold War Era," George
Weigel brings the discussion home by exploring the moral implications
of the end of the Cold War for the future course of American foreign
policy. Offered as a theologian's counsel to the strategist, Weigel's
essay argues for the inescapable moral element in international politics,
suggests a number of key moral themes that could serve as guides for
policy, and identifies important new issues that ought to be part of the
contemporary debate. His aim is to provide a strong normative framework for a foreign policy that some would label Christian realism, but
that Weigel prefers to call idealism without illusions.

The timeliness of the issues discussed in these chapters is beyond
dispute, as is the pressing need to bring some fresh thinking to bear on
them. Our hope is that this volume helpfully illuminates the moral
assumptions that, however implicitly, inform our public and academic
discourse on these matters. As we have stated, the authors consciously
draw on a rich tradition of Christian political reflection to cast light on
the issues, as well as to suggest fruitful new ways of thinking about them.
The seriousness with which they address the subject is matched by a
willingness to work with all people of good will on the common task of
better understanding and more effectively addressing the problems that
confront the whole human family in this post-Cold War era of international politics.

Part 1

Contexts

Chapter 1

The State, Transnational Relations, and Justice: A Critical Assessment of Competing Paradigms of World Order

Justin Cooper

The field of international relations is embroiled in what can be called a paradigm debate about fundamental questions of international or world order. The realist consensus, which K. J. Holsti refers to as "the classical tradition," has broken down and is being challenged by several other conceptual frameworks, including what we shall describe as variants of pluralism and globalism.[1] Although such paradigm debates in international relations are hardly new, the current installment, which arguably began with the publication of a pathbreaking article on transnational relations by Robert Keohane and Joseph S. Nye Jr.,[2] has been intensified by the end of the Cold War, as analysts face the prospect of a new world order and seek to understand what its fundamental character might be.

Underlying the current debate in the discipline are central normative questions not only about the nature of international relations but also about the structure and purpose of political authority, traditionally associated with the institution of the state, and about its long-range potential for change. Will the nation-state continue to be the paramount political structure in terms of which world order is constituted, or are we witnessing a political sea change in which the centuries-old structure of the state will be altered by transnational pressures toward the reconstitution of political authority at a higher level (or, conversely, by subnational pressures toward devolution)? Such questions are also pertinent for Christians who take seriously a created and providentially maintained

3

order for human affairs. In these terms the matter could be put this way: is the state the most comprehensive form of political organization ordained by God's created order or are other forms of legitimate political authority possible and necessary at the international level in order to respond obediently to the Lord's command to do justice?

This chapter helps answer these questions in the following three sections. First, we survey the major paradigms or conceptual frameworks in terms of which world order is understood in order to explore the basic assumptions involved in each. Second, we assess these paradigms from a critical Christian perspective to indicate strengths and weaknesses and to clarify which assumptions about the state and international society are most fruitful for a responsible conception of a future world order. Finally, we present an argument for an alternative account that is more consistent with a Christian understanding of the nature and task of political authority. By means of this analysis it will become clear that, in response to the ongoing differentiation of society, a normative conception of the development of world order should include the idea of new forms of transnational political authority that will complement the political authority of the nation-state and help ensure that public justice is more effectively carried out at the international level.

Review of the Major Paradigms

The presence of competing paradigms in the study of international affairs is nothing new. An early precursor to the contemporary debate was the eighteenth-century movement from the Abbé de Saint-Pierre's vision of a united Europe put forth in his *Project for Perpetual Peace*, to Jean-Jacques Rousseau's criticism in his *Treatise on the Social Contract*, to Immanuel Kant's attempt to fashion a synthesis in his *Perpetual Peace*, which works represent the basic streams of centralism, statism, and pluralism, respectively.[3] More recently, as international relations emerged as a distinct field of inquiry in the early twentieth century, what are often described as idealist conceptions of world organization, whether advocating a world state or a confederation of states, were challenged by Mitranian functionalism, the realism of E. H. Carr and others, and the imperialist thesis of V. I. Lenin, thereby adding other variations to the range of competing paradigms.[4]

Contemporary students of international relations who have attempted to describe the current paradigm debate have used various categories to classify the different schools of thought. These have followed a fairly consistent pattern. One recent work uses two categories to characterize the discussions that followed Keohane and Nye's challenge to the state-centric paradigm: those committed to a realist paradigm and those forging a new globalist approach.[5] A three-fold rubric, however, has become a more common way of looking at the variety of approaches, with slight variations in the precise account of each of the three paradigms. Chief among these are James Rosenau's distinction of state-centric, multicentric, and global-centric approaches; Holsti's account of the classical tradition, world society models, and world-capitalist system theories; Michael Banks's typology of realism, pluralism, and structuralism; and William Olson and A. J. R. Groom's trilogy of realist, world society, and structuralist paradigms.[6]

Although different terms are used, what each of these authors has in fact done is simply to add the Marxist-inspired image of a world system to some version of the basic realist-globalist dichotomy, thereby employing one broad category to cover all other approaches in the discipline besides realism and Marxism. For our purposes, the use of two categories, in addition to Marxist structuralism, is insufficient to disclose the underlying normative assumptions regarding the central issues of the state, justice, and political authority, which are involved in conceptions of world order. It is nevertheless helpful to note the basic questions that these commentators have highlighted in their analyses of the paradigm debate.

Three basic and interrelated issues are noted in the literature as distinguishing the various paradigms in international relations. These have been helpfully summarized by Holsti in his insightful work, *The Dividing Discipline*. As he states, "International theory has traditionally revolved around three key questions." These include (1) the causes of war and the conditions of peace, security, and order (an essential subsidiary problem is the nature of power); (2) the essential actors or units of analysis; and (3) images of the world system or society of states.[7] In Olson and Groom's account the nature of power is given separate status as a fourth issue, but the principal contribution of their discussion is the observation that the unit-of-analysis question is problematic for those approaches that reject the state as the primary actor and must therefore find an appropriate substitute for it even while continuing to deal with its undeniable role.[8] Finally, Rosenau adds an entirely new category of assumptions, which he identifies as "the degree to which change and continuity are likely to mark the course of events."[9]

Some variation of these three basic paradigms are typically distinguished according to their divergent presuppositions concerning the central issues of the unit of analysis, the nature of the international system, the basic problematic (and nature of power), and the potential for change. For our analysis, however, we shall employ an alternative and more nuanced classification scheme that addresses these issues, as well as normative assumptions about the state and international political authority. This scheme of basic approaches to world order includes six positions that can be organized into three basic categories. These categories and positions are the statist or realist paradigm, with its Hobbesian and Grotian variants, which accepts the legitimacy of the nation-state; the pluralist or polyarchist paradigm, with its Mitranian and Kantian variations, which recognizes both the state and international institutions; and the centralist or globalist paradigm, with its Stoic and Marxist versions, which works with the idea of a central authority or system.[10] Using this typology with the central questions described above, we now survey the principal presuppositions of each of the major paradigms with a view to understanding the type of world order each prescribes. For a diagram that provides an overview of this approach, see Figure 1.

The state for the realists is the central point of departure in characterizing the essential problem of international relations as that of war and the maintenance of peace, played out against a background of the organized violence of military power and its potential employment. Security and order are thus the principal preoccupations. Following from this, the essential unit of analysis is the nation-state and, in the first instance, the diplomatic-strategic behavior of states. The image of international relations assumed by realists is a system of states characterized by anarchy—understood as the absence of a central authority—and the

CENTRAL ISSUES	STATISM		PLURALISM		GLOBAL
	Hobbesian	Grotian	Mitranian	Kantian	Stoic
1. Basic Problematic [nature of power]	war & peace [military capacity]	war & peace international order [military capacity]	transitional welfare & order, war & peace [military & nonmilitary forms]	war & peace, transnational welfare & order [military & legal]	global standard, justice [legitimate authority]
2. Unit of Analysis	nation-state	nation-state	state & international institutions	state & universal association	world state
3. Image of System	states system (balance of power)	anarchical society of states	polyarchy or network	confederation of states	world political
4. View of Change	static	static	developmental	developmental	transformation

Figure 1.

balance of power. With respect to the possibility of change, realists emphasize system continuity and maintain that the development of such phenomena as nonmilitary forms of power and the increasing presence of transnational interactions in international society can be incorporated into the realist paradigm without altering its essential character. Realists regard these changes as secondary and less significant than the stability of the principal state-centric features of what they prefer to call international politics.

What distinguishes Hobbesian from Grotian realists is their assumptions regarding the nature of the state and, related to this, the degree of order that they perceive to characterize the international system. Specifically, the Hobbesian realist approach emphasizes the autonomous character of the state and of state sovereignty and therefore sees international politics as an anarchy of amoral power politics. By contrast, the Grotian position seeks to moderate this notion by noting that states operate in a shared context of rules. This paradigm thus works with what Hedley Bull has described as the paradoxical image of international relations as an anarchical society of states.[11] Both variants, however, understand the state in descriptive and prescriptive terms as the sole legitimate political authority, thereby absolutizing it as the fountain of order and justice. The existence of international institutions is acknowledged, but only as a product of the will of states expressed in treaties that they may abrogate. Such institutions are thus seen as residual, also because they lack independent military capability and therefore are not considered genuine political actors. In short, realists see a future world order that will continue to be a states system, albeit with some secondary modifications because of the increasing presence of transnational relations.[12]

Centralists or globalists, on the other hand, share as a point of departure a dissatisfaction with the balance of power as a description of and prescription for the international system. They also begin with a rejection of the nation-state as the primary unit of analysis in favor of some central structure of global scope that is seen as essential to an understanding of what the international system is or what it ought to be. At this point, however, Marxists diverge significantly from those who follow the more traditional Stoic conception of a central political authority and, thus, arguably could be placed in separate categories.

The Marxist conception of the world-capitalist system moves from a political to an economically based notion of structure, and hence the term "structuralist" is used in some of the contemporary classifications noted earlier. In this view, the principal problematic is not so much the need to maintain peace, stability, and order, but rather how to transcend an exploitative and exceedingly stable structure of production and exchange, particularly but not exclusively economic, between a rich and powerful center and the poor and weak periphery. The unit of analysis may be pitched at a variety of levels: classes, which are the social basis of states or subsystems; states, which are significant units in the organization and preservation of such relations; subsystems, such as the center and the periphery; or the world system itself, as the totality structure in terms of which the various subsystems of oppression find their ultimate reference point. Whatever the immediate unit of analysis, however, it is always defined in terms of its place in the system of production and exchange, thereby eliminating any independent political sphere. Given its basic character, this approach reinforces the image of an overall system, which in some cases may be embellished by the idea of a dominant political power or hegemon that preserves and especially benefits from the system. Finally, on the fundamental issue of change and continuity, this paradigm displays a dialectical character, combining the assumption of oppressive stability and continuity, on the one hand, with the prospect of radical change and transformation to a more humane order of justice and equality, on the other.[13]

The other centralist or globalist variant is the more traditional one of a central global political authority or world state. This approach accepts the realist account of the centrality of the war/peace problematic and the importance of military power but sees the only viable answer to be a global political authority that holds the monopoly of force and presides over a global society of interdependence. Added to this problematic is a strong normative sense of the need to institute common standards of justice based not on nationality but rather on the universal moral community of humanity. Although it rejects the nation-state, its idea of central guidance typically consists of the elements of state authority transposed to the global level. This idea radically transforms the meaning of the state into a central authority for a global polity rather than as one unit in a decentralized states system and, at the same time, eliminates any notion of a distinctive international political authority, since such authority takes on the identity of the state. The resulting image of the international system can be described as a global community of individuals and communities or simply as a world polity characterized not by the balance of power but by the rule of law. Finally, this approach is clearly based on a presupposition of the need for and possibility of radical change and transformation of the international system. Some continuity is retained in the idea of political authority organized on the model of the state.

This is overshadowed, however, by the assumption that interdependence has made central accountability both morally necessary and politically feasible.[14]

If realism is characterized by its commitment to the nation-state and globalism, at least in its Stoic variant, in its preference for a world state pluralism can be distinguished by the presupposition that international institutions of political authority as well as nation-states must both somehow be included in a world order. This means that for both Mitranian functionalist and Kantian confederalist visions the underlying assumption regarding change is one of political development, that is, the unfolding of new forms of political authority and, consequently, the modification rather than the elimination of the nation-state. In short, both views stand in the Enlightenment tradition of the possibility of progress in international relations that Kant initiated. The differing strategies of the two approaches, however—the former more gradualist and pragmatic and the latter more formal and constitutional—are reflective of different assumptions regarding the problematic to be addressed, the specific institutional changes required, and the resulting image of the system.

In the Kantian approach the fundamental problematic remains that of war and peace. In Kant's original vision, however, an historical process is postulated in which four factors work together to bring about greater peace. These include: the existence of republican constitutional states of enlightened citizens; the development of economic relations of self-interest through the outworking of the commercial spirit; the reality of exhaustion caused by the increasing costliness of war; and the formation of a world organization consistent with a universal moral community, namely, a confederation of free states under cosmopolitan law. Military and economic power thus have some impact on the process, but the key element is the establishment of an association of states through which the states' interactions are structured and that, at the same time, recognizes the multiplicity of nation-states as legitimate.[15]

This conception allows for significant units of analysis at both the nation-state level and the international level of the confederation of states, which requires the possibility of limiting state sovereignty and enforcing cosmopolitan law. The resulting image of the system is more than a states system, yet something short of a world polity, combining elements of both unity and diversity in a confederative structure. In more contemporary versions of this vision, functionalist aspects have been included by adding sectoral associations of cooperation in areas of common concern to produce a more complex arrangement that is often referred to as the United Nations system.[16]

The Mitranian functionalist or modernist paradigm, as noted earlier, begins with a fundamental commitment to the reality of and potential for change in international relations. Although this approach includes some aspects of continuity, the emphasis on discontinuity is evident in all the other basic categories. First, modernists assume that, in addition to the essential problem of war and peace, problems of economic and ecological security and transnational order have also developed, thereby expanding the international agenda. Related to this is the modernist assumption that because of both the inhibiting effects of the awesome destructive capacity of nuclear technology and the intrinsic nature of transnational relations, new forms of power now exist that operate independently of and differently from military might.

Proponents of the modernist paradigm emphasize, moreover, the development of new actors alongside the traditional nation-state. Central to David Mitrany's functionalist conception, for example, was the creation alongside nation-states of international functional authorities in specific sectors of transnational relations, institutions that he called technical and nonpolitical (but that are in fact political in the sense of being governmental). In the more contemporary modernist paradigm, the notion of nonstate actors has been expanded to include not only international intergovernmental institutions but also multinational corporations and other nongovernmental organizations that function in the international arena. In the most extreme versions of this view, the state itself is regarded as obsolescent and outmoded; however, in most instances it is assumed that the nation-state, albeit with an attenuated version of sovereignty, will be preserved, together with other new actors and institutions.[17]

Finally, on the question of the resultant image of the international system, since modernists emphasize gradual evolution and the emergent character of the developing international system, it is more difficult to describe a prevailing view. Some of the more common conceptions include a process of interactions understood in terms of a world society, broken down perhaps into issue areas; a cobweb or network of numerous crisscrossing relationships; and a world political system in which the states system is one of a number of subsystems.[18] Whatever the specific conception, however, a common characteristic is the assumption that there will be a plurality of rule-making structures and institutions that can be described as a "polyarchy" and that usually will include some altered form of the nation-state in addition to institutions at the international level.[19]

This survey makes clear that there are significant differences between the various competing paradigms of world order. Central to these differences are assumptions about the nature and place of the nation-state as an institution of political authority. These range from the realist commitment to autonomy and immutability to the globalist idea of obsolescence and transformation to the pluralist notion of complementarity and development. In the next section, these paradigms are critically assessed in order to clarify which of their assumptions are most compatible with a Christian understanding of the nature and task of political authority.

An Assessment of the Paradigms

Our assessment of the underlying assumptions of the three basic paradigms and their variants concentrates on three areas: the nature, task, and structure of political authority, specifically in relation to the international arena; the view of historical development that is presupposed; and the directional dynamic underlying the approach itself.

The realist paradigm takes an appropriately serious view of the problem of maintaining security as the essential task of political authorities in the international arena, and its proponents have rightly seen that the responsibility for this rests in the first instance with nation-states. In emphasizing, however, that nation-states with their sovereign authority are the key to peace and freedom, realists have adopted an exaggerated view of the capacity of the nation-state and have raised its status to that of the sole legitimate political authority for maintaining international order and justice. This, in turn, is related to an overly static view of historical development, which also distorts realism's image of international affairs.

This commitment to the autonomy and permanence of the nation-state is most evident in the Hobbesian variant of realism, which sees the state and its sovereignty in terms of an autonomous center of will and self-preservation. In this account, law and legitimacy are the creations of the sovereign will of the state, which typically acts in its self-interest. Enlightened self-interest will dictate cooperation with other states by means of participation in treaties, regimes, or international organizations in order to provide some semblance of order in a shared international milieu, but, similar to treaties aimed at the maintenance of a balance of power, such arrangements are seen as voluntary and mutable creations of the will of states. Such an approach results in a static outlook because, by definition, self-preserving states will never do anything that would permanently detract from their autonomous nature; thus, international institutions that help to manage increasingly important transnational relations in areas such as trade, finance, transportation, communications, and the environment are understood as secondary and residual, epiphenomena of the will of states with no basis for legitimacy in their own right. The image of the international system remains that of a states system, with no possibility of change.

This ontological individualism and its attendant theme of autonomy, which is in obvious tension with a Christian understanding of limited and normed political authority, is tempered somewhat in the Grotian version of realism, with its emphasis on a cultural context of norms and understandings that leaders of states share and assume. Such a conception of a society of states is helpful in that it introduces elements of normativity into the international arena, although in Bull's account it stops short of any notion of natural law or created order and so remains conventional.[20] In any case, the image of international relations remains that of a states system and does not take seriously the implications of the contemporary phenomenon of transnational relations for the authority and legitimacy of the nation-state.

The essence of this issue revolves around the relation between the territorially limited jurisdiction of nation-states and the transnational character of contemporary social, economic, and environmental relations, of a wide variety of types, that transcend political boundaries. Such transnational relations in areas such as trade, finance, communications and transportation are not novel and are often given a legal context by means of extraterritorial legislation or treaties. What realism does not sufficiently recognize, however, is the possibility that transnational relations in various sectors may develop to an extent that a permanent institutional capacity is required to provide the ongoing oversight necessary to ensure that international public justice is maintained. In such cases, the nation-state, with its territorially limited jurisdiction, cannot fulfill a public justice function of such transnational scope. It is, instead, necessary to conceive of some form of international government or political authority that, though brought into being by means of a multilateral treaty, can have a status and legitimacy independent of the will of nation-states. Given the assumptions of the realist paradigm, it cannot provide an adequate conceptual basis for such a possibility.

While realism fails to account adequately for the normative political implications of transnationalism, proponents of globalism are fully cognizant of this phenomenon, have emphasized its global character, and point to it as evidence of the existence of a centralized structure or of the need for its establishment. Although the conclusions of the world-capitalist paradigm and those of the world-state framework are very different, both move conceptually from the nation-state immediately to the global level without taking sufficient account of whether the actual relationships on which they base their conception are genuinely global in scope.

In the case of the Marxist-inspired view of a world-capitalist system, it must be acknowledged that there are highly regular patterns of exchange between countries in the economically advanced North and those in the less advanced South that operate on a basis of comparative disadvantage for the poorer countries and violate norms of fairness and accountability. The existence of such patterns does not in itself, however, warrant either the assertion of a totality structure that is global in character or the assumption that such relations of production and exchange are more formative and significant than those of politics, religion, or culture and, in fact, determine their overall direction.

The motivation for such analysis may be the realization of a deeply moral vision of greater equality and freedom for all of humanity and not just for a small minority. At a deeper level, however, by placing its hope for redemptive transformation in human social change, this type of analysis does violence to the actual created diversity of economic relations as well as to other types of relationships and communities. The result is a simplistic and reductionistic holism that disregards the character of the diverse phenomena it purports to explain.

A similar line of criticism can be developed in connection with the idea of central political guidance by means of a world-state or political authority. Proponents of this position assume the presence of an emerging global society that requires a global political structure for its oversight. In so doing, however, they move immediately from the national to the global level and simply assume that transnational relations are uniformly global in scope and of sufficient diversity and complexity to warrant the assertion that there exists a global society or village that requires a global state for its political oversight; however, it is not self-evident that this claim is justified.

Globalists have rightly seen that political authority is required above the level of the nation-state, but in addition to exaggerating the global character of transnational society, the globalist paradigm, when it moves beyond the nation-state, also falls into the so-called domestic fallacy; that is, it rests on the assumption that the international or global context is similar to a domestic society and, therefore, that the state model of political authority can be readily transposed to it. Such an approach fails to consider whether the structure of the state is appropriate in the unique context of an international or global arena in which not only individuals and social institutions but also nation-states are subjects, even if this arena is characterized by an extensive level of transnational relations or interdependence.[21] Underlying this oversight is, typically, a desire to give political expression to universal moral claims and basic standards of humanity that are not consistently upheld across the jurisdictions of nation-states. While such claims are universally valid, however, they require for their realization the existence of historical communities of political allegiance that bind people together into a polity capable of implementing some measure of public justice. Consequently, to postulate the presence of such a community or its imminent formation ends up, as does the Marxist vision, with a simplistic holism that fails to take seriously the variety of civilizations and religious communities that make up our world.[22]

Such hopes for world unity are often based on a fundamental belief in the potential religious or ideological unity of humanity, whether that is based on faith in a universal reason, allegiance to science and technology, belief in capitalist liberalism, commitment to an ecological humanism, or the syncretistic embrace of the common spirit of the world's religions. Whatever the direction, though, what is presupposed is the achievement of a unity that is possible only through the power of Christ, and this, in turn, can result only in an ahistorical imposition. The globalist vision is transformationalist in character and, as it moves beyond the confines of current historical development, it envisions a radical discontinuity with a present reality that must be brought into line with its paradigmatic designs.

The pluralist approach, in contrast to the radical discontinuity envisioned in the globalist paradigm of world order, is more gradualist and includes elements of both continuity and discontinuity. The recognition of the need for the development of new institutions at the international level is typically balanced by an acknowledgment that the nation-state will continue to play an important, albeit diminished, role in the emerging world order. The positive contribution of pluralism is, therefore, its movement beyond the confines of the nation-state and world-state conceptions toward reflection on the potential for novel forms of political organization that are unique to the international context. There are, however, two important weaknesses associated with this attempt: first, a lack of clarity concerning the identity of such organizations, namely, how they can be constituted and function as institutions that are political and thus can exert genuine authority; and, second, a difficulty in how to understand the sovereignty of the state in relation to the authority of international organization and vice versa.

In the modernist version of pluralism the former weakness, especially, has been evident in a variety of ways. Earlier on, in Mitrany's functionalism, for example, there was a clear focus on the development of new international functional authorities that would exercise the pooled sovereignty of member states in specific functional sectors. These institutions were referred to, however, as nonpolitical, thereby making the nature of their authority unclear. More recently, even the identity of international intergovernmental institutions has been rendered ambiguous as pluralists have, by and large, adopted a more empirical focus on how order is maintained in the international arena without reference to any public or governmental authority having the normative task of maintaining international public justice. Employing such concepts as nonstate actors or international regimes, both political and nonpolitical, pluralists have instead conflated intergovernmental and nongovernmental institutions, because all are understood to have some role in contributing to the maintenance of patterns of regularity or order in a given issue area.[23]

This focus on the process of interactions in specific issue areas, borrowing from the domestic analogy of the policy process, fails to address some basic questions, including the source of normative standards that are to guide the process of maintaining international order, its public character as a pattern of order maintained among a variety of social institutions, and the appropriate institutional form that such a process should take in order to ensure public accountability. As noted earlier, the focus on specific institutions and processes does not address, furthermore, the larger question of what gives coherence to the variety of issue areas. Underlying this methodological empiricism is a pragmatic spirit that avoids deeper questions of structural and directional norms and assumes that international order is nothing more than human conventions and arrangements. Thus it attempts only to describe the empirical character of the contemporary landscape, simply taking for granted the preeminence of Western liberal-democratic capitalism as a background condition.

In the Kantian confederalist variant of pluralism, the starting point is the existence of a unique international political institution in addition to the nation-state; however, this approach is faced with a number of challenges that arise from its character as a universal association with a comprehensive mandate that, nevertheless, preserves the principle of state sovereignty. The difficulty of achieving consensus in an association that is intended to deal with the political problem of international security has been very evident. Neither the League of Nations notion of collective security nor the United Nations approach of a standing army made up of armies of the member states has proven workable, although the efforts in the Korean and Gulf wars have involved some form of U.N. sanction. The development of the practice of peacekeeping has been a creative and useful offshoot of the original concept of maintaining security, but with the demise of a bipolar international system, it is arguable that regional security organizations, in contrast to a universal association, would be more effective in maintaining international security in their respective zones of interest, even if the initiation of security actions still required some form of universal legitimation.

The existence of a comprehensive mandate has also undermined the legitimacy of the United Nations as its membership has swelled to include a majority of states from the developing South. The scope of the resolutions passed by the General Assembly has far exceeded the ability of the United Nations to implement them in an effective or meaningful fashion. This is not to suggest that the United Nations has not performed useful functions in framing international conventions and treaties, as well as in serving as a multilateral forum for the discussion of transnational issues by means of international conferences. Rather, it is to argue that its diffuse agenda makes it less likely that nation-states will entrust any meaningful authority to an institution with such a potentially large and unwieldy jurisdictional scope.

Finally, the United Nations, unlike Kant's original vision, has spawned a large network of functional organizations that lack meaningful account-ability. In order for these to operate more effectively, it is necessary to reflect on how to introduce more useful reviews of the conduct of these bodies, which now constitute an international bureaucracy quite remote from any democratic controls. The U.N. Economic and Social Council has not really been effective in this regard, and the proposal to place these functional agencies under the U.N. General Assembly may serve only to expand its jurisdictional scope in an unworkable fashion.[24]

In short, although it attempts to balance state and international author-ity, the original vision of an international universal confederation embod-ies an overly optimistic Enlightenment, or perhaps simply Eurocentric or Western, confidence in the efficacy of a universal rationality. Such a wide-ranging international institution may be too ambitious a project, given the current development of international society, and could prove more effective if it were given a more refined mandate focused specifically on international public justice issues that are genuinely universal in character.

Having assessed the various paradigms of world order in the literature of international relations, it is clear that a Christian approach to this issue must go beyond the options presented. The goal is to arrive at a conceptual framework that takes seriously the need to account for the creational task of maintaining public justice at the international level and to do so in a manner that responsibly reflects the current historical unfolding of transnational relations.

An Alternative Framework

In light of our assessment, we must set a direction for an alternative framework that will avoid the exaggerated claims of globalism regarding international authority and community, as well as realism's exaggerated view of national sovereignty, while at the same time providing a more consistent account than pluralism does of the distinctive role of international political institutions. We, therefore, next explore the prospect of the development of a form of international political authority that is structurally unique to the international context in which it functions and that has a legitimate, complementary place alongside the nation-state. Our exploration is guided by the following assumptions regarding the nature of international political authority: it must be appropriately delimited (thereby countering the globalists); it must modify the traditional sovereignty of states (thereby countering the statists); and it must be understood in institutional and normative terms (thereby countering the pluralists).

We suggest that the best approach to follow in coming to grips with the need for international justice is to seek to relate the exercise of political authority to a more accurate account of the character of international or transnational society that distinguishes it from domestic society. Accordingly, we will pursue the notion that political authority must itself be further developed or differentiated if it is to provide the public legal integration required by a developing transnational realm. In this regard, such an approach assumes that a conception of historical development similar to that found in pluralism, rather than the overly static position of realism or the transformationalist tendency of globalism, provides for the most responsible approach to world order.

This view of political order and authority recognizes that an important characteristic of contemporary societies is the development of transnational linkages of many kinds (social, economic, ecological, etc.) that have been engendered by technological improvements in the means of transportation and communication and also by the negative impact on the ecosystem of these advancements and related changes in industrial production. By definition, such transnational relations have a scope of operation that exceeds the administrative capacities of territorially delimited nation-states and thus would seem to require new forms of international collaboration. To arrive at an appropriate account of this differentiation of societies that requires a corresponding integration for its proper functioning, however, it is helpful to draw on the insights of the social and public philosophy of the political tradition of pluralism, which includes such theorists as Johannes Althusius, Otto von Gierke, John Neville Figgis, Abraham Kuyper, and Herman Dooyeweerd, and to apply these to the transnational realm.[25]

These theorists emphasize the differentiated character of a society, which includes a variety of associations and communities, and use this as the basis for distinguishing between political and nonpolitical order and for assigning normative limitations to the authority that political institutions exercise. The task of political institutions is understood as the provision of public justice, that is, of a legally protected social space for the created diversity of persons, social institutions, and communities that interact in a given setting. Applying this approach to the transnational or international setting allows us to relate the development of society and political authority in three important ways: by distinguishing political and nonpolitical order; by allowing for the possibility that international public order may be provided by states as well as international political institutions; and by providing a normative basis for the limitation of international political authority.

It is important, first, to distinguish nonpolitical or nongovernmental forms of association and order, such as the International Olympic Committee, from those that are political and deal with the interrelation of various types of associations or with rights or needs that are fundamental to all of them. This avoids an undifferentiated view of transnational relations or interdependence and the conflation of various types of institutions that contribute to the maintenance of a general order, a tendency that is typically found in the pluralist paradigm of world order.

This approach also recognizes that the state itself is also involved through various forms of international collaboration in the differentiation of political authority needed to provide the wider scope of public order required by transnational societal differentiation. For instance, it may be possible by means of a multilateral treaty for states to effect the necessary regulation for a certain area of transnational relations. This was the case in dealing with the depletion of the ozone layer, where by means of coordinated policies put into effect by individual states—in keeping with the 1987 Montreal Protocol on Atmospheric Ozone Depletion—the problem is being addressed without the need for the creation of an international authority or institution.

Such an approach, however, also properly recognizes that when transnational activities or relations require ongoing public legal regulation and oversight by an institutional presence, the nation-state, because its territorially limited scope of jurisdiction is typically not coextensive with such activities, may not be the appropriate political accountability structure. This formulation of the issue indicates a commitment to the view that the nation-state is not the final or most comprehensive form that political authority can take and thus opens the possibility of new forms of political authority at the international level. It also assumes that certain areas of transnational relations may take on sufficient political salience to blur the traditional realist distinction between a "high politics" of military security and a "low politics" of other types of welfare concerns, whether economic, ecological, social, or technical.

We must address four additional substantive and normative issues if we are to avoid completely the pitfalls of pluralism. These are the nature of sovereignty; the identity of international government; the effective scope of international authority; and its relation to the idea of a universal moral community. Such a conception must first address the idea of sovereignty. It must work toward the development of a notion of the limited sovereignty of nation-states in order to make room for the legitimacy of other forms of political authority (as well as the possibility of a greater devolution of authority to subnational groups).

Such a conception of a reduced scope of operational sovereignty need not be construed as a contradiction in terms.[26] Perhaps the most fruitful approach is to underscore the limited task of the state as an institution of public justice, a task that may legitimately involve the permanent delegation of aspects of its legal authority as a more effective means of maintaining public justice.[27] This would make it possible to conceive of such an international institution as more than a voluntary association of states. It would also provide a clear limiting principle for such institutions, similar to the principle of subsidiarity in the pluralist political tradition: international political institutions should carry out only those governmental functions that cannot be properly administered by states, acting either alone or in concert. It would also supply a basic normative directive for such institutions, namely, one of complementarity and protection of diversity. That is, they should help to create conditions that will assist states to carry out their own tasks and do so in a manner that respects the diversity of institutions and communities in the legal order that is established.

These issues are closely related to the question of the identity of such an international institution. In order to avoid the domestic fallacy of globalism, we must affirm that international government will not necessarily be statelike in all its characteristics. Given the unique character of the international context, which will continue to include nation-states and to lack the sense of community present in most states, international government may be constituted and exercise public legal authority in ways that are both similar to and different from states.[28]

Central to this discussion, of course, is the issue of the effective scope of authority of international government. How appropriate would an institution of comprehensive authority and universal membership be, even on the model of confederalism, in contrast to institutions that have specific authority over jurisdictions that are sectorally, functionally, or territorially limited? The former would seem more consistent with the affirmation of the reality of a universal moral community of humanity; but just as it can be argued that conventional military security is effectively maintained primarily by means of states and the regional security arrangements that they form, we could likewise suggest that public legal authority in other sectors is also more effectively exercised when it is constituted in ways that seek to bring about political accountability in relation to the actual extent of social intertwinement. In other words, given the absence of a single developed global transnational community (the emerging European Community appears to be a regionally based exception), it would seem more appropriate to establish transnational modes of political accountability that are based on more narrowly circumscribed communities of interest.

Such an approach has been described by one commentator as attempting to put an "institutional roof" or accountability structure over those countries and institutions that share relations in a given field or area.[29] Given the fact that the scope of transnational activities varies and that they are not necessarily global, such an approach would suggest a number of transnational institutions of public legal authority. These would vary in membership and scope of jurisdiction from continental to regional to universal and could include such areas as the environment, trade, and communications that have a genuinely global scope of operations.[30]

This approach is also consistent with the presence of some universal confederal structure like the United Nations, and it does not contradict the reality of a universal moral community of humanity or, more precisely, the reality of universal standards of justice. With respect to the former, this approach does not imply the elimination of such a structure; it implies rather the limitation and refinement of what is now an ineffective and overly comprehensive mandate that ought to be focused more specifically on public justice issues that are genuinely universal in character. Regarding the latter, namely, universal standards of justice, such a formulation seeks to transcend a notion of justice as simply the morality of states in order to take account of the presence of other institutions and relations in the transnational realm—but without moving fully to an idea of a universal community of obligation that would require a hierarchy of sovereignty and a world state for its realization.

This formulation builds on an affirmation of God's providential created order, which provides the normative foundation for any transnational legal institution that would seek to apply such standards in its specific area of authority. The reality of such standards, however, does not require the establishment of a single, universal political institution. This type of unity will occur only in relation to a genuine and fully differentiated universal community, a reality reserved for the fullness of Christ's kingdom. What is necessary now is to place greater emphasis on the formation of a number of communities with specific functional and varying territorial bases that will set the context in which standards of transnational justice are upheld.

This leaves the question of the constitution and function of these less comprehensive structures of transnational political authority. Here it is important to take seriously the point that public justice will be maintained best by institutions that are carefully constituted with the genuine ability to hold governments and other institutions accountable and that are themselves democratically limited and accountable. On the side of continuity, such institutions would have the character of public legal institutions, including the power to tax and to make laws and regulations enforced by legal sanctions and adjudicated when in dispute. On the side of discontinuity, since such nonstate institutions would not have access to the monopoly of force and the threat of arms, they would have to rely on other nonviolent forms of enforcement, such as inspection, licensing, and withdrawal of essential services.

The limits to their authority would be ensured by the fact that such authority is functionally specific and also because it is bounded by the corresponding jurisdictions of member states. Limits would also be provided by the principles of subsidiarity and complementarity mentioned earlier and by the principle inherent in the notion of public justice derived from the pluralist political tradition. This principle emphasizes protection for the diversity of institutions, communities, and persons against the homogenizing enforcement of uniformity. Accountability would derive from oversight by an elected council or councils whose makeup would have to be determined according to some formula that balances representation based on the population of the relevant publics and representation proportional to national functional capacity.[31]

The foregoing discussion provides only some initial thoughts on the direction that a responsible paradigm of future world order might take. It is possible to summarize the argument by returning to the four paradigmatic questions: the basic problematic (and nature of power), the unit of analysis, the nature of the system, and the view of continuity versus change. Beginning with the last category, we have argued that a responsible paradigm will provide for both continuity and change, certainly allowing for elements of institutional novelty. Consequently, the units of analysis would include both the state as the primary focus of public justice and other international institutions of public legal authority. Regarding the basic problematic, such an approach argues for international public justice in the sense of both security and transnational order. It thus would allow for other forms of security, such as environmental, and also for other forms of power that may not necessarily be wielded solely by states. At the same time, this approach would distinguish power in general, which might have an impact on the formation of international regulations, from public legal authority, which would possess power properly constituted for the purpose of maintaining international public justice. Finally, with respect to the image of the system, this approach suggests a polyarchy of multiple authorities with nonidentical jurisdictions and overlapping memberships, which has been described as a "new medievalism."[32]

Whether such a system would necessarily be more secure or more harmonious than the previous bipolar system remains to be seen; however, this conceptual framework is an attempt to formulate a responsible political reply to the reality of increasingly differentiated societies and the need for the promotion of international public justice in these relationships. It does not fully answer the question of how to achieve political integration among the various international authorities that might be established, although some role for a universal confederal structure is implied. Given the limitations of theoretical reflection, perhaps this is best left until the direction of historical development is clearer.

Conclusion

It is important to have an adequate vision that takes into account the normative character of political authority and the full reality of the social differentiation that is taking place at the transnational level. A review of the major paradigmatic approaches to international relations and their basic assumptions regarding political authority and the international system has shown that the current debate is characterized by an inadequate normative understanding of the unique and limited character of political authority at both the national and international levels, as well as by a failure to recognize the full diversity of created social life in its historical unfolding. We have noted further that a more articulated understanding of the nature of political authority and of the transnational context in which it is called to do public justice is an essential ingredient for a more fruitful and responsible image of the world order that is emerging. Accordingly, we argued for the necessity of developing responsible and appropriately limited international political authority that will enhance the proper public legal protection of the social space necessary for the obedient unfolding of the rich diversity of created social life in an increasingly transnational world.

Endnotes

1. K. J. Holsti, *The Dividing Discipline: Hegemony and Diversity in International Theory* (Boston: Unwin Hyman, 1985).
2. Robert Keohane and Joseph S. Nye, Jr., "Transnational Relations and World Politics: An Introduction," *International Organization* 25:3 (Summer 1971): entire issue.

3. For a good analysis of this transition, see Stanley Hoffmann, "Rousseau on War and Peace," in his *The State of War: Essays in the Theory and Practice of International Politics* (New York: Frederick A. Praeger, 1965).

4. Examples of varying views in this debate are: E. H. Carr, *The Twenty Years' Crisis, 1919–1939* (New York: Harper and Row, 1964); David Mitrany, *A Working Peace System* (Chicago: Quadrangle, 1966); and V. I. Lenin, *Imperialism: The Highest Stage of Capitalism* (Moscow: Progress, 1970). These authors represent realism, functionalism, and Marxism, respectively.

5. Ray Maghroori and Bennett Ramburg, *Globalism Versus Realism: International Relations' Third Debate* (Boulder: Westview, 1982).

6. See James Rosenau, "Order and Disorder in the Study of World Politics," in Maghroori and Ramburg, eds., *Globalism Versus Realism*; K. J. Holsti, *The Dividing Discipline*; Michael Banks, "The Inter-Paradigm Debate," in Margot Light and A. J. R. Groom, eds., *International Relations: A Handbook of Current Theory* (London: Frances Pinter, 1985); William Olson and A. J. R. Groom, *International Relations Then and Now: Origins and Trends in Interpretation* (London: HarperCollins Academic, 1991). See also Paul R. Viotti and Mark V. Kauppi, *International Relations Theory: Realism, Pluralism, Globalism* (New York: Macmillan, 1987).

7. Holsti, *The Dividing Discipline*, 8. He ends up with five positions by adding Grotian and Kantian variants under the rubric of the classical tradition.

8. Olson and Groom, *International Relations Then and Now*, 144–45.

9. Rosenau, "Order and Disorder," 1.

10. This classification has some similarities to and borrows some of the names of categories from the conception of Martin Wight, who distinguishes a Hobbesian, Grotian, and Kantian or universalist tradition. See his *International Theory: Three Traditions*, Gabriel Wight and Brian Porter, eds. (New York: Holmes and Meier, 1992).

11. For a development of this position, see Hedley Bull, *The Anarchical Society: A Study of Order in World Politics* (London: Macmillan, 1977).

12. Some good examples of realist analysis are Hans Morgenthau, *Politics among Nations*, 5th ed. (New York: Alfred A. Knopf, 1976); Raymond Aron, *Peace and War*, trans. Richard Howard and Annette Baker Fox (New York: Frederick A. Prager, 1967); and Kenneth Waltz, *Man, the State, and War* (New York: Columbia University Press, 1959).

13. Some proponents of a Marxist-style analysis include Andre Gunder Frank, *Crisis: In the World Economy* (New York: Holmes and Meier, 1980); William R. Thompson, *Contending Approaches in World System Analysis* (London and Beverly Hills, Calif.: Sage, 1983); and Immanuel Wallerstein, *The Modern World System II* (New York: Academic Press, 1980).

14. Examples of globalist approaches include Richard Falk, *A Study of Future Worlds* (New York: The Free Press, 1975), and *Explorations at the Edge of Time: The Prospects for World Order* (Philadelphia: Temple University Press in association with the United Nations University, 1992); Johan Galtung, *The True*

Worlds: A Transnational Perspective (New York: The Free Press, 1980); Jan Tinbergen, coordinator, *Reshaping the International Order: A Report to the Club of Rome* (London: Hutchinson, 1977); and James A. Yunker, *World Union on the Horizon: The Case for Supranational Federation* (New York and Lanham, Md.: University Press of America, 1993).

15. See Immanuel Kant, *Perpetual Peace*, trans. M. Campbell Smith (New York: Macmillan, 1917), especially 30–32, 143, and 157.

16. See Inis Claude Jr,. *Swords into Plowshares*, 4th ed. (New York: Random House, 1971), chap. 4.

17. For an argument supporting the obsolescence of state sovereignty, see Richard A. Mansbach and John A. Vasquez, *In Search of Theory: A New Paradigm for Global Politics* (New York: Columbia University Press, 1981).

18. For a development of these conceptions see, John W. Burton, *World Society* (Cambridge: Cambridge University Press, 1972); Harold K. Jacobson, *Networks of Interdependence: International Organizations and the Global Political System*, 2d ed. (New York: Alfred A. Knopf, 1984); and Seyom Brown, *New Forces, Old Forces, and the Future of World Politics* (Glenview, Ill.: Scott, Foresman, 1988).

19. This term is taken from Brown, *New Forces, Old Forces*, 1, 241–43, 261ff.

20. For his approach to natural law, see Bull, *The Anarchical Society*, 6–7, 148–49.

21. For a fuller discussion of the misuse of the domestic analogy, see Hidemi Suganami, *The Domestic Analogy and World Order Proposals*, Cambridge Studies in International Relations 6 (Cambridge: Cambridge University Press, 1989).

22. For a recent treatment of this issue, see Samuel Huntington, "The Clash of Civilizations?" *Foreign Affairs* 72:3 (Summer 1993): 22–49.

23. For a good example of this, see Richard W. Mansbach, Yale H. Ferguson, and Donald E. Lampert, *The Web of World Politics: Nonstate Actors in the Global System* (Englewood Cliffs, N.J.: Prentice-Hall, 1976). For a more recent example, see James N. Rosenau, *Turbulence in World Politics* (Princeton: Princeton University Press, 1990). The idea of international regimes, as developed by Stephen Krasner, has been used primarily by those trying to revise a neorealist approach to international affairs; however, this notion has also been picked up by those with more pluralist leanings. See Stephen D. Krasner, ed., *International Regimes* (Ithaca, N.Y.: Cornell University Press, 1983).

"International governance" is another concept that allows for a variety of means of maintaining international order, including, but not limited to, international political institutions. For a development of this concept, see James N. Rosenau, "Governance, Order, and Change in World Politics," in James N. Rosenau and Ernest-Otto Czempiel, eds., *Governance without Government: Order and Change in World Politics*, Cambridge Studies in International Relations 20 (Cambridge: Cambridge University Press, 1992).

24. For a discussion of the need for reform of the supervision of the functional organizations of the United Nations by ECOSOC, see Douglas Williams, *The Specialized Agencies and the United Nations: The System in Crisis* (London:

Hurst, 1989). See also Paul Taylor and A. J. R. Groom, eds., *Global Issues in the United Nations' Framework* (New York: St. Martin's Press, 1989), especially chap. 11, "Report of the Committee of Eighteen."

25. Some of the important works representative of the pluralist political tradition include Johannes Althusius, *The Politics of Johannes Althusius*, trans. Frederick S. Carney (Boston: Beacon Press, 1964); Otto von Gierke, *Community in Historical Perspective: A Translation of Selections from* Das deutsche Genossenschaftsrecht (Cambridge: Cambridge University Press, 1990); John Neville Figgis, *Churches in the Modern State* (London: Longmans, Green, 1913); Abraham Kuyper, *Lectures on Calvinism* (Grand Rapids, Mich.: Eerdmans, 1931); and Herman Dooyeweerd, *The Roots of Western Culture: Pagan, Secular, and Christian Options*, trans. John Kraay (Toronto: Wedge, 1979). For a useful reader that includes key works from the pluralist political tradition, see James W. Skillen and Rockne M. McCarthy, *Political Order and the Plural Structure of Society* (Atlanta: Scholars Press, 1991).

26. The term "operational sovereignty" is taken from Robert Keohane, "Sovereignty, Interdependence, and International Institutions," in Linda B. Miller and Michael Joseph Smith, eds., *Ideas and Ideals: Essays on Politics in Honor of Stanley Hoffmann* (Boulder: Westview, 1993), 102–3.

27. For a helpful discussion of the legitimacy of the notion of limited sovereignty, developed in the context of a discussion of the consociation of states and international institutions and referred to as "reformed realism," see Paul Taylor, *International Organization in the Modern World: The Regional and the Global Process* (London and New York: Pinter, 1993), especially 40–42, 84, 108, and 114–17.

28. For further development of the argument that international authority should not necessarily be statelike, see Inis Claude, Jr., "The Growth of International Institutions," in *States and the Global System: Politics, Law and Organization* (New York: St. Martin's Press, 1988), 118ff.

29. This term is taken from Seyom Brown, *New Forces, Old Forces, and the Future of World Politics*, 264.

30. At the present time, it is clear that matters such as communications and climate have a scope of operation and impact that makes them global affairs. The International Telecommunications Commission has been developing regulatory powers in the field of communication. To date, issues related to global climate change are not sufficiently developed or urgent to warrant an international authority; the reality of ozone depletion, for example, has been dealt with on a multilateral basis without the need for a permanent institutional presence. For more on global communications, see Howard H. Frederick, *Global Communication and International Relations* (Belmont, Calif.: Wadsworth, 1993). Regarding the issue of ozone depletion, see Richard Elliot Benedick, "Protecting the Ozone Layer: New Directions in Diplomacy," in Jessica Tuchman Mathews, ed., *Preserving the Global Environment: The Challenge of Shared Leadership* (New York: W. W. Norton, 1991), chap. 4.

31. This discussion of representation draws on the work of Mitrany. See his "An Advance in Democratic Representation," in *A Working Peace System*, 121–30.

32. This term is taken from Bull, *The Anarchical Society*, 254–55 and 264ff.

The Ambiguities of the Search for International Justice: A Response to Justin Cooper

Alberto Coll

There is much in Justin Cooper's essay to commend it to our attention. The first part is a thoughtful critique of what he calls the three competing paradigms of world order. Each of these is a general theoretical model that seeks not only to explain the workings of international relations but also to lay down a normative framework for how statesmen should act. The paradigms or models are both descriptive and prescriptive, a problem that Cooper might have explored in greater detail, especially in relation to his own Christian alternative, which he posits toward the end of his essay. The three paradigms are realism, in its Hobbesian and Grotian versions; globalism, whether of the Marxist or Stoic ("world state") kind; and pluralism, either in its Kantian form (as in *Zum ewigen Friede*) or as in the functionalist theories of David Mitrany. After outlining the salient features of each paradigm, Cooper points out some of the key strengths and weaknesses of each paradigm, showing the extent to which each of them in its own way is incomplete both as an empirical description of international relations and as a normative prescription for how statesmen and their nations ought to behave.

In some respects Cooper has a refreshingly Rankean approach to world politics that is often missing among those who eagerly advocate sweeping structural and institutional changes in international relations in the direction of a more tightly knit global community.[1] He appreciates the rich cultural and political diversity that makes problematic the creation of such a community in the near future; moreover, he thinks that such diversity is a good thing, worth nurturing and worth the effort that would be required to preserve it even as a global community gradually takes shape. He is emphatic in his call for "protection of the diversity of institutions, communities, and persons against the homogenizing enforcement of uniformity" (Cooper, 22).

There is also in his essay a Burkean recognition of the gradual character of historical evolution. Radical change should not, and often cannot, be forced; it is best to allow it to take place over time, with some assistance from deliberate human action but never pushed forward with disregard for the historical context and the long-standing cultural and social fabric within which such change is being promoted. As Cooper writes, "some conception of historical development similar to that found in pluralism, as opposed to an overly static realism or transformationalist globalism, allows for the most responsible approach to world order" (17). This recognition separates Cooper from some of his more radical, and less patient, transformationalist colleagues in the evangelical and secular worlds. While I have described these qualities as Rankean and Burkean, Cooper indicates that their source is "the social and public philosophy of the political tradition of pluralism . . . Althusius, von Gierke, Figgis, Kuyper, and Dooyeweerd" (18), to which he is deeply indebted and which indeed constitutes a formidable body of Christian thought.

There are two chief problems with the argument, however. First, Cooper's Christian alternative is not developed with adequate clarity and seems to be torn between two competing conceptions, the world state and the Grotian paradigms. Second, there is in his discussion a baffling neglect of the problem of power in international politics, as well as of security issues.

The ambiguities in Cooper's Christian alternative are numerous. He moves toward a world-state conception of international order when he writes that "transnational relations in various sectors may develop to an extent that a permanent institutional capacity is required to provide the ongoing oversight necessary to ensure that international public justice is maintained." He then adds that "it is necessary to conceive of some form of international government or political authority that, though brought into being by means of a multilateral treaty, can have a status and legitimacy independent of the will of nation-states" (12). He steps back, however, from the full implications of this rather suggestive assertion later on in his essay when he criticizes the advocates of "central political guidance by means of a world-state or political authority" for assuming "that transnational relations are uniformly global in scope and of sufficient diversity and complexity to warrant the assertion that there exists a global society or village that requires a global state for its political oversight" (13). The tension among these different positions is never clarified adequately, much less resolved successfully.

The ambiguities persist even as he tries toward the end of his essay to sketch in greater detail a Christianly responsible paradigm of future world order. There he alludes to "a polyarchy of multiple authorities with nonidentical jurisdictions and overlapping memberships, which has been described as a 'new medievalism' " (22). Such authorities would address specific issues of international public justice and order under conditions in which the member states of international society would have yielded their sovereignty with regard to such issues to that particular authority. Cooper explains that his scheme "does not fully answer the question of how to achieve political integration among the various international authorities that might be established, although some role for a universal confederal structure is implied" (22).

Once again, the basic dilemma confronting this hazily defined Christian paradigm is revealed, in spite of Cooper's best efforts not to allow himself to be pinned down. If the new paradigm requires the creation of extensive political authorities superior to state sovereignty and a confederal structure that ties these various political authorities together, then it is very close to the world-state model. If, however, states are to yield dimensions of their sovereignty to international institutions for the purpose of addressing selected issues, such as trade or the environment, in a way that serves their long-term interests more effectively than unrestrained anarchic competition, then Cooper's paradigm hardly differs from a Grotian-cum-Mitrany world. In that case states retain the core attributes of sovereignty, including the freedom to withdraw from these functional arrangements at will and to use military power whenever necessary. Whether Cooper's paradigm is the former or the latter, it is neither particularly new nor distinctive.

Two other questions need to be raised concerning Cooper's proposed paradigm. First, what normative language or common set of moral reference points will be employed by the different participants in the project of international political justice that Cooper envisions? As he recognizes, the world's religious and cultural traditions are richly diverse. It will be difficult enough to avoid the "clash of civilizations" feared by Samuel Huntington and others and much more so to forge the kind of basic normative consensus required by Cooper's global community. Second, where will be the ultimate locus of sovereignty in such a community? Inevitably, underlying the numerous disputes about justice in such a community will be even graver disputes about the distribution of power and the right to use power in the adjudication and enforcement of justice claims. To use an American analogy, will it be the model of the 1783 Articles of Confederation or the very different one of the Federal Constitution of 1787? The difference between those two models is roughly that between the world-state and the Grotius-cum-Mitrany paradigms. Cooper is not clear about which direction his paradigm leans more heavily toward or about the way in which the more fundamental differences about questions of justice and power would be resolved once the community moved beyond those relatively simple functional issues that are the bread and butter of today's international organizations.

To Cooper's credit, he emphasizes the need for the international institutions he envisions to be accountable and limited. This is most commendable, especially since the record of some of the largest international organizations to date has not been particularly reassuring on either of these two counts. One recalls in this connection Margaret Thatcher's celebrated comment that "we have not rolled back the frontiers of the State in Britain in order to see them reimposed on us from Brussels."[2] She feared that the emerging supranational European Union bureaucracy would be neither accountable nor limited and would become a powerful, centralized Leviathan, with damaging long-term consequences for the freedom and diversity prized by Cooper. Accountability and limits become tougher problems as one moves higher up the ladder of political organization. As a political institution becomes farther removed from the individual citizens whose concerns it supposedly was created to address, the opportunities for corruption, arrogance, and abuse of power grow significantly.

While he points to the two useful principles of accountability and limits, Cooper falls short on sketching in the details. It is not clear whether the ultimate holders of accountability in his system would be the governments of nation-states or individual citizens and their nonstate associations. It is also far from clear what kinds of limits would be imposed and how such checks on the power of supranational institutions would operate. The issue of where the locus of sovereignty resides is again relevant. Either it resides in the supranational institution, in which case it will be difficult to place substantial checks on it, or else it lies with the member states, in which case they can ultimately disregard the will of the supranational institution if their vital interests are at stake.

Even if he does not tackle some of the larger and more problematical aspects of the problem of sovereignty, there is still much to applaud in Cooper's discussion of the subject. For example, he calls for delimiting the sovereignty of nation-states not only to make room for the legitimacy of supranational institutions but also to allow "the possibility of a greater devolution of authority to subnational groups" (19), a consideration that must be dear to admirers of freedom and decentralization everywhere. In fact, this is one more example of the refreshing difference between Cooper and many of his world-order colleagues. For many of the latter the best future is a global version of a Swedish welfare state circa 1950 with large doses of central planning and homogeneity. By contrast, Cooper is a genuine believer in the value and richness of individuality and small communities. For him, a more harmonious world need not mean a world of uniformity and centralized power.

The essay's second major problem is its neglect of power and security issues. Throughout the discussion, Cooper says much about justice but little about order. He writes of the need "to respond obediently to the Lord's command to do justice" (4) and "to account for the creational task of maintaining public justice at the international level" (17). Nowhere, however, does he touch on the equally important Christian imperative to maintain order in a world in which sin and chaos make this a supremely difficult and extraordinarily worthwhile task. In this he is not alone. The overwhelming majority of evangelical political philosophers, in what amounts to a partial abandonment of their Augustinian and Reformed heritage, are far more interested in questions of justice than of order, even though the weight of the Christian tradition is clear on the equal importance and mutual interdependence of justice and order. Without order, not only justice but many other worthwhile goods such as the quest for truth, beauty, and a humane society become imperiled by the lust for power and the self-destructive conflicts it generates, so it is appropriate to ask several order-related questions.

How would the international system that Cooper envisions provide military security for its members? It is important to note that, valuable and necessary though other forms of security (such as economic and environmental) are, the military kind remains paramount as a basic prerequisite for achieving the others. Without security from the types of predatory aggression by ambitious neighbors and would-be imperial powers so common in the annals of history, it is difficult to make much progress on economic or environmental problems. In the arrangement that Cooper envisions, would security be provided by a confederal institution or would it continue to be provided by nation-states acting individually and through alliances? The former option seems for the moment implausible, as well as pregnant with numerous dangers. The latter, for better and for worse, is the one with which we currently live.

Cooper neglects to mention that the process of international integration that he describes and wishes to strengthen requires for its further development the kind of international security environment that has prevailed since 1945, one in which the Western liberal democracies have held the major trump cards of military power. The resulting equilibrium of power, markedly tilted in favor of the Western coalition led by the United States, has been hospitable soil for the values of international pluralism, human rights, and peace and has kept in check forces, such as the former Soviet empire, bent on pursuing a very different vision of international order. In the coming decades the prospects for success of the laudable project for international justice that Cooper commends to our attention will rest to no small degree on whether the same or a similar coalition of democratic-liberal states continues to maintain a favorable equilibrium of military power under whose shadow no hostile aggressors will be able to prosper and the peaceful processes of international integration can proceed. It goes without saying that the United States will need to play a vital role in such a coalition if it is to succeed.

In sum, no discussion of a project for international justice seems complete that does not address the highly problematic issue of the creation and management of the structures of power and military security essential to the achievement of limited justice. To paraphrase what Hegel said of passion, nothing great in the world has been accomplished without power. Power can lead to great evil, but it is also useful and necessary for the construction and maintenance of durable structures of justice. Had Charles V succeeded in imposing political and military control over Germany during the first half of the sixteenth century, the Protestant Reformation would hardly be remembered today; and were a new totalitarian power to arise in the first half of the next century and succeed in spreading its influence over much of the globe, the ensuing international order would be radically different from that which Cooper advocates.

All of this points to the need for political theorists, especially those concerned with questions of international political theory, to turn to the great historians for some assistance in illuminating the rough outlines of the human condition over long periods of time. It is easy, and rather understandable, for international political theorists eager to transform the dominant paradigms of world politics to overlook some of the constraints posed by the sad and tragic continuities of history and fallen human nature. This is where the great historians can be of some help.

Both Jacob Burckhardt, the late nineteenth-century Swiss historian, and Sir Herbert Butterfield, one of the outstanding Christian historians of our times, would remind us of the reality and strength of evil in history and of the persistence of chaos and entropy in the historical process.[3] Even in the best of times and with the best of efforts, it is extremely difficult at the international level to achieve the stability, security, and order necessary for the attainment of a just and humane society. Burckhardt pointed to the state as one of the "four powers of history," the other three being the individual, religion, and art. Finally, both of them recognized the ambiguity at the heart of political power, as well as the inescapable dilemma facing anyone involved in the political world: power is an instrument for doing great evil but also a sword with which to protect our fragile moral achievements in a hostile world.

Perhaps Cooper needs to question the limits to international political theory itself. Not long ago the doyen of Cold War historians, John Lewis Gaddis, shocked the political science establishment by asking why, for all its great intellectual confidence in its supposedly scientific analytical processes, the discipline had failed so miserably to predict the end of the Cold War or anything remotely resembling it.[4] Christian international political theorists can find in Gaddis's question something worth pondering. While international political theory has never exhibited the predictive pretensions of behavioral political science, it can still benefit from looking beyond its boundaries and drawing insights from other disciplines such as history that are more modest in their normative claims and less likely to ignore the world as it is for the sake of the world as it should be.

Endnotes

1. See Leopold von Ranke, *The Theory and Practice of History*, ed. George G. Iggers and Konrad van Moltke (New York: Bobbs-Merrill, 1973).

2. Margaret Thatcher, *The Downing Street Years* (New York: HarperCollins, 1993), 745.

3. See Jacob Burckhardt, *Reflections on History* (Indianapolis: Liberty Classics, 1979), and Herbert Butterfield, *Christianity and History* (New York: Scribner's, 1949).

4. See John Lewis Gaddis, "International Relations Theory and the End of the Cold War," *International Security* 17 (Winter 1992–93): 5–58.

Chapter 2

On the Cusp of Sovereignty: Lessons from the Sixteenth Century

Daniel Philpott

Among the hallowed things that fell with the Berlin Wall was the sanctity of absolute sovereignty in international relations, the principle that within their borders, state institutions are untouchable, inviolable, and supreme. The rupture was not sudden, sweeping, dramatic, or intended—it is not, like the League of Nations, the design of intellectuals or, like many new constitutions, the blueprint of revolutionaries; rather, it has come intermittently, via fissures and cracks, without historic design or conceptual forethought, in response to immediate crises and sudden outcries in Somalia, Yugoslavia, Iraq, Haiti, and Rwanda. Together, though, these anomalies represent a historic trend. At least in the eyes of the permanent members of the U.N. Security Council and most European states, new types of intervention and new criteria for recognizing states are becoming legitimate, and if we look not just to military affairs but also to other diverse matters that states govern, we can see in the 1990 Maastricht Treaty the re-energizing of a different sort of departure from state sovereignty, this one begun a generation earlier when European states pooled their sovereignty over trade, commerce, and other affairs into the institution of the European Community.

Such trends are important, for these norms of sovereignty—the rules that determine what a state is, who can become a state, and what basic prerogatives a state has—define the very entities that fight, ally, trade, balance, bargain, and make peace and set the terms on which they do so. They may be thought of as the constitution of international relations; they are fundamental, and it is rare that they change, but when they do,

Christian ethicists must ask which norms of sovereignty we can endorse. At present, together with the policymakers who face this dilemma, we stare at a blank canvas, shyly dabbing here and there, but with little sense of a complete picture. Should sovereignty be absolute? For what purposes may it be overridden and intervention permitted? Which alternative institutions are just? Which of these purposes and institutions are compatible with Christian morality? Is sovereignty a purveyor of order—the essential purpose of government for Augustine and Luther—or an umbrella for tyranny? Does it preserve pluralism or shield threats to our faith? We are daunted by novelty.

We ought to hold claims of novelty, however, somewhat suspect. Few new orders are really new. In fact, I want to argue that respite for our confusion lies in modesty toward our uniqueness, for there was a time when rulers and ethicists faced dilemmas over sovereignty quite similar to our own. I am thinking of early modern Europe, specifically the period between 1517, when Luther posted his ninety-five theses, and 1648, when the religious wars were finally settled at Westphalia. Claims to absolute sovereignty opposed by a universal ideal holding all authorities accountable, deeply irreconcilable faiths and ideologies, death and turmoil novel in their scale and intensity—all troubled that century and ours. As Europe was still a Christian continent, most philosophers who reflected on this holy disorder did so from the standpoint of faith, and so today we have a full palette of Christian views, Catholic and Protestant, conciliatory and obdurate, in which to dip our brush.

The two worlds are not identical, of course: few orders are new, but no two are just the same; yet if our world is redolent of theirs, if the sixteenth century offers us proximate templates, if forgotten thinkers have labored before to describe this common landscape in moral terms, then we ought to dust off their drawings. I seek, then, to compare this earlier time with our own and ask whether philosophers then have insights for us now. I show how international relations then, like now, were contested between those who sought a system of sovereign states and those who desired an order based on a more comprehensive morality. I also describe the major Christian responses to this dilemma and suggest that one in particular—a natural law approach—is most appropriate to our day.

Westphalia and the Norm of Sovereign Statehood

Shakespeare's Richard II, forced to abdicate by his rival Bullingbrook, his divine royal aspect shattered, laments, "I find myself a traitor with the rest, For I have given here my soul's consent / T'undeck the pompous body of a king, / Made glory base, a sovereignty a slave." Despite his divine mandate, in 1399 the English king was continually threatened by baronial ambitions, and when these carried the day, he was left tragically bereft of his transcendent appointment, a "traitor" to his calling.[1] To Henry V, however, who ruled fewer than two decades later, such ambitions were not a threat. To conspirator nobles he could say with poise, "But we our kingdom's safety must so tender, / Whose ruin you have sought, that to her laws / We do deliver you. Get you therefore hence, / Poor miserable wretches, to your death."[2] By the reign of Henry VII at end of the fifteenth century, actual historical English kings could rule with the confidence that Shakespeare's Henry V did. Inside the realm, their authority was effectively supreme; they enjoyed internal sovereignty, and internal sovereignty made them completely sovereign. When Henry II had, centuries earlier, crushed Thomas à Beckett, archbishop of Canterbury, the Roman Church lost its political influence within England; at that time, the king became externally sovereign, too.[3]

Sovereignty is supreme legitimate authority within a territory. A sovereign need not be a person, like Henry V or Louis XIV or Hobbes's artificial Leviathan. It could also be the united will of the people, as Jean-Jacques Rousseau envisioned, or a distinct body of law that prescribes the authority of offices and positions, such as the United States Constitution. The key is that within certain borders, the sovereign authority is supreme: in the chain of authority by which I look up to higher authority, who looks up to yet a higher one, and so on, the holder of sovereignty is the highest—nobody may question it, nobody may legitimately oppose it.[4]

When several of these sovereigns are found adjacent—fighting, allying, trading, and so on—we have a system of sovereign states, and we may call "norms of sovereignty" those rules that define and regulate this interaction. Norms of sovereignty have three faces, each answering a question about legitimate authority. First, who are the legitimate players? An empire, the European Union, sovereign states, or something else? Second, who is entitled to participate? If states are the legitimate entity, who may become one? Nations that currently have no state? What about colonies? What are the standards for membership in the European Union? Third, what are the essential prerogatives of the participants? Are they free from intervention in all areas? Or are some kinds of policies subject to an outside authority? Which areas of policy are pooled into a larger institution? A norm of sovereignty exists when the major powers in a system agree to it and when they regularly practice it; that is, when

its tenets are generally upheld by all of those who might have the power
to violate the norm with impunity if they so desired.

Sovereignty first took shape in England and France about 1300,
although two centuries of civil war delayed its consolidation in these
places. A whole system of sovereign states existed in Renaissance Italy,
only to disappear; yet the notion of the sovereign state, systematically
articulated and widely endorsed, is distinctly modern. It was first rigor-
ously developed by Jean Bodin, Thomas Hobbes, and Hugo Grotius,
who sought to place politics beyond the realm of religious authority. The
idea of a system of sovereign states probably finds its most parsimonious
expression in the writings of Emerich de Vattel, whose *The Law of
Nations*, written in 1758, portrays a balanced, rational, ordered Enlightenment world where the only universal law is that states have an equal
right not to be hindered in their internal affairs.[5]

In the century before the Peace of Westphalia, our period of concern,
a silhouette of Vattel's world could be perceived, but its full and clear
emergence was yet distant. Today Vattel's design strongly characterizes
our world, and yet it is beginning to blur. Now, like then, we are on the
cusp of sovereignty; international relations exist between a world of
sovereign states and something else. The difference, of course, is that we
are going in the other direction. On our historical escalators, we are
passing at the same level, except that one of us is going up, the other
down.

Early modern Europe remained long on sovereignty's doorstep, approximating it but not achieving it. This had much to do with the
persistence and power of what was being left behind: the Middle Ages.
The Pauline metaphor of the body of Christ, used by publicists, philosophers, theologians, and holders of power to describe their political and
social world, captures the era well. Believers in the true faith were
members of a single organism in which all lived in common under the
same law and morals and where none were severed or independent in
their authority or beliefs; yet not all were equal in purpose and role but,
like the parts of the body, were arrayed in an inclusive division of labor,
a complex hierarchy with the pope and emperor at the head, kings,
barons, bishops, dukes, counts, and peasants each in their proper place,
and all connected by the most labyrinthine ligaments of privilege and
prerogative. Thus was society held together, just as the church is united
in the body of Christ.[6]

The body metaphor describes the archetypical medieval world between
the eleventh and thirteenth centuries. In this *corpus mysticum*, or *res
publica christiana*, there was no sovereignty. Both the Pope and the

Emperor intervened regularly in the territorial affairs of kings, nobles, and bishops and other ecclesiasts, but there were limits. The same kings, nobles, and ecclesiasts held prerogatives against the pope and emperor that they would defend even by arms; neither was any body of law sovereign. While natural law, a manifestation of eternal law, was a universal moral standard, it did not prescribe offices and powers or rights and judicial procedures; these prerogatives often had local feudal sources instead. The norm of sovereignty was, to the degree that it is amenable to a singular description, simply the lack of sovereignty, or what political scientist John Ruggie calls "heteronomy."[7]

Much of this medieval world had disappeared by the sixteenth century. By then, Britain, France, and Sweden all looked very much like sovereign states, while princes in Germany and the Netherlands enjoyed many of the prerogatives of sovereignty. As I have noted, there was also a hermetic system of sovereign states in Italy between roughly the Council of Constance in 1415 and the sack of Rome in 1527.[8] The Italian system did not persist, however, but was subsumed by its French and Spanish conquerors into the European system, and this European system was not yet one of sovereign states. Ruling redoubtably over much of the continent was the Holy Roman Empire, the last medieval entity, venerated for its pedigree, persistent in its authority, but not preeminent in any particular territory. In its shadow, German, Dutch, and Italian princes were under the authority of the emperor and pope, yet enjoyed ancient liberties that neither could challenge. There were also cities that were almost totally independent, and countless other entities with innumerably variegated portfolios of powers. Arcane lines of authority were the norm and idiosyncrasy the only regularity. All of this was complicated infinitely in 1519 when the king of Spain, Charles V, became emperor, tying into a vast medieval conglomerate the Spanish crown, the empire, the church, the Habsburg family, and Habsburg possessions in Germany, the Netherlands, and Burgundy. From this base, Charles aimed to reunite Christendom.

Europe was still distant from the world of Henry V. In one matter in particular Charles V would not tolerate autonomy within his lands, and that was loyalty to the true faith of the true church. His efforts to eradicate Protestantism, however, were defeated in the 1555 Peace of Augsburg, whose terms famously included the formula *cuius regio, euis religio* ("whose the region, his the religion"), allowing German princes to enforce their own religion, Catholic or Protestant, within their own territory. We can think of this formula as an international analogue of individual freedom of religion: each state could practice its own faith without hindrance from its neighbors or a universal government. The cross followed the flag. For the princes, this meant sovereignty, the completion of their portfolio of powers. Augsburg, however, did not last. Over the next three generations, Catholics of the Counter-Reformation would war against Protestants, culminating in the Thirty Years' War. Not until the close of this war in 1648 was something like *cuius regio, euis religio* accepted and respected and practiced.

What was this Peace of Westphalia? How did its component treaties of Münster and Osnabrück end Christendom and elevate the sovereign state?[9] In the minds of the victorious French and Swedish diplomats, it was quite distinctly a system of sovereign states,[10] and all of the victors, France and Sweden, the Netherlands and Germany, sought the detailed substance of sovereignty in provisions that would free princes from all imperial control. A norm of sovereignty, however, is more than a subjective inclination and must be legitimate (explicitly agreed to) and practiced (generally upheld). In several respects, Westphalia indeed made sovereign statehood a norm. While it did not formally dissolve the empire, it gave princes the power to make alliances—a key attribute of external sovereignty—and solidified *cuius regio, euis religio*. Although some restrictions on the practice of religion within certain realms remained, neither emperor nor pope, nor even outside states for that matter, would intervene forcefully in the religious affairs of a European state for centuries afterward, just as neither would ever again pose a threat to the power of German princes to make alliances. The treaties also created new sovereign states, the United Provinces and the Swiss Confederation. Finally, the treaties curtailed the powers of the empire and papacy—those that still existed were barren of efficacy. Fittingly, Pope Innocent X issued a bull, *Zel domus*, in which he termed the treaties "null, void, invalid, iniquitous, unjust, damnable, reprobate, inane, empty of meaning and effect for all time," and even as late as 1900, popes were still condemning international law as a Protestant science, refusing to drop Grotius's *De jure belli ac pacis* from the Index of banned books.[11]

I must qualify slightly my conclusions about Westphalia. First, the peace limited sovereign statehood to Europe and excluded the Ottoman Empire. Christendom was still relevant as a qualification for membership, if not as a source of obligation for states in their internal affairs. On the question of continuity, it is true that some anomalous imperial practices remained after 1648 and that many traits of the system of sovereign states had appeared much earlier than Westphalia; but the anomalies were just that—traces of the past—and as for Westphalia's novelty, I do not argue that it created a system of sovereign states ex nihilo but, rather, that it consolidated three hundred years of evolution toward such a system.[12] In history, perfect fissures are rare, but as historical faults go, Westphalia is about as clean as they come.

Westphalia's norm of sovereign statehood set new standards for each of the three faces of sovereignty: it made the sovereign state the legitimate political unit; it established that the basic attributes of statehood—the existence of a government with control of its territory—were now, along with Christianity, the criteria for becoming a state; and, as it came to be practiced, it meant that there were no legitimate restrictions on a state's activities within its territory. Such a sweeping transition in sovereignty, affecting so many areas, would not be seen again until the European Community came into being in 1950.

Recent Challenges to State Sovereignty

In the history of sovereignty one can skip three hundred years without omitting noteworthy change. Westphalia ended the previous century's contest over sovereignty, and its norm of sovereign statehood has remained intact up to the present. Since World War II it has been preserved in the United Nations Charter, in which probably the most frequently cited clauses are Article 2(4), which prohibits members from forcibly violating one another's "territorial integrity or political independence," and Article 2(7), which disallows the United Nations from intervening "in matters which are essentially within the domestic jurisdiction of any state." Clearly the primary sort of crime envisioned is an attack of one state on another, not the attempt to influence a state's internal matters. Article 39 makes centrally culpable "the existence of any threat to the peace, breach of the peace, or act of aggression," and Article 51 speaks of "the inherent right of individual or collective self-defense." It is true that Article 55 posits human rights and self-determination as basic goals of the Charter, but nowhere does the Charter or subsequent U.N. covenants on human rights deem intervention an acceptable remedy.

It is not altogether implausible to contend that the Security Council is legally empowered to authorize military action to enforce human rights within states. One might argue that this is consistent with the broad purposes of the Charter and that the Genocide Convention especially points to the legitimacy of intervention. This argument, though, is neither obvious nor without flaw.[13] International law is not, however, merely what is written in charters, covenants, and treaties but also includes practices that become generally accepted over time. On these practices, too, the status of sovereignty and nonintervention rests. By this logic, sovereignty has remained inviolable, at least until the end of the Cold War.

Consider the matter of humanitarian intervention, the use of force by outsiders to quell widespread starvation, genocide, or other human rights abuses occurring within a state's borders. During the Cold War, something like it took place several times: India intervened in East Pakistan in 1971, Tanzania in Idi Amin's Uganda in 1978, and Vietnam in Cambodia in 1978, each putting an end to "crimes that shock the conscience of mankind." In each of these cases, though, the intervening states did not even claim the principle of humanitarian intervention, but appealed instead to self-defense, and in none of these cases did the United Nations, or even a majority of the world's states, approve of these measures.[14] The only measures approaching intervention actually undertaken by the United Nations were the decisions in the 1960s and 1970s to authorize sanctions on racist Rhodesia and South Africa for reasons that were vaguely stated, but seemed aimed at internal matters. Yet these have been the only exceptions, and the only recognized standard for U.N. coercive action has remained threats to "international peace and security."[15]

All of this is beginning to change. Through several interventions—against starvation, genocide, and the denial of democracy—the United Nations and its proxy Great Power armies have, since the end of the Cold War, sought to restrain cruelties committed by governments against their own people. Intervention is nothing new, but that the United Nations should allow it, endorse it, authorize it, oversee it, is indeed new. Although in each case the authorizing resolution still mentioned the threat to "international peace and security"—a tribute to sovereignty's extant legitimacy—its rationale for intervention focused on an internal ill, and its resulting action certainly looked like intervention.[16] Though it is still not clear exactly what sort of action or rationale, if any, will become a precedent, the number of interventions that the United Nations has authorized in the past five years suggests an emerging customary practice, a fresh norm of sovereignty. It does not yet have the scope of Westphalia, for it deals only with one of the three faces of sovereignty— the prerogatives of the state against outsiders—but, since nonintervention has been perhaps the key *Grundnorm* of the Westphalian system, the trend is notable.

Compared to these transitions in sovereignty, the Maastricht Treaty is both more prosaic and more grand—more prosaic because it is not a novelty but an expansion of a previous revolution; more grand because this previous revolution was far more sweeping than the evolution of intervention or state recognition. The creation of the European Coal and Steel Community in 1950 was the first transition in sovereignty since Westphalia to alter all three of sovereignty's faces. For the first time since the Holy Roman Empire, a significant political authority other than the state, one with formal sovereign prerogatives, had become legitimate. The constitution of the European Community, now the European Union (E.U.), had definite criteria for membership, including a well-defined regimen for application. It also carefully distributed prerogatives among the member states and the E.U. institutions themselves. The European Coal and Steel Community curtailed the autonomy of member states only in limited areas of policy but was significantly expanded in 1957 with the Treaty of Rome, which created a common market with institutions that governed trade and regulated commerce. In 1985 the Single European Act expanded the common market and rendered many areas of policy governable by a qualified majority (rather than allowing every member a veto), thus strengthening of the institution's formal powers. Then, in 1990, the most marked expansion of the community's powers since 1957 took place with the signing of the Maastricht Treaty, which set as its goals a common currency, the further integration of monetary policy, and the development of a common foreign policy. It is not clear, however, that Maastricht will be realized in unity. We may instead witness combinations of states pooling their sovereignty in some areas of policy, with other combinations uniting in separate areas, creating a "Europe of different speeds."[17] This state of affairs, even more than intervention, may signal a return to the overlapping spheres of authority of the Middle Ages.

What do these trends in sovereignty have to do with the transition to Westphalia? Sweeping in its scope and dramatic in its founding impetus, Westphalia seems inestimably mightier than today's incremental and piecemeal steps. Westphalia did not come all at once either, however, but fell together in parts, little by little, over centuries. Today's transition in sovereignty is also limited in the approval that it enjoys, which is far from universal. Even those humanitarian interventions unanimously approved by the permanent Security Council members are often eyed suspiciously by former colonies and victims of intervention in Africa, Asia, and Latin America. Then again, in the century before Westphalia, sovereignty was also contested and was a source of conflict between beliefs and ideologies on which compromise was unthinkable. In that period, moving toward sovereignty, and in this period, moving away from it, sovereignty's defenders oppose those who would limit sovereignty on behalf of some purportedly universal ideal. With respect to sovereignty, then, the institutional and political problems and trends of early modern Europe were similar to our own—at least similar enough that what Christian ethicists said then may help us morally evaluate our plight now.

Early Christian Responses to State Sovereignty

It was the shattering of a unified world that Christian philosophers had to confront in the sixteenth and early seventeenth centuries. The new pluralism was created by two juxtaposed phenomena. First the Protestant Reformation sundered a Europe united by one church and one creed, then the discovery and colonization of the New World brought European Christians into regular contact with strangers to the faith. Together these events produced creeds whose zealots would not live side by side and elicited unsettling dilemmas with strong implications for the status of territorial boundaries. Constants were now variable, certainties eviscerated. If I am a Reformer, do I penetrate Catholic realms in order to open up their land to the truth? If I am a Catholic, do I fight to prevent further lands from being won to heresy? What about the natives who have never heard the gospel? If we send missionaries to convert them, may we fight their leaders for the freedom to preach? Do we attempt to convert through arms? Does the call to spread the gospel to hostile lands, or at least to resist idolatry, know territorial boundaries? Is political authority—my own or my neighbor's—absolute? If it is not my duty to bear arms against threats to the faith, does my faith provide any other reasons for interfering in the affairs of a foreign tyrant? In response to these new dilemmas, new doctrines on sovereignty and international relations had to be fashioned.

It was almost inevitable that the schism of a world of one unalterable truth, based on an eternal doctrine and interpreted by a universal Church, would yield equally ardent adherents to an equally incontrovertible opposite truth. Because most people believed in exclusive truths rather than in guarded, compromised, and qualified doctrines of tolerance, they concluded that they ought to restrain, or even eradicate, the devotees of falsehood. Thus arose the holy war as one tradition of response to this pluralism that also carried implications for sovereignty. All over Europe, in all of these battlegrounds between counterreforming Catholics and mainstream or radical Protestants, philosophers on one side or the other sought to defend war on behalf of their faith. Few of them addressed the question of sovereignty directly, but their thoughts on war led to unmistakable conclusions on the matter of intervention in the internal affairs of others.

What, then, urges the Christian to war? In his helpful study of just-war thought, James Turner Johnson points out that England provides perhaps the richest array of these holy war entreaties and so is worthy of special attention.[18] Defensive war, that is, war against an attack from outside, was a tenet that almost all of the holy-war thinkers endorsed and one that they borrowed from the classic just-war tradition; but they dramatically expanded its interpretation. It was not just direct, or even imminent, attacks by armies amassed on one's borders that needed to be warded off but also threats to religion, which were interpreted broadly to include the mere existence of a country—Catholic Spain, for instance—that claimed to protect an alternative Christendom. For Francis Bacon and the preacher Stephen Gosson, both Protestants, this was all the justification that was required.[19] For other Englishmen, it was not enough for the righteous Christian to defend his own faith, even against broadly defined threats, but he was also called to wage war against infidels and heretics abroad, who were little different from criminals in the domestic realm. God not only commanded this, but engaged actively on the side of his combatants. This kind of offensive war was endorsed by the late-sixteenth century scholar Henry Bullinger, as well as by Puritans William Gouge and Alexander Leighton in the seventeenth century. Bullinger put forth the old Augustinian doctrine that the magistrate is the wielder of the sword but went further than Augustine or the traditional just-war school in arguing that the state may initiate war for the sole aim of enforcing religion, even carrying out the punishment of God against the "incurable," whom he already condemned.[20] Gouge considered the primary reason for offensive war to be the "Maintenance of Truth and purity of religion."[21]

For these Protestant exhorters, Scripture, naked Scripture, was the plain source of the call to arms. Like the Israelites who defeated the Amalekites, like Abraham, Joshua, or "the best of the Kings," like the Old Testament warriors who prayed for God's direction and assistance and received it, and like all those whom God taught and commanded to fight, the righteous Christian was duty bound to fight and maybe die to quell the vile heresy of papists, anti-Christs, and infidels of all sorts. God judged them, and to carry out this judgment was a privilege for which to give him praise.[22] Because, for these Puritans, Scripture was solely authoritative (although they rarely mentioned the New Testament) and because only those who thus interpreted and relied on the Scripture could see the truth, those Christians or non-Christians who turned to other sources were by definition in error.

The holy warriors may not have actually thought that they could convert hearts with guns, but it was certainly within their purview to prevent practices that were hostile to the faith and even to enforce God's justice among those who did not obey it or even understand it. So we find little truck with any notions of universally accessible truth, the natural dignity of man, the role of reason, or a common morality. Any notion whose source lay outside the Word was a corrupt compromise with the world. This applied, too, to the developing doctrine of sovereignty and the secular doctrines of war that went with them. Gouge condemned wars fought solely for reasons of state as wars between "wicked men."[23] In a just and godly war one could distinguish clearly between the righteous and the unrighteous; the former were bathed in glory, the latter mired in ignominy. There was a Catholic version of all this, too. William Cardinal Allen, an English Catholic bishop in exile, thought that the "Catholic, Romane religion" was the only one for which war was to be waged; Protestants were rebels, the supreme commander was the pope.[24] On both sides of the schism, the doctrine looked the same—borders were immaterial when it came to following God's commands.

Not all Christians who responded to the schism did so as holy warriors. Significant thought came not only from the two extremes but also from those who saw in the destruction only tragedy and mistakes and who offered a cooler, more tolerant response. Such fifteenth-century Spanish Catholics as the Dominican Francisco de Victoria and the Jesuit Francisco Suarez and such late fifteenth- and early sixteenth-century Protestants as Alberico Gentili and Hugo Grotius, were major voices of reason. To call them voices of reason is not merely a judgment on the tenor of their work but on the content of their philosophy, for they all believed that politics and war were to be governed by moral precepts that are written on the heart and thus accessible to all reasoning beings: the natural law (Romans 2:14–15). They believed in Christian truth, but held—with some variation among them—that a certain portion of it was accessible to humans by virtue of their rational capacity and that this natural law was to be the basis of relations, the *jus inter genes*, between people of different creeds. On this ground they defended political authority as an entity serving the good of various human communities, including nascent sovereign states. The moral status of all political authority rested on this foundation, and those who failed to accomplish this purpose could justly be restricted.

What it means to serve this human good and under what conditions we may say that a government is not doing so are also matters for natural reason, which suggests that at the very minimum governments must uphold something like "the common rights of mankind."[25] In polities where the authority is negligent or unable to meet this standard, other princes may intervene and even have a duty to intervene. As the common rights of mankind are few and essential, including the rights to life, freedom from bodily harm, and basic public order, just intervention is rare. Natural law theorists considered it rare not only on grounds of first principle but also out of fear that the right to intervene would be abused by rapacious, pretext-seizing princes. Sovereignty was the presumed entitlement of all political authorities, but it was restricted in some areas, in some situations.

The duty to intervene had its moral roots in the natural and Christian duty of benevolence (the two were not separated). This is stated most forcefully by a lesser-known theorist in the natural law tradition, the sixteenth-century French Protestant, Hubert Languet. All Christians were part of the body of Christ, Languet emphasized, and this meant that "not even the least . . . can suffer violence and harm, without the others being injured and feeling pain, as the whole of Scripture teaches";[26] and because the church is in the charge of princes, "if one part of it—the German, perhaps, or the English—is in the charge of the prince of that region, but he abandons and disregards another part which is being oppressed when he could have rendered assistance, he is considered to have deserted the church."[27] Even more strongly:

> Similarly when all Christian kings are inaugurated, they receive the sword expressly for the protection of the catholic—or whole—church. When they have received it in their hands, they point to all the quarters of the world, and brandish the sword towards the east, west, south, and north, lest any part of the world should be considered exempt. When they undertake the protection of the church in this fashion, they undoubtedly understand it to be the true church, rather than a false one. Therefore they ought to furnish assistance to restore in its entirety that which they profess to be the true and pure church.[28]

This obligation extends not just to Christians but to mankind in general: "Since, Cicero says, the nature of all men is one, nature itself prescribes that man desires to show concern for another man, whoever he may be, for this very reason: that he is a man."[29]

Benevolent intervention was not merely a moral duty for the natural law theorists of this time but also a legal obligation, just as the natural law was not merely a set of moral precepts but a body of law that implied the authority to enforce it. Although the natural law did not specify exactly what sort of authorities these would be—whether princes or emperors or popes—the implication was that whoever they were, they should guarantee that it was followed. This was clearly a holdover from the medieval *res publica christiana*, where nobody's authority was absolutely supreme but everybody was to some degree responsible for justice within the realm. It was a legacy that the natural law advocates wanted to preserve. If natural law restricted sovereignty on behalf of justice, it also ruled out war across borders for the purpose of spreading religion. Religion was a matter of conscience, requiring inward assent, and thus could not be forced. On this key matter, for reasons of natural justice, this tradition differed starkly from the holy-war school, yet it allowed borders to be crossed to remedy certain ills.

The Spanish Catholics, who articulated one version of this approach, wrote in the scholastic tradition of Thomas Aquinas. As trustees and guardians of that tradition, for them the problem was one of adaptation: what would the timeless Gospel, an eternal and natural law governing an organically linked world, mean now that sovereign monarchs warred and bartered with impunity and scant ecclesial or imperial oversight? Victoria and Suarez could accept the general authority of monarchs as another type of authority whose natural basis was the good of the political community and that was to be obeyed by its subjects, but they did not have in mind the modern monarchs, rulers such as Louis XIV and his counterparts of the seventeenth and eighteenth centuries, who exalted their authority as supreme and who held themselves independent of any international obligation except that to which they consented. States were powerful but also bound by eternal duties; they were elevated but obligated—and neither Victoria nor Suarez could countenance a world without some form of substantive papal authority. Although they wanted to limit the pope to churchly powers, they included among these the rather substantial "indirect" temporal power of excommunicating heretical kings, which meant dethroning them.[30]

That the world possessed a moral unity, that authorities were bound to the natural law and to the *jus gentium*—the law of nations that was founded upon the natural law—meant that princes were sometimes required to intervene and enforce the law in another's realm. Suarez writes:

Therefore, although a given sovereign state, commonwealth, or kingdom may constitute a perfect community in itself, consisting of its own members, nevertheless, each one of these states is also, in a certain sense, and viewed in relation to the human race, a member of that universal society; for these states when standing alone are never so self-sufficient that they do not require some mutual assistance, association, and intercourse, at times for their own greater welfare and advantage, but at other times because also of some moral necessity or need. This fact is made manifest by actual usage.[31]

What reasons justified intervention? Only those rooted in natural law, not those based solely on divine revelation. Victoria's most original contribution was *On the Indians*, which he wrote in 1532 to convince Charles V that it was not permissible for Spanish armies to force American natives to convert; Suarez echoed that Christians had no title to rule the infidels.[32] Victoria, however, envisioned intervention when missionaries were harassed, Christians were persecuted by unbelievers, seekers of the faith were hindered from converting, innocent lives were threatened by human sacrifice or cannibalism, trade or passage to foreign lands was blocked, or a population was incapable of self-government.[33] Suarez, more circumspect, was wary that intervention would become a vain pretext and turn into another predatory rationale. He allowed it mainly in cases when a foreign prince forced his Christian subjects to practice idolatry. He argued that this kind of intervention was a precept of natural law, but he did not apply it to non-Christian subjects in Christian lands.[34]

It is not clear exactly how Victoria and Suarez thought that the emperor of the Holy Roman Empire should respond to the Reformation, another kind of pluralism they both thought heretical. Both clearly forbade religious wars, yet they allowed the pope to excommunicate heretics, which they considered the German Protestant princes to be, and they might have argued that the Protestants' seizure of Catholic property was a form of persecuting Christians that was forbidden by natural law. When Victoria wrote *On the Indians*, though, the wars over the Reformation had barely begun, and although Suarez attempted to refute the Lutheran heresies, he never indicated how they should be stopped. We know generally, however, that for Victoria and Suarez it was common reason, not the inflamed particularity of belief, that provided the grounds for intervention.

The Protestants Gentili and Grotius were even more insistent on using only natural law as a foundation for the justice of war. "Let the theologians keep silence about a matter which is outside their province," wrote Gentili.[35] Wars of religion were indubitably unjust for this late sixteenth-century Protestant, and he explicitly condemned contemporary ones. "Religion is a matter of mind and the will, which is always accompanied by freedom . . . Our mind . . . [is] not affected by any external power or potentate, and the soul has no master save God only, who alone can destroy the soul."[36] Violence should not be used against subjects who practiced a religion different from their rulers or against rulers who changed their religion, a prescription both for domestic and international tolerance. Yet Gentili also offered the strongest defense to date of legitimate intervention:

> But so far as I am concerned, the subjects of others do not seem to me to be outside of that kinship of nature and the society formed by the whole world. And if you abolish that society, you will also destroy the union of the human race. . . . And unless we wish to make sovereigns exempt from the law and bound by no statutes and no precedents, there must also of necessity be some one to remind them of their duty and hold them in restraint.[37]

That a Protestant would endorse this notion of the kinship of nature and society is remarkable. In this regard, he is similar to Victoria and Suarez. In the *societas gentium*, the human community in which even barbarians and infidels participate, wars could be fought to secure the "common rights of mankind." Gentili provides no elaborate list of what these rights are, although he mentions the honor of women and, more generally, the victims of "immoderate cruelty and unmerciful punishment."[38]

Hugo Grotius, often praised as the father of international law, is the most famous figure in this natural law tradition. Of its major philosophers, he is the strongest proponent of sovereignty: "That power is called sovereign, whose actions are not subject to the control of any other power, so as to be annulled at the pleasure of any other human will. The term 'any other human will' exempts the sovereign himself from this restriction, who may annul his own acts."[39] Like Bodin, Grotius thought that absolute sovereignty was the only way to maintain order in a world devoid of effective higher authority, yet even sovereigns were bound by the natural law as well as by human international law. Evidently, Grotius too wanted to maintain something of the *res publica christiana*. Any sovereign could intervene in any corner of the globe to right certain wrongs: to prevent cannibalism and the harassment of missionaries, to protect free trade and free seas, and to punish pirates, breakers of treaties, and those who traded with enemy belligerents.[40]

The enthusiasm for sovereignty that Grotius demonstrated in his 1625 *De jure belli ac pacis* was greater than that of the earlier figures in the natural law tradition and intimates a whole new tradition of which he was not yet a member. It is the tradition of absolute sovereignty, unlimited in its prerogatives, unchallengeable, boundless in its authority, ultimate, granting to one government or law supremacy within a territory and inviolability from without. This tradition was articulated best by Bodin and Hobbes, and it complements the doctrine of *raison d'etat* arising from Machiavelli and Richelieu.[41] It is Vattel's tradition, in which the only universal value is sovereignty itself. It is the tradition that triumphed at Westphalia and that came to flourish in an age of increasing religious skepticism. Even during the age of modern constitutionalism, when sovereignty devolved to laws that limited human rulers within boundaries, external sovereignty held firm.

Natural Law and the Limits of State Sovereignty

Today, when the world is still one of sovereign states, yet one in which legitimate limitations on sovereignty are also becoming thinkable, the traditions of early modern Europe offer Christians a menu of responses. Of these, it seems to me, the natural law tradition is the most morally compelling. Why is this tradition more attractive than either the holy-war or the Westphalian traditions? Religious belief cannot be coerced, and to try to force its practice on those who do not accept or understand it is to violate the natural dignity of the person.[42] Wars aimed at conversion or at preventing the practice of beliefs contrary to the Christian faith are thus not only imprudent and unlikely to succeed but are distinctly unjust on Christian grounds. The Westphalian system reaches the other extreme: its premise is that states have no obligations or claims on each other's treatment of their citizens. This the Christian must regard as a moral failure, for it is the institutional abandonment of the *societas gentium*, of a human community bound by justice.

It is ironic that I would find the natural law approach the most compelling, for of the three it was the only one that was not actually practiced in the earlier time. There are reasons, though, to think that its chances are better now than then. First, however, let me state what I think the natural law tradition implies for contemporary institutions and practices of sovereignty. These implications are, of course, large matters. Here I can only sketch its broad outlines and suggest some attendant dilemmas. The unifying intuition is that since our institutions and practices are, with respect to sovereignty, similar to those of early modern Europe and since natural law is eternally valid, then the insights of the natural law tradition into the politics of that period should provide moral guidance for today.

Intervention is the contemporary international issue to which the early modern Europeans devoted the most thought. The basic ingredients of their moral case flow readily from natural law thinking and carry over easily to our own day. Political authority is conditional on the faithfulness of government in upholding the common good. The precise contents of the common good are the subject of a centuries-long conversation within the tradition, but most natural law proponents would agree that it consists of at least maintaining the public peace and the enjoyment of natural rights, including the rights to life and subsistence, freedom of conscience, and freedom from torture and certain physical harms. The government that fails to provide these goods may become subject to intervention. Indeed, the Christian and natural obligation of benevolence suggests that outsiders have a prima facie duty to intervene. It may be limited by the means and consequences of any intervention, but it is a duty nevertheless. I argue, then, for an expansion in the *jus ad bellum* category of just-war theory to include intervention for the purpose of natural justice. The chief difference between early modern Europe—at least the earliest part of it—and today is that, then, the remaining unity of Christendom provided a source of legal authority, whereas, today, this authority is only beginning to develop through the customary law of the United Nations.

The raw materials of this theory—limited government, natural rights, a duty to intervene rooted in benevolence—continue to be upheld in modern natural law thought.[43] This we expect, for natural law would not be natural law if its basic tenets did not endure; yet, to my knowledge, few in the modern Christian just-war tradition have drawn the conclusion that these fundamental tenets imply just intervention.[44] Doubtless, there are good reasons for this, including a preoccupation with nuclear weapons and a general skepticism toward intervention during the Cold War, but if intervention is indeed a natural conclusion of natural law theory, then we should recover the tradition of Victoria, Suarez, Gentili, and Grotius.

A natural law account of justice that calls for limitations on sovereignty has implications not only for intervention but also for other novel institutions and practices. Making the recognition of new states contingent on their degree of domestic justice would be one such practice. Establishing institutions that monitor and enforce elections and human rights would be another. The European Union, however, is different. It, too, represents an evolution from sovereign states to something else. As I noted earlier, the union's complex prerogatives, the extreme version of which is a "Europe at different speeds," evoke a medieval-type intricacy perhaps even more vividly than does humanitarian intervention; but it is a different kind of evolution, one that entails not the prospect of outside enforcement but the supranational pooling of authority over certain areas of policy: commerce, trade, labor, social policy, and so on.[45] About this kind of trend, the early modern Europeans unfortunately have little to say to us. Although they were concerned with spheres of authority, the authority they had in mind was the now-archaic authority of the pope, the emperor, and other claimants. Though papal policy and church-state issues are by all means still important, they are not the central moral concerns raised by the Maastricht Treaty or the Single European Act; instead, the appropriate degree of centralization and democratic accountability are the key normative issues.

If we look at the wider Christian natural law tradition, however, we discover moral insights relevant to these issues. Through several papal encyclicals, one principle in particular has become prominent, the principle of subsidiarity.[46] As Pius XI described it in *Quadragesimo anno*, subsidiarity is the principle "that one should not withdraw from individuals and commit to the community what they can accomplish by their own expertise and industry," nor "transfer to the larger and higher collectivity functions which can be performed and provided for by lesser and subordinate bodies."[47] The subsidiarity principle is related to Alexis de Tocqueville's insight about the enervating effects of centralizing institutions, the democratic insight that people are freer (more morally autonomous) when they participate in directing their own affairs, and the communitarian insight that preserving families and communities ought to be an end of government.

Subsidiarity makes little sense apart from a substantive notion of human flourishing that guides what institutional designs ought to accomplish. We can look to the Christian natural law tradition to provide that criterion. The tradition's conception of justice is historically complex and much debated; however, it usually involves not only a peaceful order and minimal human rights (in the modern versions) but also a positive notion of human flourishing through participation in family and religious communities.[48] In addition, we need to think more systematically about exactly what level of authority is most appropriate to different policy areas. These are matters whose resolution cannot be captured in simple, unitary concepts. We can be sure, though, that subsidiarity will be at the center of the public moral debate on the nature of the European Union. Subsidiarity is written into the preamble to the Maastricht Treaty, and its inclusion in a separate article of the treaty was demanded by Euroskeptics during the debate over ratification. Its meaning, however, is notoriously vague, making systematic Christian reflection all the more imperative.

For the European Union, as well as for practices such as humanitarian intervention, the natural law tradition gives us the outline, if not the full details, of a world that is more just than our Westphalian one. This is not to deny value in Westphalia—sovereign statehood, to the degree that it commands moral force, helpfully preserves the stability of borders and restrains avaricious interference. We must take care not to erode these benefits. Indeed, in envisioning the principles of a more just world, we must generally weigh the consequences of trying to bring it about. In the case of the European Union, it is again difficult to be systematic about the consequences of revising sovereignty; we can only examine the union's institutional innovations piece by piece. About the dilemmas of intervention, though, we can generalize more readily. I can think of three guidelines in particular, and they contribute to the agenda for thinking about sovereignty.

First, what sort of injustices may justly be remedied across borders? Certainly humanitarian disasters that "shock the conscience of mankind," including massive starvation and genocide, qualify. But what about lower levels of human rights violations? Is the denial of democracy a just cause? What about self-determination?[49] The natural law tradition has not considered these questions systematically and that requires that we give them more thought.

Second, as I have argued, the early modern Christian philosophers could assume that the natural law was accompanied by a legal unity that was the legacy of Christendom and that authorized any justly constituted political authority to enforce at least some parts of the natural law in any part of the globe. Today, of course, the legal unity of Christendom is gone. Positive law—what states agree to or regularly practice—is now the only source of legally enforceable obligation. Our task, therefore, is to bring the positive law into closer conformity with the natural law. The recent practice of U.N. intervention in humanitarian disasters is a trend toward some sort of customary right of humanitarian intervention, but it leaves many questions unanswered. Should the U.N. Charter be revised to allow for humanitarian intervention more directly? Should the constitutive post-World War II criterion of "a threat to international peace and security" be preserved? Should we define the sort of cases in which intervention might occur broadly, in order to allow flexibility amidst unpredictable circumstances, or narrowly, to restrict the rationales for intervention?

Third, there is a need to define the parameters of moral prudence. That intervention is morally and legally justified does not mean that it is prudent policy or even moral policy. After all, just-war theory sets forth the probability of success and that an action will be carried out with proportionate means and without harm to noncombatants as basic standards of *jus ad bellum*.

The historical experience of early modern Europe raised acute quandaries for intervention, quandaries that have not altogether disappeared. One is that of deep pluralism: given profound disagreements over religion and morality, can we agree on a common set of moral norms? Samuel Huntington has recently argued that in the coming era the largest international conflicts will occur between "clashing civilizations," suggesting that ideological and religious warfare has not disappeared from our historical era.[50] With respect to intervention, Huntington's scenario could be realized most plausibly in a conflict between the Western permanent members of the Security Council (the United States, Britain, and France), who will argue for intervention in the name of human rights and democracy, and its non-Western members, who will claim that such values are primarily Western and serve as a convenient rationale for domination. The conflict will be more strained and common agreement more elusive the more expansive the Western rationales for intervention become. Our new dilemma is whether, in order to maintain consensus, the West should advocate intervention only in places such as Rwanda and Somalia, where the suffering is worst, or abandon consensus altogether in favor of promoting democracy and human rights more vigorously.

Another quandary involves not the conflict of values but the quest for power. Given that few historical interventions, even ones that achieve humanitarian good, are fully morally motivated, will not a norm of intervention merely lend further legitimacy to the use of arms for the more traditional aims of acquiring land and wealth? Part of this problem could be solved through multilateralism, by making legitimate only those interventions approved by the U.N. Security Council. Even some legal scholars, however, are suspicious that this too would be little more than a Great Power instrument.[51]

Whether reforming Westphalia ultimately makes moral sense will depend on whether these dilemmas are surmountable. If Victoria, Suarez, Gentili, Languet, and Grotius were right in arguing that in a world of sovereign states, sovereignty should not be absolute, then there is a moral case for investigating the prospect and attempting the project of reforming the international order—carefully, incrementally, with cir-cumspection—so that it is a bit more like the one they envisioned. The U.N.-approved interventions of the past half decade offer some evidence that now, unlike then, genuine humanitarian intervention is a real possi-bility. Despite deep pluralism, there is some evidence that at least a few human rights are universally endorsed, if not practiced. The Holocaust and more than four decades of Cold War have brought more nations around the globe to realize that there are some things that governments cannot do anywhere or at any time. For Christians, this is the truth. It is not the whole truth, but it is the part that we share with all people, the part that Saint Paul tells us is written on the human heart—and it is as valid now as it was then.

Endnotes

*I would like to thank John Owen and Timothy Shah for reading the manuscript, and the John M. Olin Institute for Strategic Studies for support while I completed the project.

1. William Shakespeare, *Richard II*, ed. Michael Clamp (Cambridge: Cam-bridge University Press, 1992), 4.1.247–50. For a discussion of Shakespeare's theory of kingship, see Ernst Kantorowicz, *The King's Two Bodies: A Study in Mediaeval Political Theology* (Princeton: Princeton University Press, 1957), 24–42.

2. William Shakespeare, *King Henry V*, ed. Andrew Gurr (Cambridge: Cambridge University Press, 1992), 2.2.170–76. On Shakespeare's understanding of international relations, especially the laws of war, see Theodor Meron, *Henry's Wars and Shakespeare's Laws: Perspectives on the Law of War in the Later Middle Ages* (Oxford: Clarendon, 1993).

3. I accept J. R. Strayer's judgment that the English and French monarchs were sovereign by 1300, though we should keep in mind that two centuries of civil war delayed sovereignty's lasting consolidation. See Strayer, *On the Medie-val Origins of the Modern State* (Princeton: Princeton University Press, 1970), 3–56.

4. Works on the concept of sovereignty are voluminous. Particularly helpful, though, are Alan James, *Sovereign Statehood: The Basis of International Society* (London: Allen and Unwin, 1986), and F. H. Hinsley, *Sovereignty*, 2d ed. (Cambridge: Cambridge University Press, 1986).

5. Jean Bodin, *On Sovereignty*, ed. Julian Franklin (Cambridge: Cambridge University Press, 1992); Thomas Hobbes, *Leviathan*, ed. and intro. C. B. MacPherson (New York: Penguin, 1968); Hugo Grotius, *The Rights of War and Peace*, trans. A. C. Campbell, intro. David J. Hill (Westport, Conn.: Hyperion, 1979); Emerich de Vattel, *The Law of Nations*, 6th ed. (Philadelphia: T and J. W. Johnson, 1844).

6. On the meaning of the body metaphor, see Kantorowicz. For other works on sovereignty, see Ernest Barker, "Medieval Political Thought," in F. J. C. Hearnshaw, ed., *The Social and Political Ideas of Some Great Medieval Thinkers* (London: George G. Harrop, 1923); Robert N. and Alexander J. Carlyle, *A History of Medieval Political Theory in the West*, 6 vols. (London: W. Blackwood and Sons, 1903–36); Otto von Gierke, *Political Theories of the Middle Ages*, trans. F. W. Maitland (Cambridge: Cambridge University Press, 1900); Gaines Post, *Studies in Medieval Legal Thought: Public Law and the State, 1100–1320* (Princeton: Princeton University Press, 1964); Michael Wilks, *The Problem of Sovereignty in the Later Middle Ages* (Cambridge: Cambridge University Press, 1963); Brian Tierney, *The Crisis of Church and State, 1050–1300* (Englewoods Cliffs, N.J.: Prentice Hall, 1964); and Quentin Skinner, *The Foundations of Modern Political Thought*, 2 vols. (Cambridge: Cambridge University Press, 1978).

7. John Gerard Ruggie, "Continuity and Transformation in the World Polity: Toward a Neo-Realist Synthesis," in Robert O. Keohane, ed., *Neorealism and its Critics* (New York: Columbia University Press, 1986), 142.

8. On the nature and dates of the Italian state system, see Martin Wight, *Systems of States* (Leicester: Leicester University Press, 1977).

9. Stephen Krasner attacks the conventional wisdom that Westphalia is the beginning of the sovereign states system and argues that sovereign states were present long before Westphalia and that medieval forms of authority were present long after. I agree that sovereign states preceded Westphalia but, as I argue below, the Holy Roman Empire ceased to exercise any meaningful authority following Westphalia. States, or the equivalent of states, effectively practiced sovereignty. See Stephen Krasner, "Westphalia and All That," in Judith Goldstein and Robert O. Keohane, eds., *Ideas and Foreign Policy: Beliefs, Institutions, and Political Change* (Ithaca, N.Y.: Cornell University Press, 1993), 235–64.

10. There is ample evidence for this in the writings of Cardinal Richelieu and of the Swedish king Gustavus Adolphus, who is rumored to have toted Grotius' writings in his saddlebags. Although both figures had died by the time of Westphalia, their ideas were prominent in the minds of French and Swedish diplomats. On the influence of Richelieu, see William F. Church, *Richelieu and Reason of State* (Princeton: Princeton University Press, 1972); on Grotius's influence on Gustavus Adolphus, see Hedley Bull, "The Importance of Grotius in the Study of International Relations," in Hedley Bull, Benedict Kinsgbury, and Adam Roberts, eds., *Hugo Grotius and International Relations* (Oxford: Clarendon Press, 1990), 75.

11. The quote is from David Maland, *Europe in the Seventeenth Century* (London: Macmillan, 1966), 161. On the pope and the banning of Grotius, see Bull, "The Importance of Grotius."

12. I share Martin Wight's view that Westphalia represents a consolidation of the evolution toward a sovereign state system. See Wight *Systems of States*, 150–52; and also Charles Tilly, *Coercion, Capital, and European States, A.D. 990–1992* (Oxford: Basil Blackwell, 1990), 167.

13. For an assessment of these issues in relation to the U.N. Charter, see Lori Fisler Damrosch, "Commentary on Collective Military Intervention to Enforce Human Rights," in Lori Fisler Damrosch and David J. Scheffer, eds., *Law and Force in the New International Order* (Boulder: Westview, 1991), 215–23, 219. On the Genocide Convention, see David J. Scheffer, "Challenges Confronting Collective Security: Humanitarian Intervention," in David J. Scheffer, Richard N. Gardner, and Gerald B. Helman, eds., *Three Views on the Issue of Humanitarian Intervention* (Washington, D.C.: United States Institute of Peace, 1992), 1–15, 10. The Genocide Convention states in Article 8: "Any Contracting Party may call upon the competent organs of the United Nations to take such action under the Charter of the United Nations as they consider appropriate for the prevention and suppression of acts of genocide or any of the other acts enumerated in Article 3." In Article III, these acts are enumerated: "genocide, conspiracy to commit genocide, direct and public incitement to commit genocide, attempt to commit genocide, and complicity in genocide."

14. On these cases, see Tom J. Farer, "An Inquiry into the Legitimacy of Humanitarian Intervention," in Damrosch and Scheffer, *Law and Force*, 193.

15. See Kelly Kate Pease and David Forsythe, "Human Rights, Humanitarian Intervention, and World Politics," in *Human Rights Quarterly* 15 (1993): 290–314, 302–3.

16. Each intervention has idiosyncrasies that distinguish it from the paradigmatic humanitarian intervention, but it still represents a departure from the Cold War norm of sovereignty in important ways. For instance, Resolution 688, which authorized U.N. action in Iraq, did not actually authorize the use of force, although the intervening powers did in fact use force to back it up. In the case of Somalia, one might argue that there was no functioning state to be intervened against; nevertheless, it was still quite a departure for the United Nations to use force without the consent of parties within the official territorial borders of a state, even one with a defunct government. In the cases of Haiti and Rwanda, the intervention was unilaterally implemented, although the authorization came from the United Nations.

17. A good history of the European Union is Neill Nugent, *The Government and Politics of the European Union*, 3d ed. (Durham, N.C.: Duke University Press, 1994). On sovereignty in the European Union, see Robert O. Keohane and Stanley Hoffmann, "Institutional Change in Europe in the 1980s," in Robert O. Keohane and Stanley Hoffmann, eds., *The New European Community: Decisionmaking and Institutional Challenge* (Boulder: Westview, 1991), 1–40. A couple of other developments in sovereignty are noteworthy. The 1990 Copenhagen Document of the Conference on Security and Cooperation in Europe lists human rights, democracy, and self-determination as fundamental entitlements and prevents sovereignty from being a hurdle to international support for them within European countries. What institutions or policies this implies is not wholly clear, but the commitment has been made. The World Trade Organization, which created a judicial body to adjudicate trade disputes, is also significant.

18. See James Turner Johnson, *Ideology, Reason, and the Limitation of War* (Princeton, N.J.: Princeton University Press, 1975), especially chap. 2. I rely almost exclusively on Johnson for my understanding of the holy-war tradition. See also Roland Bainton, *Christian Attitudes Toward War and Peace: A Historical Survey and Critical Re-evaluation* (New York: Abingdon Press, 1960), especially chap. 9.

19. Johnson, *Ideology, Reason, and the Limitation of War*, 85–105.

20. Johnson, *Ideology, Reason, and the Limitation of War*, 112.

21. Johnson, *Ideology, Reason, and the Limitation of War*, 120.

22. This sort of line is clearest in Gouge. Johnson, *Ideology, Reason, and the Limitation of War*, 121–22.

23. Johnson, *Ideology, Reason, and the Limitation of War*, 123n.

24. Johnson, *Ideology, Reason, and the Limitation of War*, 116.

25. For a helpful account of limitations on sovereignty and the idea of the common rights of mankind, see Theodor Meron, "Common Rights of Mankind in Gentili, Grotius, and Suarez," *American Journal of International Law* 85 (January 1991): 110–16.

26. Hubert Languet, *Vindiciae, contra tyrannos*, ed. and trans. George Garnett (Cambridge: Cambridge University Press, 1994), 174.

27. Languet, *Vindiciae, contra tyrannos*, 175.

28. Languet, *Vindiciae, contra tyrannos*, 175.

29. Languet, *Vindiciae, contra tyrannos*, 181.

30. For the writings of Victoria and Suarez, see Francisco de Vitoria, *Political Writings*, ed. Anthony Pagden and Jeremy Lawrence (Cambridge: Cambridge University Press, 1991); and Francisco Suarez, *Selections from the Three Works*, trans. Gladys L. Williams, Ammi Brown, and John Waldron, intro. James Brown Scott (New York: Oceana, 1964). For a good commentary on the political thought of Victoria and Suarez, see Quentin Skinner, *The Foundations of Modern Political Thought*, vol. 2 (Cambridge: Cambridge University Press, 1978).

31. Suarez, *Selections from the Three Works*, 349.

32. Skinner, *Foundations of Modern Political Thought*, 169–71.

33. J. Bryan Hehir, "The Ethics of Intervention: United States Policy in Vietnam (1961–68)" (Ph.D. diss., Harvard University, 1976), 59–61.

34. See Johnson, *Ideology, Reason, and the Limitation of War*, 167.

35. Alberico Gentili, *De iure belli libri tres* (Oxford: Clarendon Press, 1933), 57.

36. Gentili, *De iure belli libri tres*, 38.

37. Gentili, *De iure belli libri tres*, 74, also quoted in Meron, "Common Rights of Mankind," 115.

38. Gentili, *De iure belli libri tres*, 76.

39. Grotius, *The Rights of War and Peace*, 62.

40. Hehir, 75–76.

41. On *raison d'etat*, see Friedrich Meinecke, *Machiavellianism*, trans. Douglas Scott, intro. W. Stark (Boulder: Westview, 1984).

42. This position is not universally accepted within the Christian natural law tradition. Some would argue that to the degree that religious freedom is defensible, it is only on grounds of prudence. My own position is informed by the writings of John Finnis, *Natural Law and Natural Rights* (Oxford: Clarendon Press, 1980), and Pope John XXIII, "Pacem in terris," in David J. O'Brien and Thomas A. Shannon, *Catholic Social Thought* (Maryknoll, N.Y.: Orbis, 1992). Much of the debate between the two positions has centered around the interpretation of the writings of John Courtney Murray. See Keith J. Pavlischek, *John Courtney Murray and the Dilemma of Religious Toleration* (Kirksville, Mo.: Thomas Jefferson University Press, 1994).

43. See Finnis, *Natural Law and Natural Rights*; Pope John XXIII, "Pacem in terris"; Jacques Maritain, *Man and the State* (Chicago: University of Chicago Press, 1950); Paul Ramsey, *The Just War* (New York: Scribner's, 1968); and The United States Catholic Bishops, *The Challenge of Peace: God's Promise and Our Response*, reprinted in O'Brien and Shannon, eds., *Catholic Social Thought*, 492–571.

44. There are a handful of exceptions, including James Turner Johnson's own piece in this volume. Michael Walzer has also argued for humanitarian intervention, though not on the basis of the Christian just-war tradition. See his *Just and Unjust Wars* (New York: Basic, 1977), 101–8.

45. On the term "pooling," see Robert O. Keohane and Stanley Hoffmann, "Institutional Change in Europe in the 1980s," in Robert O. Keohane and Stanley Hoffmann, eds., *The New European Community: Decisionmaking and Institutional Change* (Boulder: Westview, 1991), 7–8.

46. In O'Brien and Shannon's *Catholic Social Thought*, see Pope Leo XIII's 1891 encyclical "Rerum novarum," 12–39, Pius XI's 1931 "Quadregessimo anno," 40–79, and John XXIII's 1962 "Pacem in terris," 129–62.

47. O'Brien and Shannon, *Catholic Social Thought*, 60.

48. On subsidiarity and the common good, see Joan Lockwood O'Donovan, "Political Authority and European Community: The Challenge of the Christian Political Tradition," *Scottish Journal of Theology* 47 (Winter 1994): 1–18.

49. There is considerable debate between Michael Walzer and his critics on the level of human rights violations required for intervention to be warranted. Walzer wants to restrict intervention to collosal humanitarian disasters, while his critics do not want to rule out intervention against more "ordinary cruelty." See Walzer, *Just and Unjust Wars*, 101–8; and the criticism of David Luban's articles with Walzer's response, collected in Charles Beitz, Marshall Cohen, Thomas Scanlon, and A. John Simmons, *International Ethics* (Princeton, N.J.: Princeton University Press, 1985): David Luban, "Just War and Human Rights," 195–216; Michael Walzer, "The Moral Standing of States: A Response to Four Critics," 217–37; and David Luban, "The Romance of the Nation-State," 238–43.

50. Samuel P. Huntington, "The Clash of Civilizations?" *Foreign Affairs* 72:3 (Summer 1993): 22–49.

51. See Damrosch, "Commentary," in *Law and Force*, 220–22.

Natural Law Before and After Sovereignty: A Response to Daniel Philpott

James Skillen

Daniel Philpott has shown that the constitution of international relations that took shape after the European Peace of Westphalia was not one in which states, already self-sufficient, met to declare themselves henceforth sovereign and unencumbered; rather, a treaty representing an international consensus (albeit one reached after years of warfare), gave recognition to a newly emergent distribution of political power and authority. The new arrangement of relatively independent states had differentiated itself with great difficulty from an earlier, more organic, medieval arrangement that was, as Philpott describes it, without sovereignty. It was not that late medieval Christendom had no political power and authority but pope, emperor, ecclesiastical and secular courts, lords, kings, and other authorities exercised their various powers in overlapping and often conflicting ways, quite different from the pattern that emerged after Westphalia.

The important point I want to emphasize here, drawing from Philpott's historical description, is that the new states claimed their sovereignty in an international context of assent, which, to some degree, helped constitute the rules and terms of their sovereignty from outside that sovereignty. In other words, the constitution of international relations that emerged with the birth of the sovereign states was to a certain degree transnational and nonarbitrary in character. Sovereignty was not as autonomously sovereign as the word might suggest.

We should, furthermore, note that the post-Westphalian order was one in which each new state claimed and exercised less authority than had been claimed and exercised by the intertwined Roman Catholic Church and Holy Roman Empire. At the same time, this reconfiguring of political power within multiple state borders gave each state greater capability of actually establishing public law and order within its borders. The new sovereignty represented a concentration of political power but also a delimiting and differentiating of political authority. States as well as churches (Roman Catholic and various Protestant movements) began to take on sharper definition in distinction from one another. We might say that the modern system of states exhibited a double differentiation from the medieval world of universal Christendom that had gradually proven incapable of maintaining order and peace across the whole of Europe. This double differentiation involved, first of all, the emergence of relatively independent states, each with a narrower but more clearly defined political authority than Christendom had had. It also entailed the concentration of these separate political sovereignties within mutually exclusive boundaries that were smaller in each case than the boundaries claimed by the dominant authorities of Christendom.

In the light of Philpott's argument, therefore, we can see that the proper historical starting point for thinking about the modern question of sovereignty is not with an imaginary array of autonomous and unbounded states, each of which functions solely according to its own law and recognizes nothing superior to itself. We must begin rather with the historical reality of a multinational Christendom in which wars, ecclesiastical conflicts, and overseas explorations were leading to the redefinition and reconfiguration of legitimate, competent political authority. That process of redefinition and reconfiguration led to both a domestic individualizing of political power and to an international agreement about the political reordering of Europe. In other words, the differentiation of relatively independent states from a weakening Christendom represented, simultaneously, the redefinition of the constitution of international relations. Among other things, this process gave birth to norms of sovereignty that, as Philpott explains, at least in part constituted those states from above, from outside their self-declared sovereignty.

Unlike the Westphalian era, our problem or challenge at the end of the twentieth century, according to Philpott, is not that of trying to figure out how to shift from a less differentiated, organic Christendom to a more differentiated system of states, churches, and other institutions but rather one of learning how to redefine both a domestic and international political order for an increasingly differentiated but also increasingly integrated political world. In these circumstances the sovereignty ideal that emerged with Westphalia appears increasingly unfit for global political reality, just as the earlier Christendom ideal showed itself to be increasingly inadequate by the time of the Peace of Westphalia. The modern tradition of absolute sovereignty, which, as Philpott explains, came to mean that a state is "unlimited in its prerogatives, unchallengeable, boundless in its authority, ultimate, granting to one government or law supremacy within a territory and inviolability from without" (Philpot, 53), is itself a tradition in crisis. Emerich de Vattel's maxim that the "only universal value is sovereignty itself" (53) now appears to be quite insufficient in a world where increasingly interdependent states are forced to spend more and more time defining the transnational rules of their interdependence. Clearly, at both the international and domestic levels, important constitutional redefinitions are necessary.

In this century, of course, states have been redefining themselves as they have expanded and thickened the web of international treaties through which their sovereignty is more and more restricted, and some of the treaties are helping constitute ever more powerful transnational institutions such as the European Union. It is clear that the kind of sovereignty once associated with autonomous states has been giving way for some time. Likewise, the definition of a legitimate state in its internal or domestic character has also been undergoing revision at the international level. There is less and less willingness on the part of states simply to bow before another state's inviolable sovereignty by virtue of the fact that one regime or another claims a monopoly of power within its own territory. The international acceptance of human rights standards, democratic governance patterns, and other domestically relevant criteria have, in important ways, led many countries as well as the United Nations to be less willing to refrain from interference in countries where, though members of the United Nations, governments are acting in defiance of internationally accepted standards or have collapsed altogether.

These developments suggest that, of necessity, the exercise of state power increasingly must comply with internationally agreed-on norms for domestic conduct as well as with the rules of behavior of various international treaties. To be sure, the separate states and the state system are not about to collapse or dissolve into a single, undifferentiated, worldwide political entity, but the very meaning of sovereignty, which has always to some extent been grounded in an international web of legal norms, is becoming qualified more and more by the very thickness of an international network of human relations that requires just governance across and above state boundaries as well as within them.

This is the historical setting in which Philpott argues that the time has come to try to transcend sovereignty in our thinking and to begin doing so by trying to give a normative account of the challenge to sovereignty that is already being presented by various internationally agreed-on benevolent interventions. To do this we will need to make and defend moral and legal arguments about the legitimacy of interventionist actions. How will this be possible? Philpott properly recognizes that questions of justice, authority, legitimacy, legality, and jurisdiction come to the fore in a fresh and urgent way as soon as we enter this arena, and he makes the case for returning to the natural law tradition in order to conduct such moral arguments. Can that be done successfully? How much weight can the natural law tradition bear in this post-Westphalian, and possibly postsovereignty, era?

If we look back to the late medieval period, we might say that natural law philosophy was able to serve as the framework for moral reasoning and normative political/legal judgment because it was part of a relatively less differentiated, religious-political-legal matrix, a matrix with a single, supreme, institutional authority: the church. After political and religious diversity emerged to the point where the older organic matrix could no longer function, the problem became how to delimit and reconstitute newly differentiating political-legal entities ("states") from ecclesiastical, scientific, artistic, and other realms of life. What happened was not simply that states displaced the empire while otherwise continuing to uphold a common, transcendent religious and cultural order; rather, the differentiation of modern states went hand in hand with the differentiation of ecclesiastical, scientific, economic, artistic, and educational authority.

The Peace of Westphalia sought in one way to answer the question of political-legal commonality in face of the differentiation of sovereign states. It did not go very far, however, in fashioning a common understanding of the new order as one that would eventually have to depend on transnational legal and political norms transcending simple strategies for the balance of power, nor did the sovereignty system advance a detailed, normative definition of what makes for a just state. Once that system of sovereign states gained historical dominance, of course, no state or group of states had sufficient enforcement power to impose on others a universal definition of either a just state or a just interstate system.

Today, however, the sovereignty system can no longer afford to ignore the need for normative reasoning at the transnational level. The dominant image of international politics as a balance-of-power system in which transcendent norms are either irrelevant or serve merely as a means to the primary end of advancing the national interest is only half a picture, only a half truth. The other half of the picture includes the reality of diplomats from these sovereign states struggling to devise rules that support but also, of necessity, restrict sovereignty, rules of a supra-arbitrary nature that carry real moral weight. To whatever extent leaders once believed that sovereignty was the only universal value, they must today, increasingly, invoke values that transcend absolute sovereignty. In sum, moral argument about legal and political norms is unavoidable.

Can the older natural law tradition be recovered, however, for the task of debating universal, supra-arbitrary political and legal standards when peoples and states the world over have for so long taken sovereignty for granted as the premier, normative principle of law and government? How likely is this recovery when the pressing need for international moral reasoning arises not from within Christendom but in a shrinking globe of states with widely divergent cultures and religions? The line of questioning I would follow to engage Philpott at this juncture concerns the natural law tradition's capability of dealing with the differentiated complexity of modern states and societies in the rapidly integrating world that we know today.

Natural law thinking emerged from and harks back to a relatively undifferentiated medieval and early modern world in which law had its meaning in the social, political, and religious context of Christendom prior to, or near the time of, the emergence of sovereign states. One paragraph from Philpott's essay helps to illustrate my point. In the sixteenth century, says Philpott, the approval of benevolent intervention by an outside authority was justified by natural law theorists not merely as "a moral duty . . . but also a legal obligation, just as the natural law was not merely a set of moral precepts but a body of law that implied the authority to enforce it." He continues:

Although the natural law did not specify exactly what sort of authorities these would be—whether princes or emperors or popes—the implication was that whoever they were, they should guarantee that it was followed. This was clearly a holdover from the medieval *Res publica christiana*, where nobody's authority was absolutely supreme but everybody was to some degree responsible for justice within the realm. It was a legacy that the natural law advocates wanted to preserve (50).

As this paragraph suggests, a sixteenth-century appeal to natural law (as was true earlier) was an appeal to universal, moral principles that any authority should recognize as obligatory and capable of legal expression. Whether the authorities were political or ecclesiastical, high or low, they all should feel the binding force of one natural law. The very nature of post-Westphalian developments, however, was one of institutional differentiation—not only diverse states from the empire, but states from church, and eventually economic, scientific, and educational institutions from both states and churches. The religious wars helped produce the conviction that churches should enforce a different kind of law than states. Natural law as a single, integrative norm for an entire social order served Christendom for a while, but in order to serve today as the guide to positive legal and political judgments in highly differentiated societies and the world, the natural law framework would have had to guide the historical process that led to the differentiation of political, ecclesiastical, scientific, and other jurisdictions of authority. The challenge today for normative, ethical thinking about international justice, however, is not only that the sovereignty system may be inadequate but that the dominant framework for moral reasoning about politics and law, in the West at least, is not Christian.

Insofar as Philpott is struggling to find a mode of reasoning that can openly appeal to transsubjective norms by which to guide and judge the actions of states and individuals, then a return to natural law thinking can serve as a helpful reminder of the way that Aristotelian, Thomistic, and Grotian variants of such thinking worked. Reasoning about and judging the legitimacy of contemporary political actions such as benevolent intervention, however, will require a framework that has clearly differentiated the various kinds of normative, institutional obligations that belong to human beings. If, from a Christian point of view, one cannot first make a strong case for what a state ought to be in relation to the transnational political obligations of all states and if one cannot clearly distinguish this political jurisdiction from ecclesiastical, economic, artistic, scientific, familial, and other realms, then it seems to me that it will not be possible to distinguish legitimate interventions that aim to advance international justice from mere imperial overreach on the part of the intervening power or powers.

What Christians need today is not greater sharpness and sophistication in moral reasoning within a natural law framework about, for example, particular cases of intervention but, rather, much greater normative clarity about the specifically *political* obligations of state and transstate actors in an increasingly interdependent world of differentiated states and societies. The international constitution of states—the treaty structure of the state system—demands greater detailed specification both of its own identity as a normatively ordered system of justice and of what each state should in fact be in order to be recognized as a legitimate bearer of political authority.

Philpott states that Francisco de Victoria, Francisco Suarez, Alberico Gentili, Hubert Languet, and Hugo Grotius were right in arguing that "sovereignty should not be absolute," and he wants to make a moral case for reforming our international order "so that it is a bit more like the one they envisioned" (57–58). If Philpott means that he wants to help make the case for a norm of international justice that will relativize the ideal of absolute sovereignty, then I want to work with him in the Christian effort to articulate the meaning of such a universal, transnational, God-given obligation. If Philpott's aim is, however, to take us back three or four or five hundred years into a world "like the one they envisioned," then I am afraid he will get no farther than to recall the conditions that helped to produce the victory of absolute sovereignty over an institutionally inflexible ideal of transnational justice.

Chapter 3

Kantian Ethics, International Politics, and the Enlargement of the *Foedus Pacificum*

John Hare

This chapter is about the relation between Immanuel Kant's ethical theory and his hope for a gradual enlargement of what he called the *foedus pacificum*, which I translate as "pacific union." It was Kant's astonishing prediction, in the 1790s, that liberal democracies would not fight with each other and that the resulting zone of peace would gradually expand (though not without setback and tragedy). When he wrote, there were three regimes that qualified under his criteria;[1] there are now about fifty. What is truly remarkable is that his prediction has turned out right. In the last two hundred years, there have been no wars among liberal democratic states.[2] I return to this historical claim in the final section of this chapter.

My main point is that the enlarging of the community of market democracies is, if Kant is right, also the enlarging of the zone of peace. This is one fundamental rationale for a policy of promoting democracy worldwide. It was Woodrow Wilson's rationale and it is one rationale of President Bill Clinton's foreign policy, for example, in Haiti; thus, as Clinton's national security advisor, Anthony Lake, has stated, "The successor to a doctrine of containment must be a strategy of enlargement, enlargement of the world's free community of market democracies."[3] After the Cold War, with containment no longer an appropriate focus, the rhetoric of enlargement keeps us in the same family of metaphors but suggests a generous rather than a defensive posture.

In the first part of this chapter I describe briefly Kant's ethical theory and then discuss at greater length how he gets from this theory to the optimism of his prediction about the pacific union. In that context I wish to say something about the relation of Kant's theory to the debate between realists and idealists. In principle, the distinction between realism and idealism that so pervades the literature on international relations cuts across ethical theories. In practice, the most conspicuous American realists in this century have been Kantians in their ethical theory (though not in their application of the theory to the conduct of international relations). The idealists, however, also reach conclusions similar to Kant's, even though they start from rather different premises. In the second part of this chapter I discuss what seems to me the major objection to Kantian ethical theory that has arisen in the professional literature in the last fifteen years. This is the objection from particularity. The objection can be found in some recent communitarian writings, in feminist ethics, and in the work of certain ethicists who are neither communitarian nor feminist. I claim that there is a form of this objection that succeeds. Finally, in the third part of the chapter, I try to link this objection to some hesitations about Kant's prediction and optimism about the enlargement of the pacific union. My claim is that what I call "the cosmopolitan agenda" may actually undo liberal regimes in certain circumstances or cause them to decay. I also claim that this cosmopolitan agenda can make conflict between liberal and nonliberal regimes more likely, as well as more damaging.

Kant's Ethical Theory and the Pacific Union

I will describe Kant's ethical theory in a slightly unfamiliar way in order to make vivid the difference between his theory and the objection to it that I discuss in the next section. Kant holds that the supreme principle of morality is a Categorical Imperative, which he formulates in various ways.[4] I will start with two of them, the Formula of Universal Law and the Formula of the End in Itself. I suggest later that in one very natural construal these formulas diverge. In Kant's view, however, they are different formulas or formulations of the same imperative.

The Formula of Universal Law requires that I act only on maxims that I can will as universal law. The clearest account of the formula is that it requires a willingness to continue adherence to the prescription that generates an action even if all individual reference is excluded from the prescription.[5] Kant does not put his point this way himself; this way of putting it relies on developments in logical theory since his death. It clarifies, however, at least part of what Kant means by calling his formula "the Formula of Universal Law."

Suppose, remarkably, that Julius Caesar is thinking morally about whether he should cross the Rubicon. His opponents have disregarded Mark Antony's veto, invoked martial law against Caesar, and ignored his immunity from prosecution; but if he crosses the river with his army out of his province into Italy proper, it will be an act of war. Eliminating individual or singular reference would require eliminating reference to the Rubicon, to Italy, to Mark Antony, and most importantly, to himself. We could think, then, of replacing these individual references with purely universal terms. What would guide us in this replacement is the same as what would guide us if we were moving from a singular instance of a natural phenomenon to the universal law that it instantiates. Reason works the same way in this respect in science and in morals. Suppose I throw a particular stone at a particular window at a particular time, and the window breaks. Assuming the regularity of nature, I can move to the law that whenever anybody throws a stone of this mass (specified in purely universal terms), at this kind of sheet of glass (specified in purely universal terms) the glass will break, other things being equal. This is what the scientist is after. In the same way, Julius Caesar should be able to move, according to the Formula of Universal Law, from his individual maxim about crossing the river to the maxim that anyone in this kind of situation (illegally threatened with prosecution, on the brink of starting a civil war, with at least an even chance of securing ultimate power) should make this sort of threat (universally specified) against this sort of opponent (universally specified), other things being equal. What will guide the replacement in both cases is the need to preserve in the new principle what made the old principle acceptable.

The second famous statement of the Categorical Imperative is the Formula of the End in Itself: "Act in such a way that you always treat humanity, whether in your own person or in the person of any other, never simply as a means, but always at the same time as an end." We can understand this formula better in the language I have used to describe the first formula. In its universal and maximally specific form, the maxim of my action will apply to the hypothetical situation in which the roles of the parties in the actual situation are exactly reversed.[6] Suppose Julius Caesar were in exactly the situation of, say, Pompey, and Pompey were in exactly his, would he still be prepared to will the maxim that Pompey should take his army back into Italy? Suppose the maxim involves starting a civil war, the loss of thousands of lives, and the end of the republic?

The constraint in the Formula of the End in Itself is that the maxim of an action must be such that any other free and rational agent can adopt it. Treating humanity as an end in itself is, for Kant, respecting our capacity for free and rational choice; in his term, it is respecting our *autonomy*. I am constrained, according to this formula, by the consideration that it is wrong, other things being equal, to impede the agency of others. To treat another human being as merely a means is to ignore the other as a center of agency. The best cases here are those of coercion and deception. To take an unproblematic case of coercion, if I take the hand of one of the students in my class and with it I strike the neighboring student's face, I have bypassed the first student's agency. I have treated her merely as a means, as though she were merely an organic hitting implement. The same is true of deception, because a person cannot make a free and rational choice for a situation where the nature of the situation has been concealed.

Kant goes further. He says that this second formula of the Categorical Imperative requires me to endeavor to further the ends of others, "for the ends of a subject who is an end in himself must, if this conception is to have its *full* effect in me, be also, as far as possible, *my* ends," (98, 430). I am required, that is, to share as far as possible the ends of others. How far does Kant think this possible? At least the requirement is limited by the need for the ends of the other person to conform also to the categorical imperative. I am not required, that is, to share immoral ends. To return to the example of Julius Caesar, he has to share the ends of the thousands who will die in the civil war, but he does not have to share the ends of his opponents in illegally prosecuting him. To put this in the terms used earlier, an agent has to will for the hypothetical situation in which she has the (morally permissible) ends of those affected by her actions as well as the ends she has in the actual situation.

Kant claims that reason requires adherence to the Categorical Imperative. One way he explains this is by stating that self-contradiction is involved in the failure to adhere. I do not have time here to describe his argument. I do, however, want to end this section with one more formula. Kant draws his two statements of the Categorical Imperative together into a third statement, the Formula of the Kingdom of Ends. His idea is that we are to act as though we were, through our maxims, law-making members of a "Kingdom of Ends." He characterizes this Kingdom of Ends as "a systematic union of rational beings under common objective laws" (100, 433). All rational agents are subject to the universal laws that they themselves make, and these laws require them to treat each other as ends in themselves. They thus together comprise a kingdom constituted by these laws. This kingdom, Kant says, has members and a head. The head is also a member, being a rational agent himself but he (unlike the others) is an infinite rational agent, being a maker of laws but not himself subject to the will of any other.

How does Kant get from his ethical theory to his prediction about the *foedus pacificum* to which I drew attention at the start? The place to begin, I think, is with what Kant says about the highest good. I will use mostly his work *Religion within the Limits of Reason Alone* (henceforth, *Religion*), since this is his most sustained treatment of the topic. To those who have read only the *Groundwork of the Metaphysic of Morals*, this work is a great surprise. In the secondary literature Kant has often been accused of going soft at the end of his life, or "tailoring his rhetoric" to fit the Prussian censor.[7] In *Religion*, Kant introduces a great deal of Christian doctrine, and it is hard to pin down the spirit in which he does this.[8] The highest good is the goal that our reason sets for us, and Kant gives us two versions, a more ambitious and a less ambitious. The less ambitious version is that the highest good is a system in which happiness is proportional to virtue, so that the virtuous are happy and the nonvirtuous are not. The more ambitious version is a state of the world in which all people put the previously mentioned system into operation by being virtuous; so that everyone is virtuous and everyone is happy. This kingdom is, in its universality, like the Kingdom of Ends already mentioned, but the condition is added that the members of this kingdom attain the appropriate reward for their virtue in their happiness.

There is, however, an obstacle to the highest good in the more ambitious sense, and that is, according to Kant, the human propensity to evil. He acknowledges that there is, even prior to this propensity, a predisposition to good; but the predisposition to good is overlaid with a propensity to evil. This propensity is explained as the adoption of the evil maxim, which I mentioned earlier, that subordinates duty to the inclinations. What we have here is Kant's translation, within the limits of reason alone, of the doctrines of creation and fall. The radical evil, which consists in this subordination of duty, makes necessary a similar translation of the Christian doctrines of redemption and the second coming.

First, let us consider Kant's translation of the doctrine of redemption. "Ought," Kant says, "implies can." To put this the other way around, if it is not the case that I can do something, then it is not the case that I ought to do it. We can legitimately hold people accountable only to standards that they are able to reach, but the propensity to evil means that the ground of all our maxims is corrupt. What is needed is what Kant calls a "revolution of the will" to reverse the priority of inclinations and duty. We could accomplish such a thing only, however, by willing good maxims, and this is, by hypothesis, not possible for us. If it is not the case, however, that we can accomplish the revolution of the will, it is not the case that we ought to, and then it will not be the case that we can, or ought to, live by the moral law. This is a conclusion he cannot accept.

To solve this difficulty, Kant appeals to a translation of the Christian doctrine of redemption within the limits of reason alone. "Ought implies can" does not itself imply "Ought implies can by our own devices." Kant preserves the coherence of his moral theory in light of his belief in radical evil by postulating the possibility of divine assistance, or a "divine supplement," in accomplishing the revolution of the will. In this connection he uses the language of call, election, atonement, and justification; yet all of this doctrine has to be translated within the limits of reason alone, and that means at least that Kant has to exclude reference to historical events. The process is like universalizing the maxim of an action, and the result is that the translated doctrine cannot refer to a fall in Eden or redemption on Calvary. It is a long discussion whether the doctrines translated in this way can do the work that Kant needs them to do.[9]

So far, however, we have a merely individualistic account of an interior revolution in a person's will. The highest good, in the more ambitious sense, requires a social analogue, and this creates an additional difficulty. Following Rousseau, Kant locates an occasion for our fall in the influence of the association with other people. "Envy, the lust for power, greed, and the malignant inclinations bound up with these, besiege his nature, contented within itself, as soon as he is among men."[10] It does not even have to be evil people he associates with: "it suffices that they are at hand, that they surround him, and that they are men, for them mutually to corrupt each other's predispositions and make one another evil." However much, therefore, a single individual may have done to throw off the sovereignty of evil, there is still need for an alliance of men counteracting evil with united forces in order to prevent him falling back under its dominion. We can hope for the victory of the good over the evil principle only through the establishment and spread of a society constituted in accordance with, and for the sake of, the laws of virtue. "We can already see that this duty [to work toward a universal republic based on laws of virtue] will require the presupposition of another idea, namely, that of a higher moral Being through whose universal dispensation the forces of separate individuals, insufficient in themselves, are united for a common end," (89, 97). With this new idea, we can have the prospect of the church militant becoming finally the changeless and all-unifying church triumphant (106, 115). Here is Kant's translation of the Christian doctrine of the second coming.

There is a large hermeneutical difficulty with Kant's thought that I will mention only in passing. The difficulty is in knowing to what extent he thinks this ideal is realizable in history. In *Religion*, he gives the impression that there are empirical warrants for believing in the moral progress of humanity, but the notion of noumenal history is paradoxical given Kant's usual views about the world of noumena, or things in themselves, a world that includes our rational wills. Kant scholars disagree widely. The position on one side is that Kant acknowledged at the end of his life "the fundamental temporality of human moral agency."[11] In this view Kant no longer maintains the sharp distinction between the exterior (legal) and the interior (moral) realms, which is the practical complement of the metaphysical distinction between the phenomenal (or sensible) and the noumenal (or intelligible). The highest good, which we have a duty to work toward, becomes a this-worldly ethical commonwealth. On the other side are many texts even in Kant's late work that maintain a sharp exterior/interior distinction and point to the realization of the Kingdom of God not in this world but in the next.

I am myself persuaded that Kant's overall position is that there is a disjunction between the hope for political and cultural improvement (a juridicocivil society *in accordance with* the laws of virtue), which is a worldly telos, and the hope for moral or religious completion (an ethical commonwealth *for the sake of* the laws of virtue), which is otherworldly.[12] Kant is not, in this view, holding out the prospect that human beings might cease on the earth to live torn between the two worlds,[13] but he does offer the hope for progress in history toward a political and juridical commonwealth that is in accordance with the moral law.

Little by little, those that have power will use less violence, and obedience to the laws will increase. There will arise in the body politic perhaps more charity and less strife in law suits, more reliability in keeping one's word, etc., partly out of love of honor, partly out of well-understood self-interest. And eventually this will also extend to nations in their external relations towards one another up to the realization of the cosmopolitan society, *without the moral foundation* of mankind having to be enlarged in the least.[14]

On the other hand, a perfect moral kingdom on earth is "an unachievable Idea."[15]

There are two lines of argument that lead to the hope for a pacific union. The first is a transcendental argument, the second an empirical one. In other words, while the second derives from experience, the first derives from considerations of the conditions for the possibility of experience. In the first argument, we have to believe in providence moving us toward the highest good, which is the ideal prescribed by reason. We have to believe in this since otherwise we could not, given radical evil and the fact that we are instruments of evil to each other, maintain our commitment to the ideal; but the ethical commonwealth cannot be brought about except on the basis of a juridicocivil society.[16] We can therefore have the hope that providence will bring about the latter, as a step toward the former. Kant notes, however, that a single juridicocivil society is not enough for the highest good. What is required is a combination of such societies, so that they do not become the occasion for each other's downfall. Providence therefore provides mechanisms for both transitions, both the transition to the single society and the transition to a federation of states. Part of the mechanism is commerce, part is "unsocial sociability"—the very vices of individuals and states that are used to promote their union.

The second argument, which is derived from experience, takes a look at the history of the human race, and draws comfort. It looks at the giving of the law on Sinai and then at the replacement of the particular covenant with the Jews by a covenant with God's people of any race and tribe. It looks at the gradual move toward republican forms of government and especially the widespread moral approval of the goals of the French and American revolutions. It sees in this history a reason for hope in a certain direction in which providence is moving us, although there may be setbacks and regressions.

I want to note three related things about Kant's view. First, it operates on some of the same premises about human nature as do those of Reinhold Niebuhr and Hans Morgenthau.[17] I said earlier that the most conspicuous American realists in this century have been Kantian in their ethics, though not in their application of ethics to international relations. Kant starts from radical evil, from what Luther calls the bondage of the will. Niebuhr takes a similar two-worlds view, quoting Luther and insisting that the essential characteristic of Christian love is self-sacrifice. It is reasonable to hope for love, Niebuhr thinks, in a tainted form from individuals in some contexts; but it is never reasonable to hope for it from groups. Niebuhr distances himself from both natural law (which he thinks too optimistic about our knowledge) and utilitarianism (which he thinks too optimistic about our moral nature because it tries to assert the essentially ethical nature of politics). Morgenthau attended Niebuhr's lectures at Harvard and called him the greatest political thinker of his generation. For Morgenthau, as for Niebuhr, morality characteristically demands complete self-sacrifice, and we cannot achieve this politically because we are infected by the *animus dominandi.* He quotes Luther here, just as Niebuhr does. International politics, in this view, is by definition a struggle for power.

In the light of the realist argument, Kant's position seems paradoxical. He seems to start with the premises of the realist and end with the conclusions of the liberal idealist. The key here is to see that Kant can get from his premise about radical evil to his conclusion about the *foedus pacificum* only because he adds the possibility of divine assistance. This is the second point I wish to make, for without this additional theological context, Kant is vulnerable to the realist attack against the liberals' pie-eyed optimism. Kant's liberal followers have dropped the theological context and thus made themselves liable to the charge that they have not taken seriously what the theological sources call original sin.

The third point I want to make is that both Kant and Niebuhr are strikingly rigid in their refusal to allow moral worth to local attachments. For Kant, all actions (both individual and political) are either under the good maxim, which subordinates inclination to duty, or the evil maxim, which subordinates duty to inclination. Local attachment is in itself what he calls "pathological love." He contrasts it to "practical love," which is a duty and which therefore regards all rational beings as equally ends in themselves, to be respected as authors of the moral law. I am not suggesting that Kant forbids local obedience, for example, to one's prince. He thinks, rather, that duty requires it; but duty requires it only as a vehicle, just as it requires subscription to historical revelation as a vehicle. Here, "vehicle" should not be taken merely as "means" but as "outward expression." Local attachment does not have moral value in itself.

In a similar fashion Niebuhr gives several explanations as to why, in his view, groups are inevitably selfish. Social groups, he says, are held together by emotion rather than reason. They are therefore less likely to feel moral constraints, since these cannot operate in the absence of a high level of rationality; moreover, even altruism on the part of the individual is corrupted and "slewed into nationalism," since what is outside the nation is "too vague to inspire devotion."[18] Here the implication is that love of the nation cannot be in itself a moral emotion, first because morality operates at the level of rationality, not emotion, and second because it is human beings as such ("what is outside the nation") who are the proper objects of moral respect.

The Objection from Particularity

In the second part of this chapter I discuss what seems to me the most important objection in the recent literature to Kant's ethical theory. I call the objection "particularist," and I end up endorsing it, although there are many versions of the objection that seem to me mistaken. The important question for us, however, is not so much whether the objection is right but what impact it has, if it is right, on Kant's view of the pacific union.

Aristotle does not endorse impartiality in a Kantian sense. For him, the man of practical wisdom is not required to treat all human beings affected by his action as ends in themselves. Morality is particularist in the sense that moral obligation is tied to the members of the agent's own community and reference to the agent cannot be eliminated. The question I now want to raise is whether all moral judgments are universalizable. The particularist objection claims that not all are (though in my usage, a particularist may claim that many are.) I have discussed how Kant's ethical theory, together with his anthropology, generates the hopeful prediction about the pacific union. If the ethical theory has to be qualified, however, then we should also expect certain qualifications with respect to this hopeful prediction.

I start by discounting one way in which this objection is often made. It is sometimes said that moral judgments must often be specific whereas the universalist requires them to be general.[19] We have to make here two distinctions: the first between general and specific, and the second between universal and particular. A principle is universal if it is stated in purely universal terms, without singular reference. There can be both specific universal judgments, describing situations in minute and specific detail but in universal terms, and general particular judgments, such as "All Americans are morally good." In this objection, then, there is a valid point against any account of the moral demand that fails to acknowledge the need for sensitive moral perception of the relevant details in particular situations. Kant, in his examples, is guilty of this (though not in his theory, I think, given the large role he gives to judgment). But we do not yet have a valid objection against universalism as I defined it.[20]

The particularist objection is that not all moral judgments are fully universalizable. I will call the species of moral judgment from which singular terms are not eliminable, "particular." It is helpful to see particular moral judgments as intermediate between prudence and universalizable morality. They are like prudence in that they do not eliminate singular reference. My prudential judgments contain essential reference to myself and my interests. What I prescribe for myself in prudence is, however, standardly specified in universal terms, or at least can be. Suppose Caesar makes the prudential (not the moral) judgment that he ought to cross the Rubicon. He is committed by this to the judgment that he ought to take this sort of action whenever he is in this sort of situation.[21] Note that this prudential judgment gives him a (prudential) reason for his action, and the reason is given in universal terms even though it applies to him "whenever he is illegally threatened with prosecution, with at least an even chance of securing ultimate power, etc."

Particular moral judgments are like judgments of prudence in both these ways. They contain ineliminable singular reference (though to some other particular person or persons as well as to myself), and what they prescribe I should do for that person (or persons) is specifiable in universal terms. Caesar ought, let us say, not to cross the Rubicon, because this will plunge his country into civil war. Again, this judgment gives him a reason (this time, moral) for his action. If this is a particular moral judgment, he is not committed in making it to the judgment that he ought not to cause civil war *anywhere*, but he is committed to the judgment that he ought not to do anything that will plunge Rome into civil war. He is committed not by universal morality but by his love for his country. Particular moral judgments are thus like prudence in these two respects, but they are also like universalizable morality, for they override self-interest in the interest of others. They are, though not in Kant's sense, treating others as ends in themselves.[22]

It is helpful also, I think, to distinguish four positions within a prescriptive judgment and see how universalization relates differently to them. The first two are the positions of "addressee" (the person to whom the judgment is addressed) and "agent" (the person whose action is being prescribed). Frequently, the addressee will not be explicitly mentioned, and, frequently, the addressee will be the same as the agent, but neither of these features is always the case. Third, there is the position of the person who is the "recipient" of the action. Finally, there is the position of the "action," which is what the speaker judges should or should not be done by this agent to this recipient. The people of Israel are told to leave sheaves in their fields at harvest for the aliens to collect.

It is usual to think that universalizability has to be a feature of the terms in all four positions at once, but this is not so. Universalizing a term is replacing it with purely universal terms, but it is possible to do this at some positions in a judgment and not at others. To soften up opposition to this claim, consider the case where the term in the addressee position is not universalizable. This is quite often the case with moral judgments; thus, the prophet is chosen by God to give a particular message to a particular audience, "O house of Israel, . . . Hate the evil, and love the good, and establish judgment in the gate." The prophet is not thereby committed to addressing this same judgment to anyone else who is like the people of Israel in universally specifiable repects.[23]

The Ten Commandments, I think, are a case where the terms in the addressee and the agent positions are not universalizable. This is a complex exegetical and theological question. I think God is initially prescribing to the particular people he has selected, and he has not selected them because of their universal characteristics.[24] The Ten Commandments are part of his covenant with the people of Israel. They may be supposed to apply eventually to all human beings, but my point is that for the universalist, they have moral value *only* when applied to all people. Kant objected to the Jewish claim to a special relation with God. I think that Christianity has a kind of particularism that Kant finds in Judaism but does not want to find in Christianity. In traditional Christianity, as I understand it, there is particularity not merely in God's covenant with Abraham and the covenant with David but also in his covenant with the particular people he chooses through election to graft onto the vine. If it is right that the Ten Commandments are initially part of the covenant, then they will not initially be "moral," in the thesis of universalism. On the other hand, the term in the action position is already universal. The people of Israel are not to steal or commit adultery at any time or place.

Another biblical example illustrates the nonuniversalizability of the term in the recipient position. A lawyer asks Jesus which is the greatest commandment in the law, and Jesus replies: "Love the Lord your God with all your heart, and with all your soul and with all your mind. This is the first and greatest commandment. And the second is like it, Love your neighbor as yourself. All the Law and the Prophets hang on these two commandments."[25] In the first and greatest commandment the term in the recipient position is not universalizable. The command is not prescribing that the believer should love anyone who is the same as God in universally specifiable respects.[26] What I am claiming, then, is that there is a class of moral judgments that are like judgments of prudence in the sense that they are judgments in which the terms in addressee, agent, and recipient positions are not necessarily universalizable, but the term in the action position is. Why do I want to insist that particular moral judgments are moral? For Kant they are not moral, because they are not (fully) universalizable. Three points should be made in response.

First, here Kant is not speaking for the ethical tradition as a whole. For Aristotle, our moral relations are always to the members of this family or of this polis. The universalist may claim that the special relations that we ought (morally) to honor can be justified on universalist grounds, but the present point is that the need for such universalist justification is a recent part of the tradition. In Greek philosophy and also in Judaism and Christianity we have examples of relations that are held to override in their importance any other relations and that are embodied in what I have called particular moral judgments. I gave the Ten Commandments as an example. Second, particular moral judgments can exemplify what seems to me paradigmatic of morality, namely, regard for another person for his or her own sake. To put the point this way is to claim that the two formulas of Kant's Categorical Imperative can diverge, though not in Kant's own account of the second formula. The requirement of treating another person as an end and never merely as a means can be met by a judgment that fails the requirement of universalizability (if this is taken as a requirement on all the terms in a judgment). Finally, because the term in the action position is universal, or at least universalizable, we can talk of particular moral judgments (in my sense) giving reasons for action. They give reasons because they tell Caesar, for example, that he should refrain whenever there is a certain kind of danger to Rome. As long as these last two features of particular moral judgments are recognized, it becomes a terminological question whether to call them moral or not.

The particularist is not claiming that all moral judgments are particular. If it is wrong to confine moral judgments to those that are fully universalizable (universalizable in all their term positions), it is also wrong to confine moral judgments to those that are particular in my sense. This point has been made by several feminist writers.[27] There are at least two sorts of reasons for this. First, special relations can be unacceptably exclusionary: I am not morally permitted to run over a slow pedestrian when rushing my daughter to the hospital. Second, they are liable to certain kinds of internal corruption: dividing up morality into care for the private sphere and justice for the public sphere damages both spheres. There is a necessary place both for what Selznick calls piety and for what he calls civility. "Civility governs diversity, protects autonomy, and upholds toleration; piety expresses devotion and demands integration. The norms of civility are impersonal, rational, and inclusive, whereas piety is personal, passionate, and particularist."[28] In the final part of this chapter, I look at some implications of the attempt to deny the place of piety in this sense for our thinking about moral progress in international affairs.

Particularism and the Enlargement of the Pacific Union

I now return to Kant's prediction about the pacific union and look at the difference it makes to this prediction if the particularist objection to his ethical theory succeeds. The Kantian has what I call the "cosmopolitan agenda" of detaching people little by little from their local attachments and replacing these with universalist commitments to all rational agents as such. My contention is that this cosmopolitan agenda is problematic in at least two ways: it may help undermine liberal regimes, and it could well make conflicts between liberal and nonliberal regimes more frequent and more violent.

The first difficulty is that the cosmopolitan agenda may actually undo liberal regimes in certain circumstances or cause them to decay. The story of enlargement of the pacific union from three states in 1790 to fifty in 1990 does not take into account that states have gone in and out of the union; moreover, some of the bloodiest wars of history have been fought by powers that were at one time in the union but left it. The particularist may object to what one might call "the corrosive acid of modernism." The claim here is that the cosmopolitan agenda has the effect of fostering a kind of rootlessness that in turn makes the local attachments return in a more virulent form under certain historically observable circumstances. The cosmopolitan agenda thus is not neutral, merely observing the passage of states in and out of the *foedus pacificum*; rather, the cosmopolitan agenda is itself an agent, which in some situations makes the demise of liberal regimes more likely.

For Kant, as I suggested at the end of the first section of this chapter, local attachments and loyalties come under the heading of "pathological love." They do not have moral worth in themselves. Any attempt to give them value independently of duty (understood in terms of universalizability) would show, moreover, that one was under the evil maxim rather than the good. If the particularist objection is correct, however, the moral situation is not so simple. We have, rather, both universal and particular duties. We need, therefore, to consider the possibility that the enlargement of the pacific union is caused not by the gradual weaning of the population away from local affiliation toward cosmopolitan loyalty, but rather by a fortunate balance between what I have called universalist and particularist ethical commitment. To the extent that the balance is lost and the local loyalties become so suspect as to be unmentionable in respectable society, the danger is of rootlessness and then reversion.

There is an empirical question to be examined here. In the case of countries such as Germany, Italy, Argentina, Peru, Brazil, Colombia, and Venezuela, which have passed in and out of liberal democracy, what has been the role of the cosmopolitan agenda? For example, the manifesto of the 1930 coup in Argentina lamented "the gradual process of social decomposition resulting from a system which must be brought to an end, cost what it may. Ignorance and crime have replaced efficiency and respect for law, respect for tradition, and respect for all the moral values which we have received as a dear inheritance from our elders."[29] According to one scholar's diagnosis,

> At stake were two very different ideologies and economic interests: the philosophy of the Enlightenment as opposed to that of late Spanish scholasticism, and the incorporation of Argentina into the world market as opposed to the persistence of the closed, subsistence economies of the interior. . . . These terms ["liberalism" and "democracy"] became the symbols of a minority that denied the traditional culture and destroyed the social structures and forms of government of a large proportion of the population.[30]

The philosophical and ideological differences here are likely to be meshed with all sorts of other causal factors; but this does not remove their significance. My main point is that the balance between the cosmopolitan agenda and more particular attachments was lost in this circumstance, and the result was the demise of the liberal regime. The notion of balance here is not expressible in terms of Kantian ethical theory, which regards the local loyalties as a "pathological" though perhaps necessary vehicle until enlightenment is complete.

Kant and the twentieth-century realists are alike in that they make ethics too pure (in Kant's sense) and then have to suppose too wide a gap between ethics and politics. Morgenthau goes even further in this than Niebuhr. Niebuhr claimed that while individual actions can be loving, the actions of groups can be just but not loving. Morgenthau denies that even the acts of individuals can be fully just.[31] According to him, ethics requires the sacrifice of self for others, politics the sacrifice of others for self; moreover, for humans to live ethically they would have to be rational, but in fact reason is the slave of the passions. George Kennan argues along the same lines when he states that a government "may not subject itself to those supreme laws of renunciation and self-sacrifice that represent the culmination of individual moral growth."[32]

In contrast to this approach, particularists want local loyalties to have moral force not derivatively, or merely intuitively, but in their own right. They want to attribute independent moral worth to the moral sentiments, which are often particular, not merely to reason and what reason prescribes. They also want these sentiments to be checked by universalist morality. My present point is that in order to think about a proper balance between the two, we need to see the moral value of both. Kantian ethics is not clear about the moral value of the first. To put this objection another way, Kant's prediction relied on premises about the necessary universality of moral thinking, but it is these very premises underlying behavior that undermine the success of liberal regimes based on those premises. The view is in this sense self-defeating.

The second difficulty with the cosmopolitan agenda is that it makes conflict by liberal regimes with nonliberal ones more likely and worse in some circumstances. This is not an objection to the prediction but to the joy with which it is sometimes greeted. I discuss this difficulty in terms of three objections.

First, liberal regimes may fight more bloodily against nonliberal regimes just because of the pacific union. This is one of Niebuhr's complaints about Wilsonian idealism. It turned the First World War into a crusade to make the world safe for democracy and therefore legitimated a scale of destruction that would otherwise have been intolerable. One of the mechanisms at work here is that in order to persuade liberal democracies to go to war, the enemy has to be demonized—painted in subhuman colors—so that it then becomes very difficult to negotiate a cessation to hostilities without the enemy's unconditional surrender. So much momentum, so to speak, has to be generated to get the war started that it is much harder to get it stopped. This is one of the strongest points in the work of Morgenthau and also Kennan. Idealism becomes an obstacle to successful diplomacy.[33]

Second, in relation to weaker nonliberal states, the cosmopolitan agenda can actually promote conflict in the name of individual rights. This is ironic because the agenda was initially Westphalian, in the sense that it started from the assumption that intervention is not permitted by one state in the internal affairs of another—autonomy is recognized at the level of the individual state—but the justification for this abstention relies in the end, for a Kantian, on the autonomy of the individual citizen. To put this in the language of rights, it is because the individual has rights that the state has rights. The irony is that liberals call frequently for intervention by one state in the affairs of another on the ground of individual rights. These interventions often lead to war.[34]

Third, the cosmopolitan agenda serves as a disguise for national self-interest. When regimes with an internationalist ideology fall, they often reveal an intense nationalism that had been disguised or suppressed. During the Cold War, for example, a veneer of communist international-ism disguised Soviet hegemony under the Brezhnev doctrine. This ideol-ogy made the legitimate and also the questionable national aspirations of the various states and substates in the Eastern bloc invisible. Liberal democracies can be guilty of similar disguise, and when national interest is confused with idealist rhetoric (as was the case with the British in Egypt in 1881-82), it can be much harder to withdraw from an unsuccessful policy.

In conclusion, I relate these three objections, in the same order, to Kantian ethics. First, Kant has horrendous remarks about Jewish ethical failure. For him, it was the claim of the Jews to a special (that is, not universal) relation to God that "showed enmity toward all other peoples and which, therefore, evoked the enmity of all."[35] Thus, "the euthanasia of Judaism is pure moral religion."[36] A universalist will make a similar historical judgment about Aristotle, denying that he has, strictly speak-ing, an ethics at all, for Aristotle does not embrace the requirement of universalizability, which is in this view a necessary condition for moral judgment. I think that the demonization of contemporary opponents is made easier in a similar way by the cosmopolitan agenda. Stories about the "bestial" treatment of prisoners of war by the Germans in the First World War and about "the inscrutability of the East" in the Second were used to show that opponents were not fully civilized into the standards of morality. I am not saying that regimes never violate elementary standards of decency, but demonization is made both easier and more necessary when the war is construed as an idealist crusade. The particu-larist will take a somewhat different line, and will want to find genuine moral value in the local loyalties of opponents.

Second, Kant's view of primitive peoples, those not yet in an age of enlightenment, is that their attitude to the law is "raw, uncivilized, and an animalic degradation of humanity."[37] J. S. Mill justifies coercive treatment of what he calls "barbarous nations." They do not have the rights of civilized nations, "except a right to such treatment as may, at the earliest possible period, fit them for becoming one." This view is rooted in the contention that "their minds are not capable of so great an effort [as reciprocity], nor [is] their will sufficiently under the influence of distant motives."[38] The point of both Kant and Mill is that people in these nations are not yet capable of full ethical thinking, as the philosophers construe it, because of their failure to live by fully universalizable moral commitments. Intervention is a large topic on its own, and I will not say much about it here.[39] In fact, both Kant and Mill were opposed to interventions that many of their contemporaries found acceptable. My point is merely that illegitimate intervention is made easier by the Kantian dichotomy between pathological and practical love and between peoples who have and who have not achieved the latter.

The particularist approach takes a different line. It wants to endorse some of the local loyalties in nonliberal nations and find ways in which they can be expressed without ethnic cleansing or civil war. It is no doubt tempting, looking at Bosnia or Rwanda, to wish for an end to nationalist commitment and to look forward as one's ideal to a general loyalty not to this or that nation but to the world as a whole, but the particularist will stubbornly insist that human morality is partly a matter of local attachment. What is wanted is not the demise of patriotism or its replacement by cosmopolitanism—this would be an impoverishment—rather, what is wanted is a balance, though I have not said anything about how such a balance could be achieved.

Finally, there is the danger of self-deception. I think the realists are wrong to say that the foreign policy of liberal states that uses idealist rhetoric is always mere ideology, in the sense of a disguise for national self-interest. There is good empirical evidence that states can indeed behave in accordance with certain ethical precepts.[40] The realists are right, however, to say that the idealism is often a disguise and that when it is such, it makes good policy making more difficult. The particularist will want to insist that love of one's nation can be a fully moral sentiment, though it is also peculiarly liable to corruption. There is thus a need to study the ways in which it is corrupted. This is not to say, though, that it has value only to the extent that it can be endorsed by "critical" or universalist ethical thinking. This means that reference to the interests of one's nation can be, though it need not be, genuinely ethical; it does not always need to be disguised. American foreign policy has been distorted by the perceived need to pretend that policies serving the national interest were in fact something else.[41] The particularist asserts what both the idealist and the realist, relying on their Kantian inheritance, deny, namely, that love of one's country can be a fully moral emotion even though it can also be a source of great evil.

I have not claimed that universalism is the only, or even the main, cause of the difficulties in international politics that I have mentioned in this section. My point has been, rather, that the cosmopolitan agenda has in some cases contributed to producing, prolonging, or worsening conflicts. We have seen that Kant derives his prediction about the *foedus pacificum* from his ethical theory and that his ethical theory needs revision. The actual course of international affairs over the last two centuries has shown both the strength of his account and its weakness.

Endnotes

1. Doyle draws up a list of liberal regimes according to four institutions that he considers essential: market and private property economies; polities that are externally sovereign; citizens who possess juridical rights; and "republican" (whether republican or monarchical) representative, government. See Michael Doyle, "Kant, Liberal Legacies, and Foreign Affairs," *Philosophy and Public Affairs* 12 (1983): 205–35 and 323–53 (part 2). See also his "Liberalism and Word Politics," *American Political Science Review* 80 (1986): 1151–69.

2. Doyle concedes a couple of minor exceptions; see, "Kant, Liberal Legacies," 216. If one objects, "What about 1812?" the answer is that Britain would not have met the criteria before 1832. An important qualification is given by John Owen in "How Liberalism Produces Democratic Peace," *International Security* 19 (1994): 87–125. His point is that the pacific union obtains only between those *perceived* as democracies.

3. *The New York Times*, 21 Sept. 1993. President Ronald Reagan already had proclaimed to the British parliament in June 1982 "a global campaign for democratic development" or "campaign for freedom," which he claimed would strengthen the prospects for a world at peace; see *The New York Times*, 9 June 1982. For a discussion of Woodrow Wilson's proposition that making the world safe for democracy would make "the world fit and safe to live in," see Charles W. Kegley, "The Neoidealist Moment in International Studies? Realist Myths and the New International Realities," *International Studies Quarterly* 37 (1993): 135–39.

4. Immanuel Kant, *Groundwork of the Metaphysic of Morals*, trans. H. J. Paton (New York: Harper and Row, 1964), 88, 421 and 96, 429. In the text I cite the page number of the English translation followed by the page number of the Prussian Academy edition.

5. I discuss this version of Kant's formula in the first chapter of *The Moral Gap: Kantian Ethics, Human Limits, and God's Assistance* (New York: Oxford University Press, 1995).

6. There is a continuum of specificity to generality, and Kant does not make

it clear where on this continuum he expects maxims to come. I have taken an interpretation that allows maximal specificity; but one of Kant's aims was that maxims could be easily taught, and sometimes he talks about only two fundamental maxims (the good and the evil), which are maximally general.

7. See Alan W. Wood, "Kant's Deism," in eds., Philip J. Rossi and Michael Wreen, *Kant's Philosophy of Religion Reconsidered* (Bloomington: Indiana University Press, 1991), 1–21.

8. For a defense of the claim that Kant is a "pure rationalist" who himself accepts the claims of Christian revelation, but does not think them necessary for salvation, see John Hare, review of *Kant's Philosophy of Religion Reconsidered*, in *Faith and Philosophy* 11 (1994): 138–44.

9. My own view is that they cannot; see Kant, *The Moral Gap*, chap. 2.

10. Immanuel Kant, *Religion within the Limits of Reason Alone*, trans. Theodore Greene and Hoyt Hudson (New York: Harper and Row, 1960), 85, 94.

11. Philip J. Rossi, "The Final End of All Things," in eds., Philip J. Rossi and Michael Wreen, *Kant's Philosophy of Religion Reconsidered* (Bloomington: Indiana University Press, 1991), 160.

12. I am following here the views of Michel Despland, *Kant on History and Religion* (Montreal: McGill-Queen's University Press, 1973), 307f.

13. Like Luther, Kant is doubtful about a literal millennium; compare the *Augsburg Confession*, article 17, and Kant, *Religion*, 125f, 135.

14. Immanuel Kant, *The Conflict of the Faculties*, trans. Mary Gregor (New York: Abaris Books, 1979), 165, 91; emphasis added.

15. Immanuel Kant, *The Metaphysics of Morals*, trans. Mary Gregor (Cambridge: Cambridge University Press, 1991), 156, 350; but see Kant, *Perpetual Peace*, trans. Lewis W. Beck, in *Kant on History* (Indianapolis: Bobbs-Merrill, 1963), 100, 356.

16. Kant, *Religion*, 86, 94.

17. For their respective views, see Reinhold Niebuhr, *Moral Man and Immoral Society* (New York: Scribner's, 1932); and Hans Morgenthau, *Scientific Man vs. Power Politics* (Chicago: University of Chicago Press, 1946).

18. Niebuhr, *Moral Man*, 91. See also *Reinhold Niebuhr on Politics*, ed. Harry R. Davis and Robert C. Good (New York: Scribner's, 1960), 85: "[Patriotism] from an absolute perspective is simply another form of selfishness." For a more detailed discussion of Niebuhr, Morgenthau and Kennan, see John Hare and Carey Joynt, *Ethics and International Affairs* (New York: St. Martin's, 1982), especially chap. 2.

19. See Carol Gilligan, "In a Different Voice: Women's Conception of Self and Morality," in eds., Hester Eisenstein and Alice Jardine, *The Future of Difference* (Boston: G. K. Hall, 1980); and Nel Noddings, *Caring: A Feminine Approach to Ethics and Moral Education* (Berkeley: University of California Press, 1984).

20. There are several objections in the literature to different forms of universalism that are not objections to the form of universalism I have defined. These

include the objections that we need to leave room for divergent personal ideals and that universalism leaves no room for close personal relations. See Margaret U. Walker, "Moral Particularity," *Metaphilosophy* 18 (1987): 171–85; and Lynne McFall, "Integrity," *Ethics* 9 (1987): 5–20.

21. See Derek Parfit, *Reasons and Persons* (Oxford: Clarendon, 1984), 149.

22. What is needed here is an account of what it means to care for another person for her own sake that is different from Kant's second formula. The point is again similar in prudential and particular moral judgments. Is there some unique set of universally specified descriptions that identifies me as me and could not identify anyone else, so that I could at least formally universalize my maxims of prudence? Perhaps the individual is individuated by a unique set of characteristics, some of which are not themselves universally specifiable because they contain ineliminable reference to particular regions of space and time. In any case, caring for another person for her own sake, on this account, relates me to another person whose identifying descriptions, if there are any, I do not know.

23. See Amos 5:1–15; also 7:14–15, 3:9–10. It is an interesting question whether there is always a person in the addressee position, even if this is implicit; and it is unclear whether, if there is, we should include the occupant of this position in the judgment itself. It might be claimed that we should not, because there is a complete sentence if the term is removed; but this cannot generally be used as a criterion for exclusion. For my purposes it is useful to draw attention to the position of addressee, because it illustrates the variability of moral judgments in respect to the universalizability of the terms in the different positions within them.

24. See Deut. 9:4–6. For the connection of the Ten Commandments with the covenant, see Exod. 34:28: "And he wrote upon the tables the works of the covenant, the ten commandments."

25. Matt. 22:36–40.

26. This is especially clear in the Hebrew commandment that stands behind this command, "I am the Lord your God, who brought you out of Egypt, out of the land of slavery. You shall have no other gods before me;" see Deut. 5:6–7. The God of Israel is here making a claim of special relation to his own people.

27. See Adrian Piper, "Impartiality, Compassion and Modal Imagination," *Ethics* 101 (1991): 726–57; Marilyn Friedman, "The Practice of Partiality," *Ethics* 101 (1991): 818–35; Mary Stewart Van Leeuwen et al., *After Eden: Facing the Challenge of Gender Reconciliation* (Grand Rapids, Mich.: Eerdmans, 1993); and Barbara Herman, "Agency, Attachment, and Difference," in John Deigh, ed., *Ethics and Personality: Essays in Moral Psychology* (Chicago: University of Chicago Press, 1992).

28. Philip Selznick, *The Moral Commonwealth: Social Theory and the Promise of Community* (Berkeley: University of California Press, 1992), 387; see also 387–409.

29. Cited in Peter H. Smith, "The Breakdown of Democracy in Argentina, 1916–1930," in Juan Linz and Alfred Stepan, eds., *The Breakdown of Democratic*

Regimes, part 3: *Latin America* (Baltimore: Johns Hopkins University Press, 1978), 19.

30. Guillermo O'Donnell, "Permanent Crisis and the Failure to Create a Democractic Regime: Argentina, 1955–66," in Linz and Stepan, part 1: *Latin America*, 141, 142. It is interesting to compare the transitions out of democracy in Germany; see M. Rainer Lepsius, "From Fragmented Party Democracy to Government by Emergency Decree and National Socialist Takeover: Germany," in Linz and Stepan, part 2: *Europe*, 73.

31. See Morgenthau, *Scientific Man vs. Power Politics*, 183–90.

32. George Kennan, *Realities of American Foreign Policy* (Princeton: Princeton University Press, 1954), 47–48.

33. See Doyle, "Kant, Liberal Legacies," 324. See also George Kenyan, *American Diplomacy, 1900-1950* (Chicago: University of Chicago Press, 1951), 98–100, 182; and *Realities*, 47–48. It is interesting to read M. Campbell Smith's introduction to Kant's *Perpetual Peace*, written in 1903. He says, "Wars between different grades of civilization are bound to exist as long as civilization itself exists" (p. 98).

34. Joseph Nye argues that the norms of state sovereignty are eroding because of the rapid growth in transnational communications, migration, economic interdependence, and the increasing self-assertion of ethnic groups inside the more than 90 percent of states in today's world that are ethnically heterogeneous; see Joseph Nye, "What New World Order?" *Foreign Affairs* 70 (1992): 83–96. For the more traditional liberal position, see Michael Walzer, *Just and Unjust Wars* (New York: Basic Books, 1977), 86–108.

35. Kant, *Religion*, 117, 127.

36. Kant, *The Conflict of the Faculties*, 95, 53.

37. Kant, *Perpetual Peace*, 98, 354.

38. Anthony Ellis, "Utilitarianism and International Ethics," in *Traditions of International Ethics*, ed. Terry Nardin and David R. Mapel (Cambridge: Cambridge University Press, 1992), 166.

39. There is a more detailed account in Hare and Joynt, *Ethics and International Affairs*, 151–62.

40. For a good summary, see Charles Kegley, "Neo-Idealism: A Practical Matter," *Ethics and International Affairs* 2 (1988): 173–97.

41. See Robert E. Osgood, *Ideals and Self-Interest in America's Foreign Relations* (Chicago: Chicago University Press, 1953).

Moral Rationality and Particularity: A Response to John Hare

David Lumsdaine

The prescience of Immanuel Kant's "astonishing prediction," later confirmed by powerful evidence,[1] makes close examination of Kant's thinking on lasting peace important to international ethics and to the pursuit of peace. John Hare's essay advances thinking on these matters in several ways and touches on important themes, including the relation between practical-legal and moral-spiritual considerations and how Kant's anthropology affects his political theory. Hare notes the important recourse that Kant's political and moral theory makes to God, while questioning whether Kant's formulation of religious concepts "within the limits of reason alone" can accomplish what Kant intends it to (Hare, 76). Hare also closely documents and helpfully discusses Kant's relation to twentieth-century realist thinkers. The central point of Hare's essay, however, on which I focus, is the problem of particularity in Kant's ethics as it relates to his political thought. Understanding Kant's neglect of the moral worth of particularity highlights problems in his political theory and in any thinking directly or indirectly influenced by it.

Hare argues that Kant's hopes for a more peaceful world and his plan for perpetual peace arise out of his ethics and his anthropology, but Kant's ethics are flawed by his refusal to allow moral worth to local attachments. Combining these premises, Hare argues that the flaw in the ethics on which Kant's cosmopolitan agenda is built creates two potentially grave problems. By denigrating local attachments, Kant may weaken rather than expand cosmopolitan commitments, and by setting

93

too exacting a standard, Kant's rigorous cosmopolitanism could encourage fanaticism and self-deception in liberal countries.

Despite my great admiration for Kant's international theory, I agree with most of Hare's very interesting argument. In seeking to develop Hare's line of analysis I make three further points: (1) Kant identifies a moral rationality operating, through voluntary choices as well as through systemic incentives, at what international relations scholars would call various "levels of analysis"; (2) the problem of particularity that Hare identifies in Kant is important in understanding the crucial international problems of marginalization and ethnic division; and (3) Christian orthodox theology, which, as Hare notes, Kant appropriated, though only in part, provides unique interpretive and moral resources for the conceptual and practical tasks of establishing the kind of lawful international society that can both respect particularity and make for a more peaceful and ethical world.

Moral Rationality and "Levels of Analysis"

Kant's argument sets out dynamics promoting the *foedus pacificum* at the level of interstate politics ("3rd image"), at the level of promoting republican government ("2nd image"), and at the level of education of the public and of statesmen by philosophers (arguably, "1st image"). Again, Kant discusses both the ways in which a *foedus pacificum* relies on voluntary, deliberate moral undertakings and the ways in which history providentially forces countries toward perpetual peace. Various contemporary international relations theories echo different parts of Kant's argument. One could find Kant's historical providence that would compel even a "race of devils" to cooperate in Robert Axelrod's *Evolution of Cooperation* and in other theories of "cooperation among rational egoists."[2] The constitutional aspect of the *foedus pacificum* foreshadows literature on functionalism and international law and on the growth of international organizations in this century. Kant's requirement that the *foedus* be among republics anticipates the work of Bruce Russett, Michael Doyle, and others on the democratic peace. The role Kant assigns philosophers fits in with the work of "constructivist" and other authors who emphasize the importance of ideas and values in structuring international politics.[3]

Kant's multipronged argument thus seems to be a grab bag of unrelated approaches until one sees the underlying logic that unites its different aspects (voluntary and structural) and its different levels of analysis (interstate, intrastate, and individual). The key lies in the moral concepts that are central to Kant's argument, and to understand these one must distinguish between two understandings of rationality. The word "rational" in contemporary international relations theory bears a very narrow meaning, almost the opposite of Kant's understanding of rationality. In social science parlance, rational actors are those who execute effective plans for advancing their own interests, but for Kant, rationality consists in acting in accordance with practical reason, whose maxims are the very antithesis of unfettered self-interest. Prudence and efficient pursuit of permitted or mandatory ends are part of practical reason, of course, but only a part.

Rationality understood as the efficient pursuit of an actor's own ends ordinarily cannot exist at more than one level of analysis. Kenneth J. Arrow's impossibility theorem demonstrates that, in general, where actors have preferences unrestricted by commitments to common goals, there is no way to aggregate their preferences into a self-consistent social choice function.[4] Where individuals pursue their own interests, the group behaves not as a purposive, unified, rational actor but as an object buffeted about, whose motions are mere resultants. If bureaus seek their own interest, national policy is an unintended outcome, as Graham Allison has shown.[5] If states pursue only their own interests, no one looks after the international system, which then becomes a destructive, self-help anarchy, as Kenneth Waltz has argued.[6] If rationality bears this narrow sense, then rationality at the different levels of philosophy, state organization, and the international system belong to different worlds, which cannot act in concert to promote peace (or any other end). Again, such rationality narrowly defined is at best indifferent to moral concerns and restraints.

Kant employs a wider concept of rationality, which includes moral consciousness as well as prudent, means-ends rationality. I have argued elsewhere that it is this kind of rationality that we actually find in international politics.[7] Actions have moral consequences, which must be heeded; however, only actors genuinely committed to moral principle are apt to take prudent heed of them.[8] If that is so, then states that behave morally and cooperatively may reap benefits at least equal to the costs they bear, as Kant's account of history suggests. Where the fundamental logic of action is a morally informed one, actors tend to employ the same principles of social organization in international politics that they do in domestic politics and personal moral life.[9] In that case, Kant is right to suggest that those states in which political affairs are settled by law, constitutionally, consensually, and by reason and negotiation—that is, republics and no others—are those best suited to join in a lawful, constitutional pacific union. Moreover, decision makers and citizens are apt to believe that lawful, just solutions will work out well, and this view is apt to turn out to be right. Reliance on moral principle, as Kant's essay shows, might thus give prescience to theorists. Statesmen may also thus acquire wisdom unattainable by morally indifferent calculation.

Unless these points are cleared up, the logic of Kant's argument will remain confused or erroneous from the point of view of systemic international relations theory. This confusion will also obscure the relevance of Kant's moral reasoning, including its flaws, for international relations theory and for the wise practice of international politics. If, however, the close relation between prudence and ethical principle is understood, Kant's argument becomes a coherent argument about practical politics, and Hare's critique of the excessive rigorism and antiparticularism of Kant's argument assumes its importance not only to philosophy but to international relations theory as well.

Particularity, World Politics, and Ethics

Hare develops an insightful connection between an excessively rigorist Kantian ethics that, on the one hand, dissociates principle from legitimate particular concerns, thus eroding a genuine cosmopolitan spirit, and, on the other, fosters ideological self-deception.[10] Hare argues that Kant's ethics creates radical disjunctures—between duty and desire, inner and outer, ethics and law, reason and emotion, universal and particular, selfishness and other-directed universality—that parallel Kant's philosophical disjuncture between noumenon and phenomenon. The radical disjuncture between duty and desire results in a devaluing of particular affections, to which Kant denies moral worth. This is rightly the object of philosophic criticism, Hare argues. The same flaw can also engender serious mistakes about international politics. For one thing, support for cosmopolitan principle may require nurturing local political loyalties as well. Kant's extreme emphasis on universal duty, therefore, may erode the balance of particular and universal loyalties that is required to foster public spirit, including cosmopolitan sentiments. For another, overemphasis on grounding reasons for action in universal rather than in particular interests may lead states to deceive themselves about their motives, encouraging ideological crusades in which distorted self-interest masquerades as universal principle and opponents are demonized. It is just such moralism that some realists have rightly warned against.

The problem of neglect of the value of the particular that Hare identifies also has implications in another important area of international politics: the problem of crafting international or global norms in a world of many different cultures and value systems. Any moral relativism, of course, including cultural relativism, leads us away from human decency, common sense, and common morality, and, indeed, away from respect for other cultures. Wars of aggression, genocide, slavery, and colonialism, worldwide trade in drugs, violations of human rights, government for the sake of the rulers and not for the sake of the governed, and so on, must be understood not simply as outcomes that we happen to dislike, but, with Kant, as objectively wrongful acts, violations of the rights of others and of the moral law itself. A purported multiculturalism that denies objective moral standards is self-defeating as well as wrong. Making all standards culturally relative takes away our grounds for condemning imperialistic, racist, or even genocidal acts by states supported by their own cultures and not merely for opposing milder cultural biases. Thorough-going cultural relativism makes it impossible to pass judgment on even the most tyrannical and ethnocentric absolutisms.

The recognition that cultures and states, like persons, have areas within which they may rightly determine what is and what is not appropriate is not, however, a denial of objective moral truth and moral law. On the contrary, insufficient appreciation of cultural spheres denigrates the value of all particular cultures and also tends to confuse moral law as such with the philosophy of dominant cultures. Enlightenment efforts to cast all particular obligations as merely so many instances of a universal reason best expressed in its full, general form by an elite eighteenth-century European intelligentsia made precisely this mistake. Billing philosophes of a particular time and place as universal seers and transparent vehicles for universal reason, however, only undermines comprehension of moral reason as it arises and is formulated in concrete cultures and contexts. It also leads to the totalizing assumption that abstract European philosophic formulations can free themselves from any cultural particularity. By seeking, as it were, the naked vision of truth in one's own strength, an insufficiently careful attempt at universality can end up erroneously assuming that one arrives at what is universal by stripping oneself of particulars.

The political consequences of this error include not only a tendency to cast particular disputes as cosmic battles between good and evil (with the self-deception and demonization that Hare rightly warns against) but also an implicit equation of progress with the universal advance of the commercial and political culture of the West, embodied in our day in the highly educated elites of the United States. The bias against particularity in the Enlightenment tradition (largely retained, I fear, in contemporary social science) is thus apt to lead to self-idealization, deprecation of others, and touting as moral universals the peculiar, and not so obviously successful, cultural and economic mores of contemporary elite America. Too, the norms advocated as universal standards by Western educated elites are not only less than proven universals; they may themselves, at points, be validly subject to criticism, perhaps even by less elite persons, as morally debased.

The problem of particularity that Hare and other philosophers find in Kant thus bears an important relation to disputes over the role of the West in world affairs, what values are truly universal, and the place of community standards and of local custom. Hare's analysis provides an interesting point of entry to certain critiques of Western cultural and economic hegemony—to be sure, not the kind of anti-other critique so often and so inaccurately advanced as multicultural, with its deprecation of ordinary citizens, its erosion of moral standards, and its presumption that other cultures should handle their societal and family norms much as educated elites in the United States do. It provides, rather, an entry for an honest attempt to understand the genuine values embodied in the particular ways of life of communities and peoples in our own and other societies, as well as the dangers that may arise from washing these cultures away in a tide of internationally disseminated commerce, media, and social norms.

To put the problem in these terms, though, only exposes some of the unsolved difficulties introduced when we place the emphasis on particularity. Claims of cultural particularity are used by dictators to claim that "African democracy," "Asian values," or "Soviet culture" justify the suppression of all political criticism, of open discussion of issues, and of inconvenient ethnic minorities. The recognition that casting principles in abstract terms freed of particular reference cannot by itself guarantee moral accuracy or generality may, indeed, undermine attempts to achieve reasonable impartiality, for once we recognize that we must take account of particularity, we are left with the difficult problem of judging which standards are universal and which are not. The project for a pacific union, based as it is on a conception of a universal moral order, thus faces the severe philosophical challenges that inhere in all attempts to develop a common basis for international norms of human rights, international peace, and cosmopolitan law.

To be sure, Kant's essays take a stab at tackling this problem—*Perpetual Peace* itself hews fairly close to the (highly problematic) Augsburg-

Westphalia approach, leaving sovereignty near absolute within states. The traditions of international order that find their roots in the *foedus pacificum* ideas of J.-H. Bernardin de Saint-Pierre, Jean-Jacques Rousseau, and Kant, and their later expression in the Wilsonian program, the United Nations, and NATO may, nevertheless, tend toward the opposite error: broad-gauge Western, especially American, attempts to reform the world in our own rather imperfect image. This danger arises from precisely the well-intentioned attempt that Kant, among other Enlightenment thinkers, made at a fair and universal liberal perspective. Exactly because the conceptual foundation that undergirds *Perpetual Peace* is a moral rationality that finds common moral principles applicable both to domestic and to international politics, the articulation of international norms that respect cultural differences is extremely difficult and tends toward self-contradiction. Perhaps because it is an approach that embraces both effectiveness and pure moral principle, these difficulties also show up both in moral tensions within the position as well as in the practical difficulty of gaining assent for such principles across significant cultural divides.

The approach advocated by Kant and his heirs probably constitutes the most hopeful way to achieve international peace and justice. It would be folly to write it off because of some thorny difficulties, even if these seem to have no ready solution. Yet it would be equally unwise to remain unaware of the range of ethical and political flaws that seem to be connected with the neglect of the moral value of particularity so typical of Kant and the whole Enlightenment tradition.

Kant's Peace Plan and the Gospel

Kant's essay *Perpetual Peace* stems from his properly unassuageable dissatisfaction with international relations as a state of perpetual war. Such a state of war runs contrary to moral law. Human beings are, ultimately, all part of a single human family and ought to love one another. Simply as rational, moral beings bound by the universal principles of right and wrong, we should eschew the fratricidal strife of war. Attempts to bring human societies into a state of lawfulness thus reflect the fact of human unity, as well as moral and humane imperatives. The tradition of *foedus pacificum* running from Saint-Pierre and Rousseau through Kant to Woodrow Wilson and modern liberal internationalism perhaps offers the best hope for a more just and peaceful world. Yet the neglect of the moral value of the particular, which Hare identifies as a defect in Kant's ethics, indicates that there are potential ethical and practical problems in Kant's scheme for a pacific union. I have argued, similarly, that the specific conceptions of universal law on which this tradition is built also lead to difficulties in dealing with cultural diversity and can foster neglect of small cultures and of those morally valuable aspects of life that fall short of universal law. I have tried, further, to explore the ways in which Kant's international political theory is connected to its philosophic roots. More specifically, I have considered how the problem of particularity reflects the general difficulties that Enlightenment traditions of universal law have in addressing ethnic diversity and the problem of reconciliation among diverse cultures, issues central to today's international relations and to any realistic plan for global peace.

These themes have been set out, here as in Kant's work, without utilizing specifically Christian assumptions or concepts, but further analysis requires that we show how the Gospel bears on them. As Hare points out, Kant tries to translate Biblical and Christian categories into what he believes to be universal language, stripped of the scandal of particularity, but, like Hare, I am skeptical that Kant's aparticular philosophic concepts can do the work that Kant wants them to do. I am also skeptical about their purported universality. The Scriptures and the church attest to the action of God in history, dealing with individual men and women in individual ways. God helps all mankind not abstractly but through his chosen people Israel, and his mighty acts find their completion in Jesus Christ, a particular man in whom God's fullness dwells. Jesus bears in himself the aspirations and the value, as well as the brokenness, of all human beings and of each of them in their particularity. The Gospel is accessible to ordinary untrained people from every culture because it touches each person's particularity through the life of the particular man Jesus. The universal good news is thus expressed in a form that, as Lamin Sanneh has argued, is uniquely cross-cultural. The Gospel is translatable into any language and culture, so that each may hear in his or her own tongue the marvelous works of God—without relinquishing, but, rather, renewing, his or her cultural particularity.[11]

The orthodox Christian faith carries, at its core, ideas that illuminate the problems of unity and diversity and of human division. It gives a unique key to understanding precisely the problems that confront us in our attempts to bring about lasting peace among the world's diverse and divided people, problems of particularity that Kant's attempts at a universal peace and law also encountered. The Gospel comes from the triune God—Father, Son, and Spirit—each fully himself, each fully at one with the others; and this understanding of personal unity in diversity provides a place where we might commence our search for human unity in diversity.[12] The Gospel likewise reveals in a concrete way, through one man, Jesus Christ, the presence of the one God with persons and peoples in their particularity. The central event and symbol of God's work in Christ Jesus, the cross, uniquely addresses the divided and broken human condition.

We need to continue our attempts to understand better the ways to overcome the practical difficulties with which the problem of particularity saddles any effort at world peace, justice, and law. Arguably, the most promising practical and theoretical lines for pursuing peace are those that stem from the Kantian tradition: democratic peace, the development of international society, and the creation of a network of international law and organizations (corresponding to republicanism, cosmopolitan law, and the *foedus pacificum*, respectively). A deeper understanding of their philosophic underpinnings, including the problems to which Hare has drawn our attention, is thus vital to the development of an ethical understanding of world politics. This very philosophical quest brings us back, however, to the need to look more deeply at the Christian roots of Kant's philosophical thinking, and to ponder the profound revealed mysteries of the Christian faith—the Trinity, the incarnation, the cross—as they bear on the vital political and practical human problems of unity in diversity, brokenness and reconciliation.

Endnotes

1. See for instance Bruce Russett, *Grasping the Democratic Peace* (Princeton: Princeton University Press, 1993).

2. Robert Axelrod, *The Evolution of Cooperation* (New York: Basic Books, 1983).

3. See, for instance, the work of Alexander Wendt and my own book, *Moral Vision in International Politics: The Foreign Aid Regime, 1949–1989* (Princeton, N.J.: Princeton University Press, 1993).

4. Kenneth J. Arrow, *Social Choice and Individual Values* (New Haven: Yale University Press, 1951).

5. Graham Allison, *Essence of Decision: Explaining the Cuban Missile Crisis* (Boston: Little, Brown, 1971).

6. Kenneth Waltz, *Theory of International Politics* (Reading, Mass.: Addison-Wesley, 1979).

7. See David Lumsdaine, *Moral Vision in International Politics: The Foreign*

Aid Regime, 1949–1989 (Princeton, N.J.: Princeton University Press, 1993), chap 1.

8. Donnelly argues this point in his essay on Thucydides; see Jack Donnelly, "Thucydides and Realism" (paper presented at the Annual Meeting of the International Studies Association, Vancouver, B.C., 1991).

9. See David Lumsdaine, "The Centrality of Worldviews and Normative Ideas in Twentieth-Century Politics" (paper delivered at the Annual Meeting of the American Political Science Association, New York City, September 1994).

10. This parallels the well-known argument of Louis Hartz, *The Liberal Tradition in America* (New York: Harcourt, Brace, Jovanovich, 1955).

11. Lamin O. Sanneh, "World Christianity and the Study of History: Framing the Issues, Exploring the Heritage" (mimeograph, January 1995). See also his *Translating the Message: The Missionary Impact on Culture* (Maryknoll, N.Y.: Orbis Books, 1989).

12. This point is discussed at some length by Walter Kasper, *The God of Jesus Christ*, trans. Matthew J. O'Connell (New York: Crossroad, 1984).

Part 2

Cases

Chapter 4

Identity, Sovereignty, and Self-Determination

Jean Bethke Elshtain

Nationalism is the great political passion of our time. That this is so is surprising and, for many, disturbing. Political scientists and analysts over the years predicted confidently that nationalism would cease to be a powerful force as the world moved toward ever-expanding rationalism, enlightenment, and universalism. (Religion, of course, was slated for disappearance, too, as yet another atavistic force.) Perhaps this helps to account for the shock waves ricocheting through the academic world since 1989. For the Christian, however, much of what is happening seems perhaps all too predictable in a fallen world in which human beings are always tempted by power and some among us are quite overtaken by hatred and a lust to dominate. With the "new nationalism" in mind, I want to explore the interwoven themes of self-identity, self-determination, and nationalism in the penultimate realm in which each takes shape: the world of states, would-be states, political rule, and civic life.

On National Identity and Self-Determination

There are some things we ought by now to have learned. One is that the imperial suppression of particular national identities is costly indeed, for these identities, once permitted expression, often take shape in militant, even ferocious forms. As Sir Isaiah Berlin points out, "People tire of being spat upon, ordered about by a superior nation, a superior class, or a superior anyone. Sooner or later, they ask the nationalist questions:

'Why do we have to obey them?' 'What right have they?' 'What about us?' 'Why can't we . . . ?'[1] In her excellent book on nationalism Liah Greenfield argues that "National identity is, fundamentally, a matter of dignity. It gives people reasons to be proud." Peoples historically—including our own foremothers and forefathers—fought "over respect due to them, rather than anything else."[2]

Václav Havel speaks of the "desire to renew and emphasize one's identity" as a force that lies behind "the emergence of many new countries. Nations that never had states of their own feel an understandable need to experience independence."[3] Although the nation-state model emerged historically as a Western invention with the Treaty of Westphalia in 1648, it has been embraced (or imposed) worldwide. At present, what aggrieved peoples want is not an end to the nation-state or to sovereignty and national autonomy but an end to Western colonial or Soviet or other "external" dominance of their particular histories, languages, cultures, and wounded sense of identity.

Catholic social thought has long recognized the validity and importance of self-determination, closely linking this concept with the need to work to achieve a common good and to a vision of human dignity tied "unquestionably," according to Pope John XXIII in *Pacem in terris*, to the "right to take an active part in government. . . ."[4] John XXIII, in that document, reminds us that no human being is "by nature superior to his fellows, since all men are equally noble in natural dignity. And consequently there are no differences at all between political communities from the point of view of natural dignity."[5] Is this not, however, what nationalism always violates by insisting that some states, or peoples, are, in fact, not only different from others, given their history and culture, but superior, too? Is not equal dignity of all peoples necessarily violated by nationalism?

George Orwell, for one, thought so. In his essay, "Notes on Nationalism," he traces the drastic simplifications and overwrought evocation of competitive prestige in which the nationalist, one who uses all "his mental energy either in boosting or in denigrating," indulges. Orwell calls nationalist thought obsessive and indifferent to reality, persisting on a plane far removed from the concrete truths of everyday social life. The nationalist (by contrast to the civic patriot, of whom I shall say more below) classifies people like insects and assumes that "whole blocks of millions or tens of millions of people can be confidently labeled 'good' or 'bad'" and, as well, insists that no other duty must be allowed to override or even challenge that to the nation-state. The nationalist evokes power as force—we need more of it, we can never have enough of it, somebody else is creeping up on us and may soon have more than we do—and he sinks his own individuality into an overarching identification with the collective.[6]

Orwell also endorses, however, as I do, a robust version of patriotic or civic identity, a form of identification always wary and cautious of nationalistic excess because the temptation of national identity pushes in a triumphalist direction. How does this square with the teaching of *Pacem in terris* and the U.S. Bishops' "A Harvest of Peace is Sown in Justice"? The bishops, too, endorse self-determination and claim that it

> should neither be dismissed as always harmful or unworkable nor embraced as an absolute right or a panacea in the face of injustice. . . . While full political independence may be morally right and politically appropriate in some cases, it is essential that any new state meet the fundamental purpose of sovereignty: the commitment and capacity to create a just and stable political order and to contribute to the international common good.[7]

I take the bishops, in line with their own previous document, "The Challenge of Peace," and the long tradition of papal proclamations in this matter to be lifting up a via media, a moderate but firm course charted between the Scylla of sovereign absolutism, or an absolutizing of particular national identities, on the one hand, and the Charybdis of an arrogant universalism or imperialism that runs rough-shod over self-determination and diversity, on the other. Let us examine this possibility further.

Identity with a nation goes deep. In his work, *The Political Life of Children*, Robert Coles found attachment to a homeland, or an imagined homeland, in the symbolism and imagery deployed by children. "Nationalism works its way into just about every corner of the mind's life," Coles writes. Children have ready access to a nation's "name, its flag, its music, its currency, its slogans, its history, its political life," and this personalized yet political identity shapes their outlooks and actions. Entrenched notions of a homeland are double-edged, at once inward looking, a place where one "gets one's bearings," and outward projecting, distinguishing and perhaps protecting "us" from "them," from foreigners who, all too easily, may become enemies. Both aspects of homeland and nationalist imagery turn up "in developing conscience of young people" everywhere.[8] John Keane, a British theorist of civil society, that realm of associations and solidaristic possibilities greater than the individual but beneath the state, writes:

> the birth of democracy required among its citizens a shared sense of nationhood, that is, a collective identity of people who share a language or

a dialect of a common language, inhabit or are closely familiar with a defined territory, experience its ecosystem with some affection, and share a variety of customs, including a measure of memories of the historical past, which is consequently experienced in the present tense as pride in the nation's achievements and, where necessary, an obligation to feel ashamed of the nation's failings.[9]

All of this sounds quite unexceptionable, but we all know the troubles that national identity trails in its wake and why there is so much cause for concern. If we want to focus our attention on the downside, all we need do is turn on the evening news and get the latest body count from Sarajevo, a city that before the past two years was codified primarily as the place in that little-known region, the Balkans, where the Archduke Franz Ferdinand was assassinated in 1914, triggering the events that led to the bloodletting of what used to be called "the Great War." How dismally appropriate, in a way, that here the most destructive features of the new nationalism should be manifest. We know what these are: a ruthless granulation of political entities in the name of a principle of the unimpeachable singularity of national, linguistic, cultural, even racial identities, coupled with the dangers of mixing any group with any other.

Let me suggest that we not rush to judge the Balkans, to dismiss this region and its people as primitives and fanatics. Rather, we should permit these terrible events to instruct us on the always-present dangers in nationalism and national self-identity. We can and must be thus instructed without abandoning altogether the inherent integrity implicit in the *ideal* of self-determination, an ideal tied to self-respect and to the possibility that men and women, acting together, may know a good in common that they cannot know alone.

What we see unfolding in the Balkans is a very old phenomenon, one from which our own society is by no means exempt. Do we not see, for example, in harsher forms of multiculturalism an assertion of the absolutism of particular identity? Going beyond rightful claims to self-respect and civic equality, multicultural absolutists insist that identities must not be mixed; that, quite literally, whites and blacks or men and women or homosexuals and heterosexuals inhabit incommensurable epistemological universes. This is a view that neither the civic pluralist nor the Christian can accept, for the civic pluralist and the Christian alike embrace universalist aspirations and possibilities, affirming the idea that we can and must reach out in gestures of solidarity, friendship, and citizenship to those different from ourselves.

The "ethno-cultural" version of identity and nationalism, as G. M.

Tamás puts it, is that "others ought to be elsewhere; there is no universal-
istic, overriding, trans-contextual principle 'legitimizing' mixture, assimi-
lation or diversity within the same politico-symbolic 'space.'"[10] Those
who break bodies politic "into warring ethno-cultural enclaves" disdain
nineteenth-century liberal and civic republican ideas of citizenship. These
accepted the possibility of, and, in some instances, the necessity for, a
form of national identity not reducible to ethnicity or culture as that
which is simply given. The new ethnocultural nationalism, "particularly
in the extreme shape it has taken in Eastern Europe, cannot and does not
want to answer political questions. It is mostly a repetitive reaffirmation
of identity." The only precept proffered by the ethnoculturalist is, "Be
what you are," as an essentialist prescription.[11] This, then, stands in
contrast to an alternative civic ideal, one that is chastened by the
recognition that "others are before and among me," that I am not
hunkered down, alone, with others exactly like myself.

The post-World War II popes, the U.S. bishops, and civic patriots (by
contrast with very uncivil nationalists) all recognize this latter reality.
The Christian, in fact, is obliged in this matter. Christianity is not
primarily a civic religion. It arose in opposition to empire and has from
its inception engaged in a struggle with political authority over what
rightly belongs to *regnum* and to *sacerdotium*. At the same time, the
Christian insists that human beings are always in the empire, in a political
formation of some sort or another. The claims of a body politic, however,
including the vast pretensions embodied in the classical notion of sovereignty, must always be checked and balanced against other claims.
Identity with, and obligation to, a nation-state is never absolute. We
rightly fear forms of nationalism that feed on hatred of other ways of
life, but much of the new nationalism, the remarkable outbursts of civic
energy from suppressed peoples, speaks in and through a rhetoric that
taps universal claims and concerns.

The independence movements in the Baltic states—Solidarity, Civic
Forum, and others—protested their control by the Soviet empire, first,
because it violated principles of self-determination imbedded in international law and shared understandings and, second, because it trampled
on basic human rights, including the right to participate in and help to
choose a way of life. Such appeals are at once universal and particular,
tapping old identities but energizing new political recognitions. Hopefully, peoples who proclaim their devotion to human rights as a universal
principle can be held accountable in ways in which rapacious, nationalistic destroyers, who scoff at such niceties, cannot (though one must, of
course, attempt to hold them accountable). This middle way—once

again as an alternative to warring racial and ethnic groupings or the homogenized stability of efficiently managed imperialism—seems to me the only possible course that respects claims to self-determination yet holds forth the prospect of a painfully attained and perhaps, for that reason, even more deeply cherished civic order based on universal principles or recognition.

Perhaps a concrete example of this delicate balancing act is necessary. I rely here on press reports of Pope John Paul II's visit to the Baltic states in September 1993. The situation in Lithuania was particularly delicate for John Paul because "Polish nationalists for their part have tried to exploit the alleged mistreatment of the 300,000 strong Polish minority in Lithuania"; thus, "the Pope had to be very careful not to offend Lithuanian sensibilities," he being not only the pope but a Pole associated with Polish aspirations to self-determination. It is worth reminding the reader that much of current Lithuania was once part of Poland. The Lithuanian capital, Vilnius, is Poland's Wilno, dear to the hearts of Poles everywhere, in part because it is the home of Adam Mickiewicz, the greatest Polish poet, but John Paul, while acknowledging the love Poles have for that particular place, used the Lithuanian name Vilnius and not the Polish Wilno throughout his pastoral visit, including the one time he spoke Polish—when he delivered mass in the main Polish-language church in Vilnius. For the rest of his visit, "the Pope spoke . . . Lithuanian which he had learnt for the occasion" and "this made a tremendously positive impression on the Lithuanians." The Poles "were not so pleased, but coming from the Pope they had to accept it. The Pope exhorted the Poles to identify fully with Lithuania, and not to dwell on the past—by which he meant not to endlessly recall the time when Vilnius was part of Poland. . . ."[12] This wonderful account shows the ways in which ethical space can be created or expanded for a form of civic identification sans irredentist or chauvinistic aspirations. One might say that eternal vigilance is the price of civic moderation.

Take a powerful example from the new South Africa as reported by theologian John W. de Gruchy, a long-time foe of the apartheid system. In a piece called "Waving the Flag," de Gruchy begins by telling us that he "never thought I would be seduced by civil religion. After all, part of the struggle against apartheid was against the civil religion of the Afrikaner nationalism that gave it birth." He then asks us to image his feelings of confusion as he unashamedly applauds "the civil religion of the new South Africa and experience[s] deep feelings of patriotism welling up in my soul." Now, de Gruchy continues, he has a "flag on my desk, a flag in the kitchen, a flag pinned to my jacket." He knows that there are limits, however: the fear of idolatry, warnings against making gods "in our own national image." For that reason, the flag of the new South Africa will not go into the sanctuary. "It is painful to do this—we would so much like to bring it in. But we need to do this to keep ourselves in chcck. The temptation of conflating civil religion with revelation has to be resisted."[13] This is an example—a powerful example—of how Christians are (rightly) drawn toward the civic goods embodied in a particular order, or the promise of one, but must, at the same time, refuse any moves, however tempting and apparently innocent, to forge too tight an identity between their religion and their national loyalty.

On Sovereignty and Self-Determination

This brings me to the claims of sovereignty and self-determination. After Nuremberg, such claims cannot trump all other claims in any instance of conflict. The issue of crimes against humanity and human rights has been a shaping force in the world arena and will continue to be such. Human rights may be a weak reed against deadly force but it is often the only weapon beleaguered peoples have, and it offers a lever that others can use to enforce the notion that geopolitical and cultural definitions of nationhood must, at this time in history, be open to chastening by universal principles. Of course, the church has always advocated such chastening, but as we enter the twenty-first century, a bevy of international associations promulgates and nurtures this conviction as well.

At the same time, the plurality of cultures is irreducible. A world of many nations, each with its own particular marks of self-identity, reminds us that we are not alone and that we cannot and ought not make the world one by cruelly obliterating diverse ways of life. One of the most insidious aspects of communist "universalism" was precisely its need to crush difference, "to make everything the same," in the words of Havel. Havel goes on:

> The greatest enemy of communism was always individuality, variety, difference—in a word, freedom. From Berlin to Vladivostok, the streets and buildings were decorated with the same red stars. Everywhere the same kind of celebratory parades were staged. Analogical state administrations were set up, along with the whole system of central direction for social and economic life. This vast shroud of uniformity, stifling all national, intellectual, spiritual, social, cultural, and religious variety, covered over any differences and created the monstrous illusion that we were all the same.[14]

No, we are not the same, but we do share a capacity for identification with the idea of a plural political body; we all require self-dignity; we all yearn for a decent life for our children.

This latter universalism is as different from the false universalism that Havel denounces as the night is to the day. In the words of John Paul, "a falsely united multinational society [the Soviet Empire] must not be succeeded by one falsely diversified." (Here the pope refers to the "racist pretensions and evil forms of nationalism. . . .")[15] A universalism that sustains respect for difference is a universalism aware of our human need for concrete reference groups in order to attain and to sustain individuality and identity. As a version of national identity, the form of membership I wish to commend softens but does not negate altogether the idea of sovereignty. The alternative to strong theories of sovereignty that place duty and loyalty to the nation-state above all other duties and loyalties is "sovereignty . . . in the service of the people," in the words of the U.S. bishops.[16]

Václav Havel writes of a politics of civic self-determination as a form of "practical morality . . . humanly measured care for our fellow human beings." Scoring the "arrogant anthropocentrism of modern man," an arrogance that has its political culmination in triumphalist accounts of sovereignty and nationalism, Havel opts for limited ideals of identity and responsibility.[17] Politics, in this account, has to do with having a home, with being at home, with tending to one's particular home and its place in the wider world in which one gets one's bearings. Pope John Paul has also elaborated an alternative to statist versions of sovereignty. In one early formulation he argued, "The state is firmly sovereign when it governs society and also serves the common good of society and allows the nation to realize its own subjectivity, its own identity."[18]

Insofar as I grasp the version of sovereignty here advanced, sovereignty is located neither in the state per se nor in an unmediated construction of the sovereign will of the people but, rather, in the multiple associations of civil society in dialogue with one another as subjects. This dialogue creates, or concatenates into, a political body whose legitimate purpose is to see that rules for civil contestation are followed and that the various loci of human social existence, necessary to human dignity and freedom, are protected and served. The coexistence of overlapping, porous entities is assumed. This is a dialogical, by contrast to a monological, political ideal.

With Isaiah Berlin, I "do not wish to abandon the idea of a world which is a reasonably peaceful coat of many colors, each portion of which develops its own distinct cultural identity and is tolerant of others."[19] This ideal, indeed, offers the strongest alternative to the cruelty and torment of a rapacious and narrow nationalism, on the one hand, or a watery universalism or impositional empire that either cannot inspire or cruelly commands people's loyalties, on the other. We live in a dangerous time, shaped by powerful forces most of us had no direct hand in shaping.

In a recent powerful book, Michael Ignatieff reminds us that this "new nationalism" takes many forms.[20] It can look as menacing and behave as horribly as the term "ethnic cleansing" suggests, a new name for a very old and, alas, pervasive phenomenon. It can also creep up on cat's paws in the form of sad little tales of past injustice coupled with a no-doubt unrealistic but very human desire for reparation, for putting things right somehow. We know, or are coming to know, the big stories of the shelling of cities, massacres, detention camps, and the breaking up of old multiethnic enclaves and ways of life. Writing of the "ethnically cleansed microstates that have taken the place of Yugoslavia," Ignatieff, in this wonderfully crafted and sobering journey of discovery, writes: "Ethnic apartheid may be an abomination, but for the more than two million refugees who have fled or been driven from their homes, apartheid is the only guarantee of safety they are prepared to trust" (37).

This holds for aggressors and victims alike, for we must bear in mind that who the tormentor is and who the one being tormented is shifts from week to week. Although the Serbs bear the major responsibility for the disaster in the Balkans, they are not solely responsible; indeed, the West must take its fair share of the blame for what has happened there. As Ignatieff notes: "For the West failed to save Sarajevo, where Muslim, Croat, and Serb lived together in peace for centuries. It is asking the impossible to believe that ordinary people will trickle back to the multiethnic villages they have left behind, simply in order to vindicate our liberal principles" (37).

What Ignatieff tries to get the reader, perhaps dipping into this volume in the comfort of an office or a soft reading chair in a den, to grasp is fear—the fear everywhere at work in struggles over the new nationalism, whether in the Balkans, Germany, Ukraine, Quebec, Kurdistan, or Northern Ireland, the sites that form the basis of his political ethnography. "There is one type of fear more devastating in its impact than any other: the systematic fear that arises when a state begins to collapse. Ethnic hatred is the result of the terror that arises when legitimate authority disintegrates" (24). That all-pervasive fear is unknown to us in contemporary Western democracies in its most primordial, most overwhelming form, but it is no stranger to many of our fellow human beings.

Ignatieff is not out to demonize nationalism. He recognizes, as all serious scholars of the subject must, the historically close connection between nationalism and democracy. "Nationalism, after all, is the doctrine that a people have a right to rule themselves, and that sovereignty reposes in them alone" (25). The "tragedy for the Balkans," then, was that when democracy at last became possible, "the only language that existed to mobilize people into a shared social project was the rhetoric of ethnic difference. Any possibility of a civic, as opposed to ethnic, democracy had been strangled at birth by the Communist regime" (25). For in Tito's Yugoslavia there were no competing political parties, no independent loci of social and political life—the divisions were based on ethnicity alone, with the *apparat* perched on top holding everything in dictatorial order. People had no experience of democratic contestation in and through the category of civic citizenship. What existed in the old Yugoslavia was "manipulated plebiscitary democracy that ratifies one-man rule" (54).

Ignatieff wants to disabuse us of a certain sort of liberal prejudice: the notion that what we see in the Balkans or Northern Ireland or elsewhere is an outburst of atavistic irrationalism. He carefully situates us in complex political and social contexts, helping us to understand how and why and when people are driven to extremes of ethnic identification and contestation, even as he is horrified at the result. He reminds us of just how important national belonging really is and how it has come about that nation-states remain the dominant form of constituting and maintaining political bodies, for better or for worse. He suggests it is a good bit of both. "It is only too apparent that cosmopolitanism is the privilege of those who can take a secure nation-state for granted" (13), he notes provocatively, for cosmopolitanism, a blithe "post-nationalist spirit," depends, in ways its advocates and practitioners often resolutely refuse to recognize, "on the capacity of nation-states to provide security and civility for their citizens" (13).

Ignatieff's is a vivid and sad journey. He takes us into the heart of fraught and fractured situations. He never adopts a stance of superior Western smugness toward those he interviews, encounters, sups, and drinks with. We hear voices and see faces. For example, we hear a skinhead in the old East Germany (where, by the way, the most virulent forms of antiforeign sentiment have broken out, not in the old West Germany with its nearly half century of democratic civic life). Ignatieff's interview with "Leo," who embodies contemporary skin culture, is filled up by Leo's talk, at once rageful and riddled with pathos. "If you see the world from his point of view," Ignatieff writes, "he comes from the only country in Europe that isn't allowed to feel good about itself" (83). Germany is still required to atone for its sins, but young men like Leo were born well after the Third Reich and they are tired, apparently, of bearing the stigma of "Germanness." Perhaps Leo, then, is an example of what happens when a country "loses peaceful ways of being proud about itself, when the language of national pride is forced underground, when patriotism is hijacked by criminals" (83). For Leo, "This isn't home, this is just misery" (84), and out of the darkness of that misery he lashes out.

Ukraine, Quebec, Kurdistan—we follow Ignatieff on his mordant quest. The fears of his respondents come alive for us. The great tragedy, he concludes, is that ethnic nationalism, as a quest for sure and certain identity, must fail because it does not allow people to be truly themselves. They must lose their individuality in that of the group. It becomes an ethnic crime to fall in love and to marry outside the group. It becomes an ethnic crime to think in and through categories other than ethnicity. Nationalism, Ignatieff hastens to assure us, is not what is wrong with the world: "Every people must have a home, every such hunger must be assuaged" (249). What is wrong is the "kind of nation, the kind of homeland that nationalists want to create and the means they use to seek their ends" (249). If hatred of others is necessary in order to achieve your own group solidarity, you are on the road to bitter disappointment and in thrall to a likely cycle of recrimination and revenge. Ignatieff concludes,

> I began the journey as a liberal and I end as one, but I cannot help thinking that liberal civilization—the rule of law, not men, of argument in place of force, of compromise in place of violence—runs deeply against the human grain and is achieved and sustained only by the most unremitting struggle against human nature. The liberal virtues—tolerance, compromise, reason—remain as valuable as ever, but they cannot be preached to those who are mad with fear or mad with vengeance (248).

That is Ignatieff's sober lesson for us, here in the waning years of the twentieth century. To those who preach wholly abstract sermons about peace and harmony and goodwill, Ignatieff would probably say: "Grow up. What we must come to realize is that nationalism is the chief political passion and force as we enter the twenty-first century. How will we in the stable and privileged West respond? With moral superiority and more preachments or with a tough-minded preparedness to engage, in order, just perhaps, to help those who seek and need our help to arrive at least at those conditions of some safety from depradation that alone might help them to learn or relearn the lessons of tolerance and moderation."

Sometimes, as I suggested above, the new nationalism is a story in miniature. Consider the fate of Karlovy Vary, also known as Karlsbad, the belle epoque spa famous in literature, frequented by the likes of Nietzsche, Freud, and, in an earlier generation, Goethe and other luminaries. Karlovy Vary is in the Sudetenland, "a region once home to 65,000 Jews, 800,000 Czechs, and three million Germans."[21] When the Germans annexed the Sudetenland, they sent the Jewish population packing. Next the "Czechs eliminated Germans. Eduard Benes, the pre-Communist post-war president, decreed their expulsion in 1945. At Potsdam, the Allies approved. As Germans fled toward Bavaria, Czechs took revenge: They murdered 40,000 Germans; many died at the end of a rope."

This episode was long-buried in the communist deep freeze, but since 1989, "the expulsion has become a national nettle. . . . Czechs know that every Sudeten German wasn't guilty of Hitler's crimes." Oskar Schindler, by the way, was a Sudeten German. Although President Václav Havel has condemned the Sudeten expulsion, the current regime wants to keep the episode closed. In the meantime, children of Jewish and German victims of expulsion and murder are seeking, one by one, the return of their family houses. These are people with real names and faces and quite specific and—in the grand scale of things—small stories and claims. Each is heartbreaking, of course. The current policy permits Jewish families with claims to regain their houses; but German families cannot. The German descendants do not understand why their troubles count for nothing. One says, "My only crime, was that for 800 years my ancestors lived in that place." They want repeal of the 1945 expulsion decree. They want a chance to get their property back. They want to return to their homeland, not just homes in Karlovy Vary but villages long emptied—ethnically cleansed—of their kind, but it will not happen.

Not every wrong can be righted. Not every injustice can be reversed. Perhaps, at this juncture, Hannah Arendt's insistence that forgiveness is the greatest contribution of Jesus of Nazareth to politics should be noted. Perhaps there is nothing left for the expelled and expropriated people of German descent to do but to forgive. This gesture is made possible, in part, by President Havel's recognition of the past injustice they suffered, but forgiveness from the side of the aggrieved itself helps to make possible forms of soul searching and recognition from the other side. Forgiveness is the hardest thing of all to do, of course, but it may be the only way to forestall quaffing the bitter brew of injustice suffered and recompense sought even unto future generations. The nationalist principle does not take us very far at this point; it can only deepen rage, not sustain forgiveness. Forgiveness, I fear, is a possibility utterly eclipsed by the new nationalism, whether writ large or small. We should all grow more fearful if I am right.

Endnotes

1. Isaiah Berlin, "Two Concepts of Nationalism," *New York Review of Books* (21 November 1991): 20.

2. Liah Greenfeld, *Nationalism: Five Roads to Modernity* (Cambridge, Mass.: Harvard University Press, 1992), 487–88.

3. Václav Havel, "The Post-Communist Nightmare," *New York Review of Books* (27 May 1993): 8.

4. Pope John XXIII, *"Pacem in terris,"* in *The Encyclicals and Other Messages of John XXIII* (Washington, D.C.: TPS Press, n.d.), 347.

5. Pope John XXIII, 350.

6. George Orwell, "Notes on Nationalism," *The Collected Essays, Journalism, and Letters of George Orwell*, 4 vols., ed. Sonia Orwell and Ian Angus (New York: Harvest, HBJ, 1968), 3: 362–63.

7. U. S. Bishops, "The Harvest of Justice is Sown in Peace," *Origins* 23:26 (9 December 1993): 458.

8. Robert Coles, *The Political Life of Children* (Boston: Atlantic Monthly, 1986), 60, 61, 63.

9. John Keane, "Democracy's Poisonous Fruit," *Times Literary Supplement* (21 August 1992): 10.

10. G. M. Tamás, "Old Enemies and New: A Philosophic Postscript to Nationalism," *Studies in East European Thought* (Netherlands: Kluwer Academic, 1993), 120.

11. Tamás, 121.

12. I here rely on Anatol Lieven's account, "The Pope's Balancing Act," in *The Tablet* (18 September 1993): 1208–9.

13. John W. de Gruchy, "Waving the Flag," *Christian Century* (15–22 June 1994): 597–98.

14. Havel, "Post-Communist Nightmare," 8.

15. "Pope Sees False Nationalism Tearing at Europe," *The Tablet* (4 December 1993): 1599.

16. "The Harvest of Justice is Sown in Peace," 453.

17. These insights and words are found throughout Havel's works. The reader might want to consult both early and late essays. See *Václav Havel, or Living in Truth*, ed. Jan Vladislav (London: Faber and Faber, 1987); and Václav Havel, *Disturbing the Peace* (New York: Alfred A. Knopf, 1990.)

18. Cited in Timothy Garton Ash, *The Use of Adversity: Essays on the Fate of Central Europe* (New York: Random House, 1989), 43. From a homily at Jasna Gora in 1983.

19. Berlin, "Two Notes on Nationalism," 21.

20. Michael Ignatieff, *Blood and Belonging: Journeys into the New Nationalism* (New York: Farrar, Straus and Giroux, 1994). Page numbers in parentheses refer to this book.

21. All quotes are drawn from the story, "Czech Republic Fields Demands of Germans, Jews for Lost Homes," *The Wall Street Journal* (15 July 1994): 1, 6.

Nationalism, An Initially Non-Liberal Assessment: A Response to Jean Bethke Elshtain

Vigen Guroian

Early in the summer of 1990 I visited Armenia for the first time. This was on the heels of the massive protests and rallies of 1987–88 and the terrible earthquake in December of 1988. In Armenia the conviction and expectation was that Gorbachev would fall from power—as indeed he did fifteen months later—and talk everywhere was of independence. Out of a century filled with great tragedies for the Armenian people a nation would be born. Even the cautious and conservative Armenian Orthodox Church had begun to shift its position and support the popular nationalist movement.

How could I help but embrace these Armenian aspirations for sovereignty and self-determination? It looked as if the dream of my grandparents was coming true. I was wary, however, of the excesses of the nationalist fervor in Armenia, and the dangers that I had identified from a distance before my visit looked even more troublesome up close. My harshest criticism was reserved for the Armenian church. Though the spread of public opinion on the national question gave reason for cautious optimism, the unmistakable mark of expediency in the church's shift from partner of the central Soviet authorities and of the old communist regime in Armenia to sacralizer of the new nationalism was worrisome indeed, for it seemed clear that in return for special privileges the Armenian church was going to follow old habits and offer itself up to the new political regime as its loyal handmaid. While the church's conspicuous neglect of its spiritually starved people was distressing enough, more troubling still was the prospect of a compromised Armenian church that in the future would be unwilling or unable to call back the nation from the extremes of Armenian particularism and nationalism.

How I related to Armenian politics and how my views were perceived by those with whom I spoke was hardly less unsettling. In the American context, I thought of myself as a Burkean conservative. In Armenia, I was called down, even by people deeply committed to democracy, as a typically deracinated American bred on a bloodless liberalism. "What gives you Americans the right to use this word 'nationalist' against us?" exclaimed Levon Melikyan, a teacher of architecture and self-described Christian Democrat. "Do you think love of country is bad or that we should not have the freedom that you as an American already enjoy?"

One evening, Onnig Vatyan, a former Armenian athletic star and now a school principal, drove me to the home of his sister and nephew, with whom I was staying. En route Onnig was stopped at a checkpoint. It was not necessary to understand the words that were exchanged. Onnig was trying to explain why he was out past curfew. The Russian soldiers were deliberately harassing and humiliating him in front of an American. When we were released, Onnig turned to me. In the dim light of the street lamps I saw on his face a grimace of intense, inner rage straining for utterance. "Vigen," he blurted out, "my dear friend, is this any way for human beings to live? We are like animals in a cage at the will of the zookeeper." I dug into my limited Armenian vocabulary and responded in the only way I knew how. "Onnig," I said, "every man has need of freedom, here also in Armenia." Onnig nodded, "Yes, Vigen, just so!"

The next morning Onnig drove me to his school. First, he proudly showed me the small museum of ancient artifacts that had been assembled through the generous donation of an Armenian-American philanthropist. These were the tools with which Onnig would transmit to his young charges the Armenian history, culture, and identity that had been suppressed for so long. Then he led me out onto the playground. He pointed to a trench that had been dug alongside the school building. This would be a firing range to train the youth how to defend the Armenian land from Russians, Azerbaijanis, Turks, or any other enemies that would deny them their Armenian heritage and identity.

Armenia is a microcosm of the nationalist struggles and turmoils that affect so much of the old Soviet empire and mock our talk of a new world order. None of this comes as much of a surprise to those, like myself, who are connected by lineage, church, language, history, memory, and sentiment to peoples that were repressed under communism. For others in the academy, however, and for many so-called policymakers, it has been a shock. They just cannot understand why these people will not be reasonable and tolerant and show respect for democracy above everything else. Even observers with a strong commitment to human rights, who are initially sympathetic, grow uneasy when they see that these movements for self-determination and nationhood are mixed up inextricably with uncompromising attachment to the land, pride of nationality, and an apparently inexhaustible animosity toward historic enemies.

Of course, there have been notable exceptions to these rather typical reactions and responses. In her essay, Jean Bethke Elshtain cites Sir Isaiah Berlin, who in an article published twenty years ago—long before almost anyone anticipated the extraordinary events of the past decade—gave this kind of nationalism a name. He called it "bent twig" nationalism. The metaphor was intended to draw attention to a type of nationalism that is a reaction of repressed peoples to national humiliation and subjugation. Berlin argued that this kind of nationalism has its own value (independent of democratic principles) with the potential of being an important healing agent for old wounds.

Berlin's liberal credentials are hardly subject to question, so his analysis has had the added effect of engendering among some of his students and admirers a tolerance of nationalism and even attempts to show that nationalism need not be antithetical to liberalism and democracy. Yael Tamir's recent book *Liberal Nationalism* is a case in point.[1] Tamir looks again at the historical relationship of nationalism and liberalism in their origin and development. She embraces Berlin's description of the psychological and historical reasons why bent twig forms of nationalism arise, but Tamir goes beyond a descriptive account to develop a normative theory of what she calls liberal nationalism. This theory establishes principles of autonomy, citizenship, cultural pluralism, and guarantees of the rights of minorities as criteria for judging whether a particular nationalism approximates the ideal.

Tamir justifies her normative theory with a typically liberal assessment that we live in a world in which few nations are any longer ethnically homogenous and notions of peoplehood based in language, common religion, and ethnic stock are more often the product of imagination than an empirical reality. Based on this assessment, she proposes liberal nationalism as a kind of half-way house between the old nation-statehood that is closely associated with political sovereignty and forms of nationhood and cultural sovereignty that are democratic and cosmopolitan. Tamir's analysis is studious, subtle, and admirably nuanced. Undoubtedly, however, my Armenian friend Levon Melikyan would see it as just a reformulated version of the same old imperious and imperialistic attitude of Western liberals who want to tell others how to behave.

In her essay, Elshtain also proposes a "middle way" between a potentially reactionary and triumphalistic cultural nationalism, on the one hand, and a bloodless liberal rationalism, on the other. She is appreciative of the diversity of human culture grounded not just in reason but also in history, and she presents us with a historicistic and pluralistic theory of nationhood and politics that yet manages to make a strong case for upholding universal human rights. Elshtain describes this middle way as an "alternative to warring racial and ethnic groupings or the homogenized stability of efficiently managed imperialism" (Elshtain, 110).

Elshtain's historical empiricism, especially, makes for a richer and more realistic discussion of nationalism than Tamir's, and for this reason my critical discussion of her essay does not imply radical disagreement. I do wish to advance the view, however, that proposals for a middle way such as those of Elshtain and Tamir are not of much help at this stage. Presently, we are faced with situations that reflect unmanageable mixes of cultural nationalism, liberal democracy, populism, authoritarianism, and totalitarianism. Many of these situations simply are not yet amenable to a middle way. Many ways are possible as forces long pent up now contend with each other in ways that defy what we in Western liberal democracies take to be normal political processes. Our insistence on balance and compromise often blinds us to our propensity to read our own history into the struggles we observe. Too much of the analysis in the West draws on distinctions between good guys and bad guys that are nothing more than positive and negative projections of our history and experience of liberalism and the demons that have tempted or threatened it. The national and political struggles in Russia, Ukraine, and Armenia entail very different historical choices and outcomes.

More important than considerations of timing, however, are the assumptions that liberals bring to bear on their analysis of nationalism. I thus want to consider bent twig nationalism by initially bracketing out our liberal democratic prejudices, contradicting much of what lies behind the rhetoric and commitments of communitarians, neoliberals, and neoconservatives who are sympathetic to it. Their sympathy comes front loaded with an agenda for vindicating and advancing liberal democracy, or whatever might be saved of it in so-called postmodernity.

Elshtain draws upon Michael Ignatieff's analysis in his recent book, *Blood and Belonging: Journeys into the New Nationalism*, and rightly takes encouragement from Ignatieff's confession that liberals such as himself need to augment their analyses of nationalism with greater historical empiricism. One would like to think also that Ignatieff's change is a harbinger of greater openness among Western liberals to voices and events in the East that challenge their quick condemnations of nationalism and easy assumptions about democracy as a political good. A contemporary case in point is their misinterpretation of Alexsandr Solzhenitsyn.

Solzhenitsyn was lionized by liberals in the 1960s and early 1970s. But when he came to the West as an exile from his own land and without "proper manner" proceeded to ruthlessly unmask the spiritual and ethical bankruptcy and historical illiteracy of liberal moralism and idealism, the early positive assessments quickly stopped. In his famous (or infamous) Harvard commencement address of 1978, Solzhenitsyn made it unmistakably clear that he was not a man of strict liberal civic faith, and for this the press and the academy began to depict the greatest living twentieth-century heir of the Russian polyphonic novel—directly in the tradition of Dostoevsky—as antipluralist, antidemocratic, antisemitic, and an advocate of authoritarianism.

To this day, Solzhenitsyn continues to insist on the inductive study of history, religious tradition, and culture rather than the accepted liberal models of deductive reason in politics. His gravest and most unforgivable sin, however, is that his God is God and not Demos. Lucky for many in the West, Andrei Sakharov was around to fill the void left by the anathematization of Solzhenitsyn. This is not the appropriate occasion for probing what made Sakharov a more attractive and acceptable figure than Solzhenitsyn, but Elshtain has supplied a suitable analog in Václav Havel, whom she describes as an enlightened nationalist or civic patriot committed to democratic liberalism and someone worthy of our admiration. Most Western liberals who are suspicious of or even negatively disposed toward Solzhenitsyn would agree with her judgment concerning Havel. She accurately describes Havel's civic philosophy as dialogical, in contrast to the monological character of modern totalitarianism. Unlike many in the West, Elshtain, much to her credit, also recognizes Havel's deep and fundamental concern with religion and morality as first-order realities of human existence. He describes himself as an opponent of what he calls "the arrogant anthropocentrism of modern man."

Havel deserves this praise, and yet even he is misunderstood by secular liberals, only in his case these misinterpretations reflect and reinforce a favorable bias that holds him up approvingly as a good liberal and civic patriot. Havel's beliefs, however, are more complicated than that. Naive affirmations that he is a champion of Western-style democratic liberalism are the reverse side of the coin that depicts Solzhenitsyn as an extreme nationalist with an authoritarian bent. In point of fact, even though Havel's Czech nation is tied more closely historically than is Russia to the Western tradition of democratic liberalism, his worldview shares many fundamentals in common with Solzhenitsyn. Elshtain taps near to these commonalties, but I would have said more and with reference to Solzhenitsyn, for Havel's roots as a dissident and opponent of Marxist-Leninism and communism make up a more complex story than the one that has been told about him by his liberal admirers in the West.

What do Solzhenitsyn and Havel believe and say in common? To begin with, both criticize modernity and the spiritual bankruptcy of advanced liberalism.[2] Both Solzhenitsyn and Havel trace the crack-up of modernity and the crisis of politics back to the crisis of faith and meaning created by the modern Promethean experiment with atheism. Even in the 1960s and 1970s Havel recognized that the new nationalism that was coming up through the cracks and rubble of a collapsing order was the valid expression of people who wanted to dig out from under the rubble. Like Solzhenitsyn, he set this in the context of a much larger phenomenon affecting both East and West, the slow death of modernity. In the East it is the rubble of Marxist-Leninism, while in the West there is the cracking up of the secular liberalism born of the Enlightenment.

Like Solzhenitsyn, Havel also insists that in order to recover their identity and determine for themselves what they want for political systems, the peoples of the former communist lands must return to their Christian roots with its anthropology of the human person created in the image of God. Without this anchor the so-called democratic virtues of tolerance, compromise, and justice are like debris tossed about on a stormy sea. Over and again, one can assert that these virtues are true; but this will not make them any more capable of countering the ethnic pride and extreme nationalism that threaten violence against neighbor and historic enemy. In 1978 Havel wrote: "To cling to the notion of traditional parliamentary democracy as one's political ideal and to succumb to the illusion that only this 'tried and true' form is capable of guaranteeing human beings enduring dignity and an independent role in society would, in my opinion, be at the very least shortsighted."[3]

That Havel has proven a friend of parliamentary democracy in no way negates his openness to new and other forms of political life and governance. This is based in a strong sense of history and, like Solzhenitsyn, on a ready ascription of first priority to the deeper relationship of faith and politics. Both men know the histories of their peoples and both also recognize that even if democratic forms are preferable for their societies, the success of home-grown democratic institutions is not guaranteed by building them out of just any old democratic debris that comes floating in from America and Western Europe. Democracy, no less than nationalism, has its corruptions, and these occur when the inherent dignity of human beings is loaded on a ship without ballast or anchor.

I know that this assessment, critique, and response do not provide the answers we all seek in a world that is so frightfully disturbed, and I want to thank Elshtain for such a clear and inviting essay, but she must surely agree that what she or I might have to say does not in the end matter all that much. Far more important are the words and deeds of persons in troubled lands who have committed their lives and all that they possess to the renewal of national life no less than to democracy and who are able to see beyond the present dangers and work for the restoration of civilization. Perhaps we ought to permit ourselves to hope that the solutions reached in formerly communist countries will derive not from old expected political formulas but, rather, from larger visions of the human good that unapologetically embrace the conviction that God, not man, is the source and fountain of freedom, justice, peace, prosperity, and love, and that God, not man, is also the judge of all that we do.

I would thus end not with prognostication but with the words of an Armenian patriot and nationalist. In October of 1989, soon after his release from a Soviet prison for his political activities as a member of the liberationist Karabagh Committee, Rafael Ishkhanian issued his now famous article, "The Law of Excluding the Third Force." In it Ishkhanian wrote:

> I think man's purpose in life is to achieve perfection. To go from bad to good, to change toward the perfect. I also think the same should be true for a nation . . . to realize the mistakes of our past, to make fewer mistakes in the future. . . .
>
> Our path to becoming a sovereign and independent nation will become barren if we forget our Christian faith. . . . If we try to do everything without relying on our maker, we will fail. . . . We need a return to Christianity like the air we breathe. . . .
>
> I am convinced that we can survive . . . if we move not with emotions and a sense of vengeance but with reason. . . . In this case God will help us. And if we survive, become strong, and do good deeds, our lands will be reunited to us too.
>
> But . . . if we become prisoners of our emotions, of the call of revenge, this piece of land too will be taken and we will be a lost nation.[4]

Endnotes

1. Yael Tamir, *Liberal Nationalism* (Princeton, N.J.: Princeton University Press, 1993).

2. For an informative discussion of these commonalities, see Edward E. Ericson, Jr., *Solzhenitsyn and the Modern World* (Washington, D.C.: Regnery Gateway, 1993), especially chap. 13.

3. Václav Havel, "The Power of the Powerless," in *Open Letters: Selected Writings 1965–1990* (New York: Vintage Books, 1992), 209.

4. Rafael Ishkhanian, "The Law of Excluding the Third Force," in *Armenia at the Crossroads: Democracy and Nationhood in the Post-Soviet Era,* ed. Gerard J. Libaridian (Watertown, Mass.: Blue Crane Books, 1991), 10, 36, 38.

Chapter 5

Humanitarian Intervention, Christian Ethical Reasoning, and the Just-War Idea

James Turner Johnson

If the end of the Cold War has found policymakers in the United States, as well as those in other countries and the United Nations, poorly prepared to deal with the conflicts and associated problems that have since arisen, it has also revealed the lack of moral discourse specifically tuned to these problems. The reason in both cases is the same: the Cold War preoccupation of the policy community and moralists alike with the U.S.-Soviet rivalry, the problems of nuclear weapons, and a conception of the world in terms of two major spheres of influence (the First and Second Worlds) with a very diverse remainder (lumped together as the Third World). In addition, for some moralists (and perhaps some in the policy community as well) who thought of the problem of conflict in the world as principally caused by the Cold War itself, the end of that contest was supposed to usher in a new era of international and domestic peace and harmony. Still further, for those observers of history who depicted the Cold War as the result of defects in an international order based on the state system, the end of U.S.-Soviet hegemony was supposed to lead to a decrease in the power of states, an increase in the power and prestige of the United Nations, and perhaps even the dawn of a genuine world government.

The reality of the last few years has, of course, proven dramatically different. Local conflicts that, under the conditions of the Cold War, would have tended to be managed by the superpowers or their allies in

127

order to avoid the possibility of their leading to a broader war have in the new international context turned out to be essentially intractable. Local forces largely have been left to fight out their differences, and the international community has been presented with repeated cases of armed conflict-created humanitarian need on a massive scale. In this new context the policy communities in the United States and elsewhere continue to scramble for a coherent and practical approach, while the United Nations has added a Chapter VII peacemaking role to its traditional Chapter VI peacekeeping functions. Moral discourse as well must be rethought if we are to address the dimensions of this new context.

The present chapter brings an analysis specifically rooted in Christian ethical tradition to one outstanding problem of the new international context: how to deal with massive humanitarian need caused by domestic armed conflicts. More specifically, I am concerned here with the moral issues attaching to the interventionary use of military force in the alleviation of such need and the interplay between national, international, and nongovernmental interests and obligations in the employment of such force. My framework of analysis is that of the just-war idea as developed in Christian ethical thought, with particular attention to two important thinkers, Saint Augustine and Paul Ramsey.

Christian Just-War Thought and the Idea of Intervention

The central questions on the morality of intervention by force across national borders are those defined by the classic just-war ideas of just cause and right authority, the core ideas of the *jus ad bellum*. The theological roots of these two ideas in Christian thought set the basic context for a moral examination of the problem of intervention and laid the groundwork for a justification of interventionary action. "[I]t is the wrong-doing of the opposing party which compels the wise man to wage just wars," Augustine wrote in *The City of God* (19:7).[1] Later Christian tradition, citing another statement from Augustine, explained what this would mean: "Those wars are customarily called just which have for their end the revenging of injuries, when it is necessary to constrain a city or a nation which has not wished to punish an evil action committed by its citizens or to restore that which has been taken unjustly" (Augustine, quoted by Gratian in *Decretum*,[2] part 2, causa 23, quest. 2, canon 2). Who might justly take up arms to carry out this function of what one writer has called "vindicative justice"?[3] Medieval Christian just-war thinkers found the answer in Romans 13:4: "For [the prince] does not bear the sword in vain. He is the minister of God to execute his wrath on him who does evil." On this basis the theorists constructed the classic just-war concept of right authority as limited to sovereign temporal rulers—those with no superior.

Medieval just-war thought defined just cause for resort to arms as including not only vindicative justice—in the standard formula, "retaking something wrongly taken" and "the punishment of evil"—but also as including the right of defense. All three of these justifying causes had been recognized in classical Roman thought, but Christian doctrine gave them a particular coloration. This was true especially for the concept of defense. Early Christian thought accepted as standard the idea that Jesus' teaching forbade self-defense. What, though, of the defense of others? Ambrose of Milan focused the question with a paradigm: a Christian is walking on a remote road, carrying a weapon to defend himself against wild animals he might meet on the way. He instead encounters another innocent traveler in the process of being attacked by an evildoer. Ambrose did not challenge the accepted doctrine that if the itinerant Christian were himself the victim of the assault in progress, he could not defend himself. (The Christian "when he meets an armed robber . . . cannot return his blows, lest in defending his life he should stain his love for his neighbor"; Ambrose, *On the Duties of the Clergy*, 3.4.27.)[4] in this case, however, the harm was directed toward another. What is the Christian's responsibility then? Ambrose's answer broke new ground: "He who does not keep harm off a friend, if he can, is as much in fault as he who causes it" (Ambrose, 1.36.179). The Christian's obligation in such a case is to defend the innocent victim of injustice, using force if necessary, but only in the degree needed to prevent the attack from succeeding; and the Christian is further restrained in the use of force by reflecting that the evildoer too is someone for whom Christ died.

Augustine took up and further developed this concept of the Christian duty in love to defend the innocent against violent harm and other forms of injustice.[5] In his thought this duty explicitly became the justification of Christian participation in military service, for while a Christian might not defend himself from harm, he has an obligation in love, Augustine argued, to defend his threatened neighbor (Augustine, *On Free Choice*, Book 1, chap. 5).[6] Military service provided an organized way to do this. Medieval writers before Thomas Aquinas took this argument as established doctrine, but Aquinas removed an inherent tension in the doctrine by arguing that in natural law there is also an obligation to protect oneself—without which protection one would not be able to defend others (Thomas Aquinas, *Summa Theologica*, 2/2, question 64, article 7).[7] From his time forward the standard position of Catholic ethics has been to maintain the right of self-defense.

The above reasoning, together with contributions from other theologians and canonists, provided the basis in normative medieval Christian thought for the core ideas of just cause and right authority in the use of force. These core ideas, in turn, were joined with other concepts both from the church and from other sectors of medieval culture to define the just-war idea in its classic form, both *jus ad bellum* and *jus in bello*. In the context of intervention, though, the central questions are those of justification and authority. The former, as we have seen, coalesced in Christian thought around the requirements that use of force be to recover something wrongly taken, to punish evil, or to defend against attack. The latter took shape in the form of the definition of the prince, understood as a temporal ruler with no earthly superior, as the one who could rightly authorize use of force, but this latter idea also included a sense of the prince's obligation to use such force in the face of evil; that is the plain sense of the regularly cited proof-text, Romans 13:4. This understanding of right authority for use of force, together with the idea that the principal justifying purpose of force was vindicative justice, clearly included armed intervention among the possibly justifiable uses of force by sovereign authority.

If we look by comparison at the status of contemporary international law on these questions of justification and authority, some striking differences may be observed. First, on the matter of just cause, twentieth-century international law from the League of Nations Covenant through the Pact of Paris to the United Nations Charter has sought to restrict the use of force by individual states to defense alone. The relevant restrictions remain in Articles 2 and 51 of the U.N. Charter. While aimed at restraining war between states, the form of the restriction also applies to interventionary use of force across international boundaries, whatever the reasons. The effect of this effort at restricting the incidence of use of force has, however, been somewhat mitigated by a broadening of the idea of defense in customary international law to include responses to behavior other than an actual attack by force, a broadening that has in effect absorbed the other two classic just causes, retaking something wrongly taken (as in the Argentine argument that its attack to recover the Malvinas/Falklands was defensive) and punishment of evil (as in the core idea behind strategic deterrence). On the matter of authority for the use of force, the very same elements of positive international law that have restricted just cause to defense have set limits on the right of individual states to undertake to use force on their own authority. At the same time, the authority taken away from individual states was relocated in regional alliances and in the United Nations itself.

Anyone conversant with the reasoning behind the classic Christian definition of the authority to use force as vested in the prince with no earthly superior and, by extension, in the sovereign state must question whether the responsibilities of sovereignty can ever rightly be passed on to a body operating by consensus or majority vote without veto, such as is the norm in contemporary international organizations. These obligations are implied in the grounding of the right to rule in the concept of the prince as minister of God to rule in God's stead. Exactly what this might mean for a contemporary state must, of course, be explicated. My point, though, is that the obligation that this concept places on the sovereign ruler, however this may be spelled out for contemporary cases, cannot be alienated by being passed on to a nonsovereign international body. The individual sovereign's responsibilities remain so long as there is, as the medieval theorists put it, no earthly superior—that is, until there is a sovereign power higher than present states.

Returning to the matter of just cause, by comparison with the classic Christian perspective summarized above, the international legal effort to prevent all non-defensive resorts to force by states leaves out some extremely important possible justifications for employing force in the service of justice. In particular, by leaving out the concept of punishment of evil—vindicative justice, in the term noted above—it undercuts the right to use force for the benefit of others when one's own state is not directly threatened. In other words, the core of Christian just-war reasoning on just cause for use of force is considerably more open to interventionary action to restore justice and punish evil than the main line of twentieth-century positive international law has been; indeed, in one sense—that of the early Christian consensus against self-defense, before it was modified by Augustine and dismissed by Thomas Aquinas— use for force for defensive purposes is the least justifiable purpose for Christians.

It is significant that the recovery of a specifically Christian form of just-war reasoning in the last four decades has focused the idea of just cause for resort to force around the idea of securing justice rather than defending one's own nation-state. For Paul Ramsey, the theologian who more than any other must be credited with initiating this revival, this is the characteristic reasoning that he established in the second and third chapters of *War and the Christian Conscience*, where the focus is on Augustine. In his later collection of essays, *The Just War*, he tied the political use of power specifically to the establishment and preservation of justice and a few pages later rooted an argument for the justification of intervention in sustaining or increasing "politically embodied justice."[8] This connection between the political use of military power (by Christians and others) and the purpose of justice permeates his just-war thought.

Such purpose, though seriously truncated, is all that is allowed in another major landmark in recent just-war theory, the 1983 pastoral letter of the American Catholic bishops: "War is permissible only to confront a 'real and certain danger,' i.e., to protect innocent life, to preserve conditions necessary for decent human existence, and to secure basic human rights. . . . [I]f war of retribution was ever justifiable, the risks of modern war negate such a claim today."[9] National defense, central in positive international law, is not explicitly mentioned here and would presumably need to be justified by the considerations listed. The classic just-war reasons for use of force also suffer here: defense is redefined in terms of protection of "innocent life" generally, preserving "conditions necessary for decent human existence," and securing "basic human rights"; retaking something wrongly taken is flatly rejected in the concluding sentence; and punishment of evil is not mentioned at all. Though the Catholic bishops' aim in this statement was to restrict the moral justification for resort to war between states, their statement on just cause for use of force opens broad possibilities for interventionary use of force for humanitarian purposes.

The Ethics of Intervention: Paul Ramsey's Argument

Despite the opening to interventionary use of force in the service of justice found in classic and contemporary Christian just-war theory, the problem of intervention as such has largely been ignored in recent Christian ethical writing on the use of force. The American Catholic bishops in their most recent statement on the ethics of the use of force explicitly touched on the question of intervention,[10] but a far more systematic exploration of the relation of a justice-based Christian just-war argument to the matter of intervention by force is Paul Ramsey's 1965 essay, "The Ethics of Intervention."[11] This essay was written as a contribution to the last serious American moral debate over intervention, which took place thirty years ago over American military involvement in the conflict in Vietnam. Though Ramsey clearly was writing with the case of Vietnam in mind, his argument was intentionally theoretical and general, in keeping with his opening statement, "In politics the church is only a theoretician" (19).

Ramsey begins with the assumption that military intervention in the cause of justice is "among the rights and duties of states unless and until supplanted by superior government"—a state of affairs Ramsey did not believe had yet come to pass (20). He goes on to address the implications of this for the United States, arguing that this country "has had responsibility thrust upon it for more of the order and realized justice in the world than it has the power to effectuate." He continues this thought by posing a dilemma: "[F]or us to choose political or military intervention is to use power tragically incommensurate with what politically should be done, while not to intervene means tragically to fail to undertake the responsibilities that are there, and are not likely to be accomplished by other political actors . . ." (23).

His solution was to tilt toward intervention; the responsibility to act even with limited abilities outweighs the argument to stand aside. "If intervention can sometimes be immoral as well as tragically ineffective, so also can nonintervention" (24). This responsibility rests with states, he stresses again, and "can be withdrawn from the nation-state only by an actual re-ordering of the structures of world politics" (25). Since the United Nations does not represent such a reordering, the responsibility remains with the states (25–27).

With the basis thus established, what remains for Ramsey is to lay out the "grounds for the possible justifiedness of intervention" (27). He distinguishes two sorts of such grounds: ultimate and penultimate. The former he also terms "just war intervention," identifying four elements that must be present in order for this ultimate ground for intervention to exist (27–33). First, says Ramsey, "the statesman must make a decision about the politically embodied justice he is apt to sustain or increase by his choice to intervene or not to intervene." Second, he must make "an assessment of order as one of the ends power must serve"; Ramsey goes on to pair this criterion with justice as both being "terminal goals in politics' act of being *proper* politics" (emphasis in the original). Third, whether to intervene must be measured by the degree to which it serves both the national and the international common good, which "are not always the same." Ramsey comments in this regard that the statesman "is not called to office to aim at all the humanitarian good that can be aimed at in the world. Instead, he must determine what he *ought to do* from out of the total humanitarian *ought to be*." Finally, the statesman must consider the requirements of the domestic legal system as well as international law and institutions in the calculus of whether to intervene in a specific case. The requirements of justice, order, the national and international common good, and the domestic and international legal systems thus constitute Ramsey's four "ultimate" criteria for determining the justifiedness of intervention.

It is clear from his discussion of these four considerations that Ramsey thinks they must all be satisfied, but that not all are likely to be satisfied completely or even equally well. There is in fact a priority ranking among them, with justice and order teamed at the top, followed by the domestic and international common good, then by the requirements of domestic and international law (with the emphasis on the former over the latter). Ramsey comments:

> Not all justice is legal order. The legalities comprise, of course, mankind's attempt to impose some coherence upon the order of power. But such coherence flows also from the justice that may be preserved, beyond or beneath the legalities, in the relative power positions of the nations (30).

This passage seems to suggest that a principled realism in the service of justice trumps the requirements of law, especially international law; indeed, he follows this passage with a discussion critical of that Christian opinion of his own time that held up international law as the reference point for identifying justice and order in the relations among nations. He noted specifically the lack of congruence between arguing for civil disobedience (justice over law) in the domestic arena while finding "no warrant for ever going beyond the law in international affairs where the legalities are far more imperfect and where the social due process for significantly changing the legal system is even more wanting" (31).

As Ramsey explores further the relation of justice and law in the international arena, though, he avoids the most radical implication of this argument: unilateral action taking no account of international law. He rather wants to couple the two, giving as his example of good statesman- ship President John F. Kennedy's handling of the Cuban missile crisis. There, Ramsey says, Kennedy acted concurrently "in the order of power" and "within the established legal institutions." Kennedy thus placed "his political action *beside*, and in this sense *outside*, the legalities" (31–32). Backing still farther away from the radical position of justice over the legal order, Ramsey concludes this section by citing *lex*, *ordo*, and *justitia* "as all alike the terminal objectives or goals of politics, yet almost never entirely congruent ones" (33).

Exactly what he has in mind in the justice-law relationship Ramsey makes a bit more clear in his discussion of the "penultimate" or "secondary" justifications for intervention (33–38). He identifies two of these: counterintervention and intervention by invitation. The relation of these to the ultimate or just-war justifications is that the ultimate ones must be satisfied first: "The penultimate justifications finally depend upon the validity of particular decisions made in terms of just-war intervention" (33). Now, since this is the priority, it is especially interesting that the two secondary justifications, counterintervention and intervention by invitation, are precisely the cases allowed in international law. If one country has already intervened in the affairs of a second, then a third may intervene to oppose the original intervention; further, if a country requests another's assistance, then that is not the form of intervention forbidden in international law. The key in each case is the doctrine of national sovereignty, which sets up the major argument against intervention in the first place. The first case assumes that it is not a violation of the victim's sovereignty to intervene on its behalf to throw out an aggressor; the second case assumes that when one is invited to intervene, that is not a violation of sovereignty.

In terms of Ramsey's argument, placing these two important legal justifications for intervention in the role of secondary justifications, as opposed to the just-war justifications, has the effect of giving more stress to the role of justice, a first-priority or ultimate justification, over mere law, which may or may not embody justice. His critics undoubtedly read in his argument an unwelcome tilt in the direction of power politics, and, indeed, such a tilt is there. Within Ramsey's system of thought, however, the emphasis on justice made this a special kind of power politics, one that Ramsey in this essay and elsewhere liked to call "proper politics," namely, a politics informed by justice. Justice is of the *esse* of politics, Ramsey argued both in this essay and elsewhere (29).[12] For Ramsey there simply was no disjunction between the requirements of such politics and those of morality; both, informed by justice, aimed at the same thing.

Ramsey's essay "The Ethics of Intervention" is notable for having been given as an address to a conference of religious leaders but originally published in *The Review of Politics*. Normally, he employed different styles of discourse with these two audiences, stressing the ethic of self-giving neighbor love with the former and what he called the "internal requirements of proper politics" with the latter. These were linked in his own mind by a conversionist understanding of the relation of grace to history that he drew from the thought of his mentor H. Richard Niebuhr's interpretation of Augustine. In this understanding Christian love transforms natural justice and redirects it toward its proper end— God and his will for history, so the quest for justice in politics, including the politics of international relations, is the most proper Christian response to grace, and it is at the same time the most proper response of statecraft to the requirements of political life. The two are not separate, though they are distinguishable.[13]

A Christian ethic of intervention for Ramsey, then, begins and ends with the requirements of justice, but a justice rooted in the transforming power of divine love. Across this fundamental base he places the requirements of order and law, citing them as the triad of *lex*, *ordo*, and *justitia*. In medieval political theory based on Augustine, however, the standard triad was *pax*, *ordo*, and *justitia*. The role of *lex*, law, was to institutionalize an order based on justice, which together would produce peace. Justice, order (including law), and peace together in this right relation produced the common good. Ramsey's understanding of the relationship among justice, order, law, and the common good is somewhat different and more complicated, but the fact that he defines his own approach through them reveals from another perspective his debt to Augustine in his approach to politics and the political use of power. There is much to be learned from this for a Christian ethical analysis of military intervention for humanitarian purposes, but I believe doing so requires both beginning a bit earlier and carrying the argument a bit farther than Ramsey does in this 1965 essay. That is the task of the following section.

Humanitarian Intervention and Christian Just-War Reasoning

The above discussion identifies two related but different lines of reasoning in Christian just-war thought bearing on the justifiedness of interventionary use of military force for humanitarian reasons. While just-war tradition has been shaped as well by other influences not specifically Christian, I focus here on the Christian arguments and their implications. One fundamental type of Christian rationale for intervention to provide humanitarian assistance derives from the paradigm from Ambrose cited above, the parable of the Good Samaritan that it reflects and extends, and the genesis of the idea of noncombatant immunity that Ramsey finds in Augustine's thought on Christian love. The obligation that flows from this is an obligation to assist the neighbor in need, including shielding that neighbor from harm, by force if necessary. This is an obligation that looks outward, toward the need of others, rather than inward, including the possible costs to oneself and one's own community of providing such assistance and protection.

This line of argument connects directly to that tradition of Protestant

Christian ethics that is focused on personal self-giving love of neighbor as the central norm for the Christian life. The concept is not, however, uniquely Protestant. A contemporary example of love-based reasoning applied directly to the question of military intervention is provided by the most recent statement of the National Conference of Catholic Bishops on the moral parameters for the use of military force. This statement specifically links military intervention "to ensure that starving children can be fed or that whole populations will not be slaughtered" to "St Augustine's classic case: love may require force to protect the innocent."[14]

The Christian argument for intervention based in the obligation of neighbor-love clearly is connected to the just-war conception of noncombatant immunity, which derives from the same source. It also clearly reaches beyond the usual just-war understanding of this concept, which involves the obligation to avoid direct, intentional harm to noncombatants in a war already known to be just by the standards of *jus ad bellum*. The argument for intervention differs in two ways. First, it extends the obligation to avoid giving harm to noncombatants into an argument for protecting noncombatants from harm caused by other persons or by natural disasters. Second, it makes this obligation into a *jus ad bellum* justification for resort to force rather than keeping it simply as a *jus in bello* guide to how force should be employed. Both changes can find possible warrant in the original Christian reasoning from which the idea of noncombatant immunity is derived, but they go considerably beyond the way in which the just-war tradition has developed this idea historically.

The second major type of Christian justification for interventionary use of military force, exemplified by the argument of Paul Ramsey examined above, originates in the idea of justice. Here it takes the form of an obligation to assist the establishment of a just order in individual human communities and in the relations among nations. This kind of reasoning takes secular as well as Christian forms. In Christian ethics it has historical ties to Augustine's conception of the increase of justice deriving from the transforming effect of divine *caritas* in history, as we see in Ramsey; but there are other roots as well. This kind of argument also may be traced back to the social-justice concerns of the Hebrew prophets of the eighth century B.C.E. (see Jer. 7:5–7), and, since Thomas Aquinas, the argument from justice has chiefly been stated in natural-law terms.

In its classic just-war form the argument for the use of force in the cause of justice was encapsulated in the passage from Romans 13:4, which medieval Christian theorists took to define both authority and just cause for resort to force. In this conception it is an inalienable responsibility of the prince to act as God's agent to punish evil and restore justice in the world. For medieval writers this responsibility was not discharged only in defense but might require the prince to initiate the use of force against an evildoer, not only within the territories over which he was sovereign but potentially also through invading the lands of another sovereign.

Both these lines of argument, found in Christian tradition and also in contemporary Christian thought, tend to establish an obligation to intervene, by military force if necessary, to provide aid and protection to victims of natural disasters and armed conflicts. In practice, though, this obligation must be laid alongside others from different sources, some of which reinforce intervention and some of which tend to deny any right to intervene. Among the reinforcements of the justifiedness of intervention are obligations found in internationalist conceptions of world order and in humanitarian international law. Broadly, the former have the effect of reducing the power of sovereignty in the face of broadly based international efforts at cooperation, including international action across state borders. The growth of United Nations peacemaking (Chapter VII) operations, which may take place by action of the Security Council without an affected state's consent, exemplifies this contemporary trend.

The growth of humanitarian international law, building on the humanitarian law of war but also including international statements and agreements on human rights, provides another sort of rationale for interventionary action, in effect defining the occasions in which Chapter VII actions, or even unilateral interventions to correct gross humanitarian or human rights abuses, are allowed. These elements in contemporary international law point in the same direction as the Christian rationale for intervention described above and tend to counteract efforts in the twentieth-century law of war to limit use of force to defense. Other sorts of obligations point in the opposite direction, however. I will identify three kinds of conflicting obligations, that is, duties that tend to prohibit or restrain the right to intervene, even for strong humanitarian reasons: obligations to the international order; obligations to the political communities involved, including one's own; and obligations to the victims and other members of societies targeted for intervention.

Obligations to the International Order

Among the obligations to the international order two are important for the question of intervention: maintaining the territorial ideal of sovereignty and protecting the concept of international consensus. In the modern period the doctrine of the inviolability of borders has spoken to two concerns. First, it has been a means of rejecting, in the name of secular sovereignty, ideological claims rooted in religious beliefs and the legitimacy of war waged to support such beliefs. Second, it has defined sovereignty in terms of the extent of territory, a criterion both theoretically unambiguous and transparent to all concerned, rather than on the basis of such factors as ethnicity, language, or religious belief. It has assumed the possibility of multiethnic, multilingual, multireligious states defined by their geographic boundaries existing alongside others that might include members from the same ethnic, religious, and linguistic groups.

The conflicts in the former Yugoslavia and in Rwanda well illustrate the decay of this ideal of sovereignty in the international order. From another direction, there is the danger posed by cross-border subversion in the name of militant religious belief, as we have seen both in the Middle East and in South Asia. The argument for military intervention across borders in the name of justice, whether supported by Christian reasoning or by a broader appeal to international human rights law and an internationalist conception of the power of the United Nations, clearly raises some of the very dangers that the territorial ideal of sovereignty was designed to counteract. Prointervention arguments may open a Pandora's box of undesirable interventions and increase the number of conflicts creating humanitarian need.

The second obligation to the international order that tends to restrict intervention, namely, protecting the concept of international consensus, to some degree serves as a corrective to the most radical implications of the justification for humanitarian intervention. Intervention that is supported by a robust consensus of nations and is undertaken by a coalition of forces representative of that consensus and answerable to its leaders provides a way to distinguish between interventions that are supportive of justice, peace, and order and those that fly in the face of these goals. At the same time, it must be understood that the requirement of such a consensus sets limits on what one nation may do unilaterally. Among contemporary cases, Bosnia and Rwanda illustrate this in different ways and to different degrees. Both countries exhibit great need for humanitarian assistance, both require at least some degree of military presence to provide such assistance, and in both, provision of such assistance is hampered by the absence of a robust consensus on the action to be taken. Yet any unilateral action of a single nation is apt to be strongly criticized, as we saw in the early response to the French intervention in Rwanda. Having a good reason to intervene and the right intention to go along with it are not enough; there is also an obligation to secure a supportive international consensus.

Obligations to the Political Communities

Among the obligations to the political communities involved, I want to focus on the disjunction between the arguments for interventionary humanitarian assistance that derive the right to intervene from the need of those persons requiring assistance and the traditional arguments in political philosophy that posit the primary responsibility of the political community to be the good of that community's own citizens. If the existence of particular states is justified by the benefits they accord their citizens, then it is natural to ask whether there is any obligation to try to extend such benefits to members of other states, particularly in the case of serious humanitarian need. The main line of political theory in the West, including the liberal tradition on which the Western democracies are based, answers in the negative: it would be good if such benefits were available to all, but the state's obligation is first of all to secure them for its own citizens.

Christian moral reasoning on this issue is not of one voice. While it begins with the idea that Jesus' command to love thy neighbor establishes an ethical obligation, it then divides along two lines. One line of reasoning defines priorities for action in terms of the degree of human need (a position traditionally identified with Protestant liberalism, but now found also among Catholics), and the other defines the obligation to love in terms of responsibilities set by the order of closeness established by natural relations (the position of traditional Catholic moral theology). The former tilts in the direction of internationalism and for intervention in support of humanitarian need; the latter gives priority to the needs of the domestic political community and nations closely linked to one's own. The conflict of obligations here allows for intervention to provide humanitarian assistance to others but sets limits based on the needs of the community that would intervene. The balance between these may vary over time and from case to case.

Obligations to Those in Targeted Societies

Finally, I want to draw attention to the implications for intervention of obligations to victims in need of humanitarian assistance and other members of societies targeted for intervention. While the other kinds of obligations identified above have to do with whether there exists a *jus ad bellum*, that is, the right to use military force for interventionary purposes to support humanitarian ends, this last point has to do with *jus in bello* responsibilities. These involve questions regarding the forms of force used, the manner of use, and the subjects of such force. The problem is that within the context of the interventionary use of military force for humanitarian purposes, the presence of such force may itself become the cause of greater harm to humanitarian values and further victimization of the very people whose assistance was the object of the intervention.

There is a tendency in the context of intervention to broaden the implications of noncombatant immunity to include protection of the victims or potential victims of a conflict or a natural disaster in which one is not involved as well as to justify intervening in such cases by military force if necessary. The problem is that military action is seldom pure in its effects. I believe it is a misuse of the just-war principle of noncombatant immunity to make it into a *jus ad bellum* category, and, thus, into a rationale for the resort to force. During the Cold War this same kind of misuse of noncombatant immunity was sometimes employed to argue that in contemporary conditions no war ever can be just, because all wars will violate the rights of noncombatants. I thought that argument mistaken as well, but it should now be placed alongside the argument for the obligation to intervene based on the need to protect noncombatants, since it points in exactly the opposite direction. The experience of United States forces in Somalia shows that an interventionary foreign military force, even one present for the laudable purposes of protecting humanitarian relief efforts, ensuring the delivery of relief supplies, and establishing a rule of order to safeguard the rights of people victimized by the conflict, can itself become a magnet for increased violence and greater victimization of the local population, or even a source of violence contributing to such victimization.

Like the conflict between concern for one's own people and those in urgent humanitarian need, the conflict between the obligation to provide humanitarian relief and the obligation to avoid increasing the danger to victims in need of such relief does not necessarily lead to a rejection of intervention by military force for humanitarian purposes. It does show, however, that such intervention may not always be the moral path and, further, that it should always be undertaken carefully—whatever the degree of humanitarian need.

Conclusion

In short, Christian ethical reasoning in the just-war tradition defines an obligation to intervene, by military force when necessary, to provide relief in cases of urgent humanitarian need, whether caused by local conflict or by natural disaster. A similar conception of obligation may be found in contemporary concepts of international law and international relations. The obligation is not, however, absolute but must be balanced against a variety of other obligations and be tempered by them. If the conflicts among these obligations are satisfied and the primary justifications required by the *jus ad bellum* established, then the same just-war reasoning that applies to other uses of force should be brought into play. The task then would be to determine whether the use of military force for interventionary humanitarian purposes is actually in order and how such force should be employed if indeed it is justified in the particular case. These are questions that should be examined in moral debate as well as in the framework of policy discussions. In both contexts they call for much more serious consideration than they have had up to the present.

Endnotes

1. Saint Augustine, *The City of God*, in *Basic Writings of Saint Augustine*, vol. 2 (New York: Random House, 1948), 481.

2. Saint Augustine, *Corpus Juris Canonici Gregorii XIII*, 2 vols. (Graz, Austria: Akademische druck-u. verlagsanstalt, 1955).

3. Alfred Vanderpol, *La doctrine scolastique du droit de guerre* (Paris: A. Pedone, 1919), 250.

4. Saint Ambrose, *On the Duties of the Clergy*, in Philip Schaff and Henry Wace, eds., *A Select Library of Nicene and Post-Nicene Fathers*, vol. 10 (Grand Rapids: Eerdmans, 1955), 71.

5. See Paul Ramsey, *War and the Christian Conscience* (Durham, N.C.: Duke University Press, 1961), 15–39.

6. Saint Augustine, *Of Free Choice of the Will* (Indianapolis, Ind.: Bobbs-Merrill, 1964), 11.

7. Saint Augustine, *Summa Theologica*, vol. 2 (New York: Benziger, 1947), 1471.

8. Paul Ramsey, *The Just War: Force and Political Responsibility* (New York: Scribner's, 1968), 11–13, 28.

9. National Conference of Catholic Bishops, *The Challenge of Peace: God's Promise and Our Response* (Washington, D.C.: United States Catholic Conference, 1983), sect. 85.

10. See National Conference of Catholic Bishops, "The Harvest of Justice is Sown in Peace" (Washington, D.C.: United States Catholic Conference, 1994), sect. 2.E.4.

11. Paul Ramsey, "The Ethics of Intervention," in *The Just War*, 19–41. Page numbers in parentheses refer to this essay.

12. See Paul Ramsey, "A Political Ethics Context for Strategic Thinking," in Morton A. Kaplan, ed., *Strategic Thinking and Its Moral Implications* (Chicago: University of Chicago Center for Policy Studies, 1973); and James T. Johnson, "Just War in the Thought of Paul Ramsey," *The Journal of Religious Ethics* 19 (Fall 1991): 183–207.

13. For a further discussion of Ramsey's use of the ideal of love and his conversionist theology, see Johnson, 185–97.

14. National Conference of Catholic Bishops, "The Harvest of Justice," 3.E.4.

Crusading for Humanity?
A Response to James Turner Johnson

Alexander Webster

Whatever the outcome of the current United States military intervention in Haiti, I think it is safe to predict that its purported justification on humanitarian grounds, among others, will continue to frame the public moral debate among contemporary advocates of the classic Western justifiable war tradition. Thanks in no small measure to distinguished scholars of that tradition such as James Turner Johnson, humanitarian concerns now loom as significant as other potential *casus belli*. My response to his essay focuses on whether this freshly minted augmentation of the *jus ad bellum* criteria of morally justifiable wars is, in the long term, for good or for ill.

Before advancing three critical objections to Johnson's argument, however, I wish first to pinpoint the sudden rise of militant humanitarianism in the post-Cold War new world order. It is my contention that the turning point occurred not in the Middle Ages, nor in early modern Europe, nor in the nineteenth century, but as recently as April 1991, in the aftermath of the Persian Gulf War, when Operation Desert Storm metamorphosed into Operation Provide Comfort for the brutally oppressed Kurds in northern Iraq. The civil war in Somalia helped to solidify this shift. After the initially peaceful United Nations intervention in Somalia proved ineffectual against marauding gangs and Somali clans, the U.N. Security Council decided to expand Article 2, Paragraph 7, of the Charter, which explicitly denies the United Nations authority to "intervene in matters which are essentially the domestic jurisdiction of any state."[1] Invoking the term "humanitarian" some eighteen times,

U.N. Security Council Resolution 794 authorized military intervention to ensure an adequate distribution of food and medical supplies to the starving and ailing masses. Elements of the 10th Mountain Division from Fort Drum, New York, then undertook Operation Restore Hope. What began under President George Bush in autumn 1992 as an exercise in "peace-making" soon expanded under President Bill Clinton, however, into a disastrous adventure in "nation-building." This was now a "humanitarian war," in Adam Roberts's oxymoronic phrase, to disarm the roving Somali warlords and rebuild that benighted nation's political and economic infrastructure.[2]

Now this "military mission escalation syndrome" has surfaced again in the current U.S. military occupation of Haiti. In his televised address to the nation on 15 September 1994 President Clinton cast a wide net indeed in an attempt to justify the impending invasion of this impoverished Third World nation: "Now the United States must protect our interests, to stop the brutal atrocities that threaten tens of thousands of Haitians, to secure our borders and to preserve stability and promote democracy in our hemisphere, and to uphold the reliability of the commitments we make and the commitments others make to us."[3] However we may assess the merits of the specific pieces in this grab bag of reasons for risking the lives of American fighting men and women, as well as of the expressed intent of restoring Jean-Bertrand Aristide to the elected presidency of Haiti, what must surely impress traditional just warriors is the unprecedented inclusion of halting inhuman atrocities and promoting democracy in a foreign land not currently at war with the United States.

Enter Johnson's cautious, carefully argued, nuanced essay. He presents, in my estimation, a reasonable case for a hopeless cause—a valiant, though, I regret to say, unpersuasive attempt to update and enlarge the classic Western justifiable war tradition to allow for at least some of the current spate of military interventions, undertaken ostensibly for the sake of humanity. There are three specific weaknesses or lacunae in the argument that warrant our attention.

Objection 1: A Radical Expansion of Just Cause

Johnson properly focuses his argument on the familiar *jus ad bellum* criteria of just cause and right (or legitimate) authority. He perceptively contrasts the traditional Christian delimitation of just cause ("to recover something wrongly taken, to punish evil, or to defend against attack"

[Johnson, 130]) and the strictures in modern international law against "all nondefensive resorts to force by states" to the very recent efforts of his mentor at Princeton, Paul Ramsey, as well as the U.S. Catholic bishops, to broaden this category considerably to allow for "the idea of securing justice rather than defending one's own nation-state" (131). The problem is that Johnson generally supports this trend!

The celebrated 1983 peace pastoral of the National Conference of Catholic Bishops speaks glowingly of war "to protect innocent life, to preserve conditions necessary for decent human existence, and to secure basic human rights." Johnson concludes, impassively at first, that the bishops' perspective "opens broad possibilities for interventionary use of force for humanitarian purposes" (132), but seems to miss the potential enormity of countless interventions by more powerful states in the affairs of less powerful states for rather slippery idealistic reasons. To his credit, he does acknowledge toward the end of his essay that "prointervention arguments may open a Pandora's box of undesirable interventions and increase the number of conflicts creating humanitarian need" (139).

Johnson also detects at least a "tilt toward intervention" in Ramsey's 1965 essay, "The Ethics of Intervention," but this is little more than a variation on the Ambrosian/Weberian maxim about moral responsibility in distasteful dilemmas: "the responsibility to act even with limited abilities outweighs the argument to stand aside" (133). This interventionist impulse may seem morally intuitive, or at least plausible on occasion, but it still requires the means of being channeled properly. Unfortunately, neither Ramsey nor Johnson provides more than a fuzzy calculus for measuring these alternative moral choices.

I would also challenge Johnson's conclusion that Ramsey's emphasis on "a justice rooted in the transforming power of divine love" (136) is at "the core of Christian just-war reasoning on just cause for the use of force" (131). Ramsey's vision pertains not to just cause, or that which may immediately precipitate a moral military action, but rather to the third classic *jus ad bellum* criterion of right intent, or the long-range goal or end of military action. The two categories are neither synonymous nor necessarily closely related. For example, a nation that resorts to war with a presumably unjust enemy for causes that have little to do with the pursuit of human rights in another sovereign state must still seek to deal with that enemy fairly, justly, and, if it is self-consciously Christian, lovingly. It must do so also with a view toward, in Ramseyan terms, "transforming" that enemy or, in more traditional Orthodox Christian language, "transfiguring" him.

Fortunately, Johnson questions the concurrent tendency to extend the classic Christian definition of right authority from the sovereign ruler to the sovereign state and, even worse, to any "nonsovereign international body" such as the United Nations organization (131). On this point, too, though, I would differ from Johnson by rejecting these developments altogether. As I have argued elsewhere, the Eastern Orthodox version of the justifiable war tradition formed during the Byzantine era knows nothing of sovereign secular states. The only morally legitimate authority to which an Orthodox Christian owes allegiance, including possible military service, is that which allows a "proper spiritual ethos" to prevail in society, that is, full freedom of religion for the church—and specifically, the Orthodox Church—to flourish.[4] The foreign policy interests of secular states such as the United States of America do not, by this standard, automatically command support from Orthodox Christians as Christians. Support must be earned, if indeed it can, on other grounds, that as citizens they find convincing.

Objection 2: Leaping from the Permissible to the Imperative

Johnson correctly dismisses the recent attempt by some Christian just warriors to fold the *jus in bello* criterion of noncombatant immunity into the just-cause category of *jus ad bellum*. This argument for humanitarian intervention, he observes, "extends the obligation to avoid giving harm to noncombatants into an argument for protecting noncombatants from harm caused by other persons or by natural disasters" (137). Johnson's nuanced rejection of this intellectual sleight-of-hand does not go far enough, however, and his presentation of this argument is, in my estimation, more persuasive than his rebuttal. What Johnson leaves unstated is this: the proponents of this position simply assume what must be demonstrated—namely, that a principle of nonmalevolence in one instance may be automatically transformed in the second into a principle of positive moral obligation.

In addition, even if one assumes a justification for military intervention on humanitarian grounds, it would not ipso facto make a particular military action morally imperative or universally binding on international actors such as the United States. The perennial problems of limited material and human resources and, in the present era, an easily erodible national popular will point to the need of powerful military states to prioritize their prospective interventions without, however, resorting to hypocritical or partisan selectivity. Another principle thus is required to apply the humanitarian interventionist impulse to specific cases. This is what John C. Bennett referred to as a "middle axiom" that would be used to determine when a mere possibility ought to become an obligation.

Johnson himself seems to sense this need when he astutely observes that the obligation to intervene is not "absolute but must be balanced against a variety of other obligations and be tempered by them" (142). Still, he makes the presumptuous leap from the permissible to the imperative by calling intervention an obligation. Also to his credit, Johnson points to the disjunction between a universal obligation to respond to the needs of the downtrodden in other countries and the responsibility of states to give priority to advancing the good of their own citizens and of nations closely linked to one's own. The balance may, he adds, tilt to one side or the other "over time and from case to case" (140). According to Johnson, Ramsey also touched on this point in his priority ranking of the four moral elements in potential cases of military intervention on humanitarian grounds (133–34), but placing justice and order in the forefront of consideration does not, in itself, suffice to inform a nation precisely when it ought and ought not to intervene militarily.

As an aside, I find what John Langan and others call the "criterion of comparative justice" even less helpful in cases of *jus ad bellum*.[5] The problem consists in whether to lend lethal military might to one, albeit somewhat less, unsavory side in a violent conflict between morally deficient combatants. But why is intervention by outside powers so imperative in those cases? To support an arguably lesser evil, such as the Bosnian Muslim government against an arguably greater evil such as the Bosnian Serbs (or the Bosnian Croats), or Jean-Bertrand Aristide against Lieutenant General Raoul Cedras in Haiti, is hardly to pay homage to the virtue of justice.

Objection 3: Making the World Unsafe for the Sake of Democracy

Consider the following quotation from another time and place: "Most of transmarine Christianity is being destroyed by the pagans in crushing defeat and, like cattle, they are every day being murdered, and the Christian race is being exterminated."[6] This emotional appeal could, *mutatis mutandis*, have issued today from the Bosnian government in Sarajevo or from friends of the persecuted tribe in Rwanda or from the Clinton White House on behalf of Aristide's supporters in Haiti. The fact that it did, in fact, appear in a letter from Pope Gregory VII to the German King Henry IV in the 1070s should give us pause. It was part of the pope's campaign to summon a crusade, an army of some fifty thousand men to be led by the Roman pontiff himself, to combat the Muslims' siege against the Orthodox Christians in Byzantium and Muslim territorial control of the Holy Land. The medieval Crusades are, we all know, an easy target for contemporary moral unctuousness, but I have resorted to this *reductio ad crusadem* for a serious purpose. Protection of human rights and the safeguarding of democracy—its establishment, restoration, and strengthening—have replaced Christianity as the inspiration for the current wave of crusades by the West. Whereas, however, medieval Christianity had, in turn, a readily discernible content (notwithstanding the East-West schism) and was a substantive entity worthy of some measure of protection, the regnant secular ideology today promotes what is merely an abstract or formal political procedure.

Democracy entails the freedom to choose in a variety of social and political situations, but the democratic principle is indifferent to the objects of those choices. Free elections in the nascent democracies of Lithuania, Serbia, and Haiti, for example, have yielded, respectively, the likes of old-fashioned communists, communists-turned-socialists, and Jean-Bertrand Aristide (the political poet of the heinous custom of "necklacing" one's opponents), proving thereby that a democratic polity does not automatically confer wisdom on a newly enfranchised electorate. It is one thing to die or to send one's soldiers into battle "for the faith"; it is quite another to die or to send one's soldiers into battle, for something as theoretical, inchoate, and lacking in substance as "democracy"—even liberal democracy, with its presumed grounding in some set of human rights.

The linkage between democracy and human rights as just grounds for military intervention also is not always self-evident. Some appeals to humanitarian concern emerge from a situation *in extremis* and project a sense of urgency lacking in other contexts; here democracy is not an immediate concern. But the U.S./U.N. mission in Somalia should provide a stark reminder that even a relatively simple peace-making intervention to secure the fundamental right to life, in a country where millions were on the verge of death by starvation, may escalate, with disastrous consequences, into a far more complex nation-building mission in the name of democracy. Considerable vigilance is required of public policy-makers to prevent such escalations and to resist the "military mission escalation syndrome." To be sure, if the promotion of democracy provides a somewhat amorphous reason for intervention, the protection of fundamental human rights offers at least a more substantive objective. Even on this score, however, the new world order, like the old, seems to lack a consensus as to which rights are fundamental and hence worthy of protection by military might. The category is ripe for abuse by ideologically motivated military powers, including the United Nations itself. Surprisingly, Johnson neglects the prodemocracy component of arguments for humanitarian intervention, despite its prominence in most recent summons to battle. Further, he treats the omnipresent human rights component with an unwarranted and uncritical equanimity. He does, fortunately, however, acknowledge the "obligation to secure a supportive international consensus" on any anticipated intervention (140). This, at least, reflects a prudence conspicuously lacking among the more militant advocates of humanitarian intervention, of whom Johnson wisely seems wary.

Endnotes

1. Kumiko Matsuura, *Chronology and Fact Book of the United Nations: 1941–1991* (Dobbs Ferry, N.Y.: Oceana, 1992), 280.
2. Adam Roberts, "Humanitarian War," *International Affairs* 69 (July 1993): 440.
3. *The New York Times*, (16 September, 1994): A10.
4. Alexander F. C. Webster, "Just War and Holy War: Two Case Studies in Comparative Christian Ethics," *Christian Scholar's Review* 15 (1986): 359.
5. John Langan, "Justice or Peace? A Moral Assessment of Humanitarian Intervention in Bosnia," *America* (12 February 1994): 9.
6. Quoted in A. A. Vasiliev, *History of the Byzantine Empire, 324–1453*, 2 vols. (Madison: University of Wisconsin Press, 1952), 2: 396.

Chapter 6

Universal Human Rights and the Role of the State

Paul Marshall

The international human rights system has often been ignored, condemned, and violated, but something more insidious is now occurring. At the 1993 United Nations World Conference in Vienna, the "Bangkok Group" sought to undermine action on human rights. At the February 1994 U.N. Human Rights Commission hearings, Sudan spearheaded another assault. The new pretext is the ongoing debate on "universality" versus "culture."[1] Authoritarian governments have always delayed and lied at U.N. hearings, claiming that their enemies lie and that reporters are duped. More recently, however, they have begun to accuse their critics of Western cultural bias. They no longer try to argue that their conduct meets human rights standards; in the name of culture, they try to destroy those standards.

China, Vietnam, Indonesia, Iran, Syria, Burma, and Singapore produced the Bangkok Declaration in April 1993. It demanded that human rights be addressed "in the context of national and regional peculiarities and various historical, cultural and religious backgrounds."[2] At face value this call is innocuous. The question of context is a long and difficult issue, and no serious commentator doubts that human rights implementation properly varies from country to country. The Europeans call this a "margin of appreciation," but the Bangkok group did not "contextualize." They simply rejected any criticism, using the claims of culture to squash their opponents. Chinese Deputy Foreign Minister Liu Huaqiu inadvertently clarified this point when he stated: "Nobody should put his rights above those of the state";[3] but hundreds of millions of other Chinese, including the underground churches and the students in Tiananmen Square, do not think their persecution is somehow part of the national culture.

In the February and March 1994 Geneva meetings of the U.N. Human Rights Commission the attack was rejoined. Malaysia, supported by China, Syria, Nigeria, and India, attempted to curtail the powers of the U.N. Special Rapporteur on Religious Intolerance. Then Sudan condemned Gaspar Biro, the Special Rapporteur on Sudan. Biro had reported on that country's child slavery, torture, extrajudicial execution, transfer of populations, application of Sharia law to non-Muslims, and use of food to compel conversion to Islam. Sudan tried to whip up international Islamic sentiment by accusing Biro of blasphemy for supposedly making the United Nations a higher authority than Islam. The Sudanese press compared Biro to Salman Rushdie, and there was even talk of a *fatwa*, or death threat, against him. Abdelaziz Shiddo, the Sudanese Minister of Justice, asked: "who am I to follow: God . . . or . . . the UN . . . ?" This is a good question, but a disingenuous one. Most of Sudan's acts have no justification within Islam or any other culture. The appeal to context is simply one more attempt by a cruel government to legitimize itself. Shiddo surreptitiously acknowledged this when he simultaneously tried to deny most of the accusations.

This call for context is really a pretext. The actual policies of many of these countries have no particular grounding in long-standing non-Western traditions, and the opponents of these governments, not to mention those whom they persecute, by and large have at least an equal claim to bear the mantle of cultural context.[4] These signs of recent international pressure do highlight, however, the great need for an understanding of rights that is capable of robust defense, and, if possible, universal application, for there are other, more cogent, theoretical threats and complex situations than these meanderings of tyrants. There is, for instance, the genuine fact of cultural diversity, something that is especially important to indigenous people. In tribal groupings the cultic aspect of life typically pervades all aspects of the culture, and even sharing the crops is part of communal ritual. In this situation the religious freedom of individuals to dissent from the views of the tribe also puts them beyond access to the food. In Canada native peoples are asking that traditional native spirituality once again become part of the ceremonies of self-government, but most native peoples there are Christian, and a substantial portion of them find that some (though certainly not all) aspects of native spirituality violate their faith. The proper response to these situations is not easily discerned, and they are real questions of culture and rights.

Facing these types of questions many years ago in his work on human rights for UNESCO, Jacques Maritain sought to bypass such theoretical differences altogether. He asked and suggested:

> How is an agreement conceivable among men assembled for the purpose of jointly accomplishing a task dealing with the future of the mind, who come from the four corners of the earth and who belong not only to different cultures and civilizations, but to different spiritual families and antagonistic schools of thought? Since the aim of UNESCO is a practical aim, agreement among its members can be spontaneously achieved, not on common speculative notions, but on common practical notions, not on the affirmation of the same conception of the world, man and knowledge, but on the affirmation of the same set of convictions concerning action.[5]

This hope now appears to have been disappointed. Political disagreements, and many philosophical disagreements, reflecting as they do real differences about the nature and purpose of human life, are producing consistent differences not only with respect to epistemology and points of departure but also on the practical meaning and implementation of rights themselves.

In the face of these threats, the major Western political responses have been conspicuously weak. On the political front, the U.N. human rights groups have stood their ground against Sudan, which has backed off some of its wilder claims. While there is backroom resistance to pressure for supposed contextualization, there is no coherent, long-term effort (in Geneva the Irish delegation resisted strongly but received little public support), and without an effective counterstrategy each new assault further threatens to weaken the human rights system.

Things are also difficult on the theoretical front. There is the question of Islam, which certainly shapes views of rights and is likely to do so much more in the future. There is the growth of ideologies in the West, particularly forms of relativism and what is called "postmodernity." It is both strange and disturbing that an organization such as Amnesty International, in its Amnesty Lectures, has taken to collecting the musings on rights of postmodern philosophers such as Richard Rorty and the (later) John Rawls, whose self-confessed parochial views are likely to have the effect of undercutting the very universality that Amnesty International strives for.[6]

Slightly closer to home we have the almost paradoxical situation that many of those calling for a more stringent view of human rights abroad are also those taking a more cautious view of rights domestically. In the United States, books with titles such as *Rights Talk: The Impoverishment of Political Discourse* and *Old Rights and New* are appearing.[7] The whole thrust of what liberals call the "communitarian movement" is to emphasize the importance of communal obligation over a narrow focus on individual rights. Meanwhile, Alasdair MacIntyre raises the historical objection that it is "a little odd that there should be such [rights] . . . in light of the fact . . . that there is no expression in any ancient or medieval language correctly translated by our expression 'a right' until near the close of the middle ages. . . ."[8]

A. I. Melden discusses at length the question of whether there was a knowledge of rights in the ancient world. His conclusion was agnostic: "Whether any of the Greeks had any such conceptions of moral agency, without which it would make no sense to speak of moral rights, is so far unproven."[9] In order to reach this conclusion, of course, he believed he had discredited the supposed proofs currently on offer. Isaiah Berlin pointed out that even the Marquis de Condorcet had maintained that rights were "absent from the legal conceptions of the Romans and the Greeks; this seems to hold equally of the Jewish, Chinese, and all other ancient civilizations that have since come to light."[10] While there is still considerable controversy concerning when and how the notion of subjective rights developed, there is also, despite Latin shadings, a growing agreement with Brian Tierney's judgment that it "was a characteristic product of the great age of creative jurisprudence that, in the twelfth and thirteenth centuries, established the foundations of the Western legal tradition."[11] As MacIntyre notes, from the previous absence of the word, or even of the concept, "it does not of course follow that there are no natural or human rights";[12] but if such rights are held to be universal, it does raise the question of why they should have such a parochial history.

When we deal with the problem of universality and rights we are addressing something that is both politically and theoretically urgent. It is also clear that we need to be careful in saying what we mean by rights and be specific in saying what type of rights it is that we wish to defend. In this chapter I do not try to outline a view of universal rights or a universal view of rights. What I do try to do is suggest that the dominant Western theoretical means of defending legal human rights by appealing to a notion of innate human rights suffers from major problems and, moreover, is all too susceptible to the criticism that it is a species of Western individualism. I then suggest an approach to rights that is less tied to the parochialisms of current Western Enlightenment thought and more tied to the Christian tradition, and I illustrate it through some examples. These examples in turn suggest that universal legal human rights are most likely to be found among what are called "negative rights," rights that are met when the government refrains from doing something. I begin by outlining some of the problems connected with the current dominant Western view of rights.

The Diverse Meanings of Rights

A vague concept of rights pervades the modern consciousness.[13] In some instances it reflects a commitment to a precise view of rights per se, as distinct from a view of duties, responsibilities, prudence, ethics, or charity. In many more cases, however, it has simply become a common word with which to express our general concerns and hopes. Someone who claims that "everyone has a right to decent housing" might mean that this is a consequence of some specific inherent human right, or even that a proper interpretation of the law requires it, but they are more likely to mean nothing more than that people should have decent housing and that it would be just and fair for the rest of us to try to make sure that such housing is available. Someone who complains that they "have a right to be spoken to face to face and not behind their back" may mean that this is a claim innate to human beings or that some employment contract specifies this as a working condition, but they are very likely simply to mean not much more than that friendship, trust, or good working relations need open communication. In short, the term often loses any specific content and becomes a loose term of approval or disapproval, commendation or criticism, advocacy or denial. In general, then, the expression "rights" is used in three broad senses.

1. to express a belief that human beings have a general responsibility to respect one another or that we ought to act toward each other in some particular way;
2. to refer to actual legislation granting and protecting such rights (i.e., "legal rights," "positive legal rights") or to the need for such legislation;
3. to express a precise view that human beings have "innate" or "inherent" rights—a view distinct from, and often at odds with, utilitarianism, natural law, or justice.

We need not dwell here on the first of these categories, but the relation between the other two is important in the contemporary human rights debate. Innate human rights (alternatively described as or included in the expressions "natural rights," "inherent rights," "subjective rights," "moral rights," or "prepolitical rights") are thought to be a particular type of claim, somehow intrinsic to human beings, that entitles people to protection by or provision from others, perhaps including states. Legal human rights, on the other hand, are guarantees contained in positive law and capable of sustaining a legal appeal.[14] This distinction is hardly a subtle one; nevertheless, confusion does occur. Occasionally, these two types of rights are treated as identical, but more common is the assumption, often inarticulate, that the two necessarily have some close connection. This usually occurs through a melding of vocabulary where, for example, certain claimed items, usually acknowledged as absent in current positive law, are articulated variously as individual rights or equality rights, with the overall purpose of justifying their establishment as legal human rights. The two meanings of "rights" are melded and the defense of the former is assumed to be a defense of the latter. This gloss pervades our political vocabulary and much of our public policy discussions. For example, in President Bill Clinton's claims about health care the two meanings of "rights" are melded, since the defense of the former is assumed to be a defense of the latter. Those who are, correctly, concerned with the protection of some human rights in positive law often assume, incorrectly, that such protection can be justified, or, at least, should be justified, only by some appeal to innate human rights. They argue for rights on the grounds that people have rights.[15]

A view of innate rights, however, does not necessarily have much of a relation to a defense of and a justification for the type of rights now found in international legal codes or fought for by organizations such as Amnesty International. It is perfectly possible to accept a theory of moral, innate, or natural rights without believing that this implies very much at all about what legal rights there should be. It is possible to accept innate rights without wanting to promulgate such rights in law. Conversely, it is possible to defend legal rights in law without believing in innate rights or even to hold to one set of innate rights while advocating a different set of legal rights. This is so not just in the obvious sense that innate rights are general principles while legal rights would need to be particular applications of those general principles; rather, innate and legal rights are developed according to different sets of principles; the argument does not proceed from one to another, but often in spite of one to the other.

Examples of this distinction are not uncommon in medieval natural rights discussions. John Wyclif held that *dominium*, approximating a personal right of property, was found in the state of nature; however, he argued on the basis of Christian charity that such strong claims of individual property should not be developed in positive law.[16] The law should instead develop principles that better help the poor. His contemporary, Richard Fitzralph, also believed that *dominium* existed in the state of nature but he maintained that in law the lordship of things should be held by those who were just, for we have fallen from that which was naturally given.[17] A type of natural right governed natural relations, but virtue was a crucial criterion for positive law. The probable author of the *Tractatus de legibus*, Durandus of St. Pourcain, stressed that property was a natural right, but he added that this right was based naturally on virtue. Consequently, it would not be in accord with nature but actually against nature for a bad person to claim goods as his own over against a better person. The right of the more virtuous should prevail. He also thought, probably correctly, that it would be difficult, if not impossible, to give legal structure to this gradation of the virtuous. He thus concluded that positive law, in contrast to natural law, should establish property rights for all.[18]

When William of Occam sought to defend a natural right of use, his purpose was not to try to establish property rights in law; rather, he was arguing that the friars, in order to maintain their vow of poverty, did not and should not have legal rights to private, or even common, property.[19] The Franciscans argued that a legal right of property would undercut a natural right of use. Essentially, they wished to exclude such a legal right so that, effectively, they could remain in a state of nature; they could be legally as well as literally poor. Thomas Aquinas's famous arguments for natural common possession did not lead to a defense of legal individual possession; rather, he argued that in social relations the latter was more convenient and so should be legally maintained. Common natural right was not an insuperable barrier to this, for while individual possession was not taught by natural law, neither was it forbidden by it.

These instances illustrate that the claim to natural rights has not been tied historically to companion claims for legal rights. There has not been a historical tie, and there does not seem to be a necessary tie. Clearly, one could believe that there is a moral right to be told the truth without believing that in any or all instances it should be backed by the requirements of positive law. Historically, we can see that this reticence has applied to a wide range of rights.

Not only have innate and natural human rights been used to justify something other than legal rights or legal human rights but they have also appeared in opposition to what are widely regarded as proper legal human rights. I am not suggesting that they are always in opposition, but that frequently they have been. This can be illustrated starkly by the debates on slavery in Spain in the early part of the sixteenth century.[20] The Spaniards, rather than trying to catch slaves, usually attempted to trade for already enslaved people on the coast of Africa. This activity could, in principle at least, be justified if one could show that it was possible for people to have become slaves on legitimate grounds.

In the ensuing arguments about the slave trade, natural rights theories played an important part, but their part was one that tended to justify rather than oppose slavery. Those who held to the type of natural rights views propagated by Gerson held that rights were like property, indeed, that a prepolitical right to property was the very epitome of a right. People thus owned themselves, owned their rights, and could dispose of them. As rights were thought to inhere in the human person rather than in the civil order, a person could legitimately sell them, give them away, or forfeit them, as, for example, the losers in an unjust war. People could thus alienate all their rights and become slaves, or people without rights, in a legitimate way; hence, certain people could justly be slaves, and trade in such slaves would be acceptable. These were slim grounds, but grounds they were, and they were used. Indeed, they were similar to the grounds that Thomas Hobbes later used to justify political absolutism in a situation where, purportedly, an entire people, in order to receive protection, traded away its rights in a social contract. They are also similar to modern arguments stressing autonomy in matters of euthanasia or drug use.

Early modern natural rights theories present us with a picture of the political order as a collection of people (with or without some rights) standing against a political sovereign that is the embodiment of the willed transfer, or alienation, of their rights. Political theory of this sort tends to become a contractual exercise in balancing or otherwise accounting for the relationship of the authority of the sovereign and of individuals. Since the basis of a contract is thought to be human will, the contract theory leads to attempts to unravel the relation of human will as it stands against, and both opposes and submits to, itself.

It is important to note that this dialectic between individual and sovereign can go either way. In such a scheme individual "powers, goods and liberty" could equally be a foundation for personal and social freedom as for authoritarianism. Since the rights of individuals are dialectically related to the acquired rights of the sovereign, this relation could yield justifications for authoritarian regimes and frequently did in early modern natural rights theories. This is true for Francisco Suarez, Hugo Grotius, and Samuel Pufendorf, as well as for Hobbes. As Richard Tuck says, "Most strong rights theories have in fact been explicitly authoritarian rather than liberal. Hobbes is representative, not exceptional."[21] In these rights theories people are faced with a call to restrict their actions in ways that they believe is in their own interest. We then are left facing the assertion of our own wills as in a mirror, and what we face is the contradictory appeals both of a literal *an-arche*, where our wills are unbound, and of the ghost of Jean-Jacques Rousseau's general will, where there is no appeal against the state/society/people because we face only our own wills and need have no appeal against ourselves.[22] Natural rights can function in either way.

Objections to an Individualist Notion of Rights

Clearly, then, the inherent-rights view is only one notion of the value of humans and their need for respect and protection, and it is quite a parochial one. Most people in history who have argued for love, respect, and the welfare of others have not done so on the basis that others possessed inherent rights. One reason they did not do so is connected with the nature of an inherent right and with human relations. When we deal with a right, we cannot deal with a person's right just in abstraction, but we must also involve this person's right to a certain thing and, when we do so, we involve those who should respect this right and, perhaps, those who should enforce it. A statement of right necessarily specifies a particular type of relation between all these. It is difficult to see how what is in fact a relation between several persons and things in differing circumstances could be found as inherent in any one of them or even in each of them considered distinctly.[23] A right is always a relationship between more than one and so cannot be inherent within one.

Historically, we find that discussions of rights originate within political relations and develop as the political order itself has developed. Actual law has played a considerable role in shaping rights not only in the sense that for rights to mean much in practice they have to find expression in law but also in the sense that theorizing about rights has often been a response to, and taken place within, developments in law.[24] Rights exist in specific political settings and cannot be understood as characteristics of particular individuals. If this depiction is correct, then in fact an assertion of inherent rights truncates a relation and treats it as an individual characteristic. The content of the relationship is then provided by supposed individual attributes such as autonomy, agency, and interests. The result is a depiction of communities as mere collections of individuals and communal relations essentially as intercourse between rights-bearing individuals.[25] The question of what is good conduct tends to be subsumed under questions of what someone has a right to do, and the question of what others owe to us gives content to the question of what we might owe each other.

For these reasons Søren Kierkegaard regarded a concern for rights, even rights for all, as motivated by self-love. Simone Weil thought rights had "a commercial flavour; essentially evocative of legal claims and arguments. Rights are always asserted in a tone of contention. . . ."[26] Mary Ann Glendon maintains that not so much rights themselves as a near exclusive fixation on them has hobbled American politics and poisoned its social relations. Current American rights talk is conspicuous in "its starkness and simplicity, its prodigality in bestowing the rights label, its legalistic character, its exaggerated absoluteness, its hyperindividualism, its insularity, and its silence with respect to personal, civic, and collective responsibilities." It produces "near-aphasia concerning responsibilities . . . without assuming . . . corresponding personal and civic obligations." It gives "excessive homage to individual independence and self sufficiency" and concentrates on the "individual and the state at the expense of the intermediate groups of civil society."[27] This, in turn, makes it

> extremely difficult for us to develop an adequate conceptual apparatus for taking into account the sorts of groups within which human character, competence, and capacity for citizenship are formed. . . . For individual freedom and the general welfare alike depend on the condition of the fine texture of civil society—on a fragile ecology for which we have no name.[28]

If we leave aside those rejections of rights made in bad faith by tyrants and we concentrate instead on a genuine concern about the false universalization of certain rights doctrines, then I think we will find that the objections are not against whether there should ever be torture or whether states may ever engage in arbitrary arrest and detention but about a certain kind of Western individualism masquerading as a universal view of rights. In many ways it is actually a critique of liberalism understood as a secular individualism, as "a set of beliefs which proceed from the central assumption that man's essence is his freedom and therefore that what chiefly concerns us in this life is to shape the world as we want it."[29] It is this sort of criticism that animates genuine Asian critiques of rights views.[30] In those societies the notion of individual rights is often equated with Western individualism and its concomitants: crime, pornography, the breakdown of the family, laziness, and irresponsibility. It is also the type of concern that is raised by Glendon and MacIntyre as well as communitarian thinkers such as Jean Bethke Elshtain, Michael Sandel, Robert Bellah, and Charles Taylor.

The objection to this type of individualism is both wide and genuine, and it is an objection used both by social theorists concerned with protecting a social ecology and by tyrannical rulers desiring to justify their own repressive agendas. This objection, however, is based on the misidentification of human rights in general with the particular doctrine of innate rights prevalent in the West and the view of the priority of individual will that goes with it. This in turn is precisely the type of misidentification that Western liberalism projects and seemingly encourages in its own attempt to equate human rights with itself. Liberal claims and Asian critiques feed on one another.

In this situation we would do well not to leap to a defense of universal human rights unless we are clear what it is that is really being attacked and what it is we really wish to defend. If an attacker of the idea of human rights really has Western liberalism in mind, then we might do well simply to agree with much of the critique. Conversely, if Western liberals try to portray their view of rights as the universal one, then we would do well to disagree with them. A failure to do either might as likely undercut universal rights as protect them, since it would reinforce the equation of human rights with innate rights and with a parochial liberal agenda. On the positive side, what we need to do is try to articulate a view of rights that is less tied to Western secular individualism and more tied to the actual nature of rights in law.

The Function of Human Rights in Law

Alasdair MacIntyre suggests that "the possession of rights [presupposes] the existence of a socially established set of rules," so that "the existence of particular types of social institution or practice is a necessary condition for the notion of a claim to the possession of a right being an intelligible type of human performance. . . ."[31] MacIntyre believes that this implies that rights can have only a local character. He is not necessarily correct in this, but it does imply that rights can exist only in political settings and cannot be understood as characteristics of particular persons. Similarly, the normativity of rights should not be thought of as an expression of some hypothetical prepolitical condition, such as a "state of nature," a "veil of ignorance," or a "calculation of interests," nor even as preexisting rights that need positive legal articulation, as in some natural law theories. They must be argued for in a political relation where they come to expression in law in the context of, and often subject to, a variety of other political norms.

Another area where the relation between legal rights and moral rights has been conflated concerns the basic or foundational character of human rights. One of the key features of rights, emphasized by nearly all authors, is that they are somehow basic (fundamental, foundational, or inalienable) and should normally win out over other considerations; hence, my contention that human rights are not ethical entities and thus should not transcend other political norms but rather be developed in law subject to such norms is likely to draw a worried response. Will this not undercut a—perhaps the—vital feature of rights, namely, that they provide firm guarantees about and limits on governmental policy? If, as I suggest, justice, prudence, expediency, or the common good may be a factor in political decision making that determines rights, then rights seem to lose their solid foundational character and become subject to the whims of legislatures and executives.

Such a response confounds the role of moral rights in argument and political rights in law. In stressing the relational character of rights we have not described the function of legal guarantees themselves but rather ways of argument about what legal guarantees there should be. We have not inquired about the role of law but only about how we decide what rights should exist in law. If, as I have tried to indicate, there is no need, often little to gain, and sometimes much to lose in granting moral rights a foundational status in a discussion of the basis of legal rights, this still says nothing about the essential place of human rights in law. This character need not lie in any claim that they are epistemically or ontologically basic or that they are the beginning point of a consideration of the nature of a just state; rather, the stress on the foundational character of human rights should be that they are legally and politically important. Legal human rights should be legally basic.

The crucial character of these rights can thus be recognized and implemented in law without attributing to them a purported priority in a process of decision making or judgment. Such legal rights safeguard people from being oppressed by governments that are pursuing particular policies and goals. They provide a limit over which governments cannot trespass, or over which they can trespass only with great difficulty. As their purpose is to control and direct governments, such legal rights would, of course, need to have a power or authority more basic than other forms of government activity, including government laws. What is key in this development is not that rights be understood as basic moral concepts but that they should be entrenched as parts of basic law in a regime where that basic law counts for something. This means that the law should recognize rights and that the government should be subject to this law in such a way that its policy is consistently and stably directed toward the meeting of human rights and is restrained from violating human rights in other aspects of its policy.

There is yet another conflation that often bedevils our rights discussions, namely, the confusion between the legal protection of rights and the existence of (constitutional) charters of rights. While a charter can be a good means of protecting legal rights, it is only one among several possible mechanisms. There are various ways to provide legal safeguards for these rights. As Johan van der Vyver explains:

> The primary function of a bill of rights is . . . on a par with other constitutional strategies for the limitation of state authority. Such strategies include the principle of representative government in a democratic dispensation; decentralization of the instruments of government in a federal structure with autonomous regional and local bureaucracies; distribution of state authority through the separation of powers; . . . surveillance of administrative acts by an ombudsman; subjection of the powers of government to the rule of law; and shielding a defined category of fundamental freedoms against legislative and executive encroachment in a bill of rights regime.[32]

What this implies is that a good theory of rights and of their protection is a good theory of the state and of its task and limits; hence, we should look for what is universal in rights in terms of how we understand the nature and proper limits of the state's authority. The key feature of rights is that, regardless of whether there might be certain advantages to the state and to others in acting otherwise, there are certain areas of human life where the state is obliged to act in a certain way. Many Christian theories of the state have long emphasized this point, though without needing to resort to the language of rights. Earlier arguments in defense of freedom of religion that were based on the impossibility of coercing conscience are a good case in point. They suggest that what the state cannot do, it should not do.[33] Likewise, arguments from natural law take this tack, as does the two-realm theory in the Lutheran tradition and the notion of sphere sovereignty in Reformed thought.

Christian legal philosopher Herman Dooyeweerd sought to delineate the boundaries of the state's competence by showing that other spheres of life resist external compulsion. The state cannot alter the laws of physics. It cannot by threat create love in a family. It cannot by decree alter the laws of science, nor can it dictate the theories of scientists; if it tries, it will certainly fail or destroy science in the process (and therefore fail). The nature of scientific work is that it must be pursued freely or else it will simply die. Similarly, the resistance of the human conscience to external pressure demarcates the limits of state competence and, therefore, of legitimate state action. Dooyeweerd extended this principle to the internal life of associations such as the church:

> Of course, the State can temporarily prohibit the formation of private associations. But it cannot arbitrarily change the internal structural principles of the societal relationships. . . . A civil judge's sentence can do no more than pronounce the civil unlawfulness [of an association] and sentence it. . . . But within its original sphere of competence an organized community can never be compelled to accept a civil judge's decision.[34]

Similar themes can be found in the natural law tradition and in more recent Catholic notions of subsidiarity.[35] They are arguments for what are now called human rights in the sense that they compel a recognition that there are areas of life that are off limits to the state and, conversely, that these are areas where either the individual or some other association such as a church, union, or professional association has its own sovereignty. They maintain that the very nature of the state requires it to relate to these nonstate entities in a particular way. I suggest that a theory of human rights developed from such theories of the state is likely to be more fruitful than one that seeks to proceed from a view of innate individual rights. This point can be illustrated in a discussion of economic rights, perhaps the area where the question of the universality of rights has come most to the fore.

The Debate on Economic Rights

Because of concerns about universality, several commentators, most notably Maurice Cranston, have criticized the notion of economic rights as not really being a rights conception at all.[36] Cranston argues that civil and political rights are "universal," "paramount," and "categorical" but that economic rights are none of these and are simply of a different "logical category."[37] Others have criticized economic rights on the grounds of the correlativity of rights and duties of the substantial differences in enforcement costs. Such rights have drawn criticism also from those who argue that since they do not limit government action but instead call for specific government action that may not be possible, they demean the whole idea of a right.

The argument from paramountcy is that political rights are of immediate and overwhelming importance, whereas some of the economic rights proclaimed in the U.N. Declaration of Human Rights, including the infamous right to periodic holidays with pay (Article 24), may well be desirable but are hardly the *sine qua non* of a just political order. The argument from the correlativity of rights and duties is that whereas a right to freedom of speech requires everyone else in the world to respect that freedom, it is not clear who is responsible for fulfilling economic rights. If I say that my neighbor has a right to housing, is it my duty to provide such housing?

The other arguments cluster around the contention that a government can fulfill genuine political rights at any time simply by doing nothing, which is why such rights are often called "negative rights." If this is true, then a government has neither grounds nor excuse for not fulfilling this right immediately. It can also afford to do so since it costs nothing and can in principle be done wherever the state has power. Such rights are not subject to the limits of scarcity. As Charles Fried puts it: "If I am left alone, the commodity I obtain does not seem to be a scarce or limited one. How can we run out of people not harming each other, not lying to each other, leaving each other alone?"[38] Such rights can always be afforded and so can be truly universal and, hence, categorically asserted.

Critics of economic rights argue that since "positive rights" require a particular type of action, they also require a specific allocation of resources and thus, necessarily, are subject to the demands of scarcity; hence, there will be times when even a well-meaning, just and committed state will simply lack the necessary means to guarantee certain purported economic rights. Since such rights suffer from questions of costs, they are not truly universal and cannot be asserted categorically. Castigating Sudan for torturing its opponents is of a different order from castigating it for not providing a guaranteed minimum income.

One final argument is that whereas political rights are limits, economic rights are goals. Limits must be obeyed, whereas goals must be aimed for, and lumping these two very different categories together can undercut political rights. If an economic right is asserted as a genuine right on a par with political rights and it is also acknowledged that it cannot be fulfilled immediately or perhaps even in the future, then we have admitted that a state legitimately need not immediately fulfill its rights obligations. If this is so, then states can, and often do, use this argument to justify all their violations of rights, including detention without trial or restrictions on speech and religion. After all, rights are only something to which we aspire.

These same states will also use their economic programs to assert that they in fact are promoting many human rights even though they deny political and civil rights. As a consequence, as Cranston points out, "affirmations of so-called human rights which are not human rights at all is to push *all* talk of human rights out of the clear realm of the morally compelling onto the twilight world of utopian aspiration."[39] The U.S. State Department's 1981 *Country Reports* on human rights began to exclude economic rights for precisely this reason: such rights are "easily abused by repressive governments which claim that they promote human rights even though they deny their citizens the basic rights to the integrity of the person, as well as civil and political rights."[40]

Those who defend the idea of economic rights respond to each of these criticisms and distinctions.[41] They argue, for example, that some economic rights can be of paramount importance. The question of holidays with pay may not be the most fortunate example, but the right to food is. Surely, nothing can be more vital than access to food since without it other rights disappear very quickly. The question of whose duty it is to fulfill the right can be taken care of by accepting that it is the duty of the state to fulfill the economic right and that it is the duty of the rest of the population to pay its share of taxes so that the state can do so.[42] On the general question of costs, scarcity, and universality, the advocates of economic rights respond that political rights also require action and so also have costs that governments may not be able to meet. Maintaining laws costs money for police, lawyers, and prisons. Political rights of participation also cost money. Democracy is expensive since it requires elections, parliaments, and publicity; furthermore, protecting rights from attack by others in and outside the society also requires major resources and, through military expenditures, is often the major budget item. Similarly, a government may not itself restrict your speech, but this may be of little help if your opponents consistently do so and the government either will not or cannot do anything about it. In sum, there usually need to be specific government initiatives for political freedom to be real. Consequently, questions of scarcity and costs also arise with political rights. In fact, claim its proponents, all the qualifications that apply to economic rights also apply to political rights, and so both can and should be labeled rights.

This debate has now continued for some forty years. The issues could be made clearer, however, if, as I suggested above, we focus less on the bare notion of an inherent or innate right and instead consider rights in terms of a theory of the state. This should lead us to use a different set of distinctions. In particular, we should separate the distinction of positive and negative rights from that of political and economic rights. Not all political rights are negative; some, such as free elections, require specific government action and can be very costly. Not all economic rights are positive; a government commitment to refrain from interfering with some type of economic action can be as cost free as any specifically political claim. If we combine the two sets of distinctions, we have instead a three-fold division: negative rights, either political or economic; positive political rights; and positive economic rights.[43]

As I have stated, negative rights such as the rights to free speech, freedom of religion, and freedom from arbitrary detention are rights that require forbearance from government: they require governments not to do anything. Since they are not dependent on scarce resources, these rights can always be met and so can be considered categorical and universal. A counterargument could be a situation where a government cannot control its own minions, such as unauthorized death squads composed of police or military personnel. In such a situation the government factually cannot fulfill the requirements of even a negative right. While this is true, it should be noted that in this circumstance the government is simply failing to be a government. It is not merely that it is derelict in some area within its sovereignty but that this area has begun actually to lie beyond its sovereignty—it is an area where it cannot in fact govern, an area beyond its factual jurisdiction. The situation described is a collapse of government per se. Clearly, we cannot always give a guarantee that in any given area there always will be a government that is capable of governing, so in this sense, negative rights cannot always be fulfilled. But this would be an amazingly stringent, indeed impossible, condition—that rights would be guaranteed even if there were no functioning government. What we can say is that if there is a government capable of governing, then negative rights can be met. This is a universality not shared by the other forms of rights.

Positive political rights are rights of a political kind, such as a right to vote or to a fair trial or to be defended from enemies, that require specific government actions and resources. Since even a well-intentioned government may be unable to meet such requirements, such rights are not as universal or categorical as negative rights. They suffer in principle from the same limitations caused by scarcity as do positive economic rights. These rights are, however, specifically related to the task of government. Even those who think that some economic rights, such as a right to eat, may be more important than some political rights, such as a right to vote, believe that it is necessarily a government concern to be involved with criminal justice or democratic procedure. There is no other body that we believe should carry out these functions. In this sense, though there may be differences about priorities, there is agreement that these are specifically government functions and that governments have a responsibility to carry them out at some point. It may also be added that though these functions—certainly national defense—cost money, in most cases the costs are smaller than those of claimed economic rights. Consequently, though positive political rights have something in common with positive economic rights, they are usually more feasible and certainly more intimately tied to the particular task of the state.

Positive economic rights have the problems of scarcity connected to positive political rights, though the former are usually more expensive. Also, unlike positive political rights, they refer to needs that can in principle be met by bodies other than government: they have no exclusive tie to government; while they may be desirable, they are not of necessity government functions. This difference becomes manifest in the fact that no democratic country has given economic rights other than a programmatic character. The notion of rights that actually seems to operate in most jurisdictions is not a harder, justiciable, and enforceable demand for rights guarantees nor a stress on inherent rights but, rather, a softer sense reflecting a view of welfare rights as ideals, where rights are seen as exhortations to governments to take the issue with the utmost seriousness.[44] Almost no jurisdiction is willing to give economic guarantees the kind of status that they extend to political rights.[45]

Conclusion

We should not leap to the defense of a notion of individual innate rights even in order to protect human rights from the relativizing pressure of tyrants. To do so would universalize a parochial Enlightenment view. We should instead consider the nature of the state and the proper limits of state action. Resources for this consideration can be found in a variety of Christian traditions that, while they have their differences, point to very similar themes.

Our discussion of economic rights illustrates the type of analysis that may be possible. It suggests that negative rights refer to necessary features of just government, positive political rights refer to policies that are both usually feasible and necessarily governmental in character, and positive economic rights refer to policies that governments may pursue.[46] Since negative rights are necessary features of a just government, they must in that sense be considered universal, and if this is the case only for negative rights, then arguably only these rights are universal.[47]

I believe this line of argument weakens one of the strongest criticisms against the universality of rights, namely, that it is just one more example of Western individualism. Though I cannot say that I have shown an avenue to universal rights in the modern world, I have indicated three things: that negative rights have a good claim to universality, that such rights are better defended by means of a theory of the just state than by appeals to a notion of inherent rights, and that resources for such a theory of the state are present in several Christian traditions.

Endnotes

*Research for this paper was funded by a Strategic Research Grant from the Humanities and Social Sciences Research Council of Canada.

1. This section incorporates my column " 'Cultural Context' Usually a Pretext" for News Network International of 12 April 1994. My thanks to NNI for permission to reprint it here. On the recent pressures in Malaysia, Singapore, and Vietnam, see Paul Marshall, "Asian Values No Justification for Repression," 7 September 1994; and "Vietnam Pursues Investment Through Less Graphic Religious Repression," 18 October 1994.

2. Marshall, "Cultural Context," "Asian Values," and "Vietnam."

3. Marshall, "Cultural Context," "Asian Values," and "Vietnam."

4. On claims for human rights within Islam, see Reza Afshari, "An Essay on Islamic Cultural Relativism in the Discourse of Human Rights," *Human Rights Quarterly* 16 (1994): 235–76.

5. Jacques Maritain, *Man and the State* (Chicago: University of Chicago Press, 1951), 77.

6. See Barbara Johnson, ed., *Freedom and Interpretation: The Oxford Amnesty Lectures 1992* (New York: Basic Books, 1993); and Stephen Shute and Susan Hurley, eds., *On Human Rights: The Oxford Amnesty Lectures 1993* (New York: Basic Books, 1994).

7. Mary Ann Glendon, *Rights Talk: The Impoverishment of Political Discourse* (New York: Free Press, 1991); and Robert A. Licht, ed., *Old Rights and New* (Washington, D.C.: American Enterprise Institute, 1993).

8. Alasdair MacIntyre, *After Virtue* (Notre Dame: University of Notre Dame Press, 1981), 66–67.

9. A. I. Melden, *Rights in Moral Lives* (Berkeley: University of California Press, 1988), 147.

10. Isaiah Berlin, "Two Concepts of Liberty," in *Four Essays on Liberty* (New York: Oxford University Press, 1969), 129.

11. Brian Tierney, "Villey, Ockham and the Birth of Individual Rights," in John Witte and Frank S. Alexander, eds., *The Weightier Matters of the Law: Essays on Law and Religion* (Atlanta: Scholars, 1988), 1–32. See also Tierney, "Origins of Natural Rights Language: Texts and Contexts, 1150–1250," *History of Political Thought* 10 (1989): 615–46; Michel Villey, "La genese du droit subjectif chez Guillaume d'Occam," *Archives de philosophie du droit* 9 (1964): 97–127; Louis Vereecke, "Individu et communauté selon Guillaume d'Ockham," *Studia moralia* 3 (1965): 150–77; Richard Tuck, *Natural Rights Theories: Their Origin and Development* (Cambridge: Cambridge University Press, 1979); Arthur Stephen McGrade, "Rights, Natural Rights, and the Philosophy of Law," in Norman Kretzmann, Anthony Kenny, and Jan Pinborg, eds., *The Cambridge History of Later Medieval Philosophy* (Cambridge: Cambridge University Press, 1982), 738–56.

12. MacIntyre, *After Virtue*, 65.

13. I have discussed this point more fully in my "Two Types of Rights," *Canadian Journal of Political Science* 25 (December 1992): 661–76.

14. Occasionally, the vocabulary of rights involves a discussion of positivity and negativity derived from Isaiah Berlin's famous distinction between "positive" and "negative" liberties in his "Two Concepts of Liberty." In this chapter, I use the term "positive rights" to refer to the debate over those rights that require government inaction ("negative rights"), as well as those rights that require government action ("positive rights"). I also use the expression "positive legal rights" to refer to rights in positive (i.e., enacted) law.

15. Particular illustrations of this gloss are given in Paul M. Sniderman, Joseph F. Fletcher, Peter H. Russell, and Philip E. Tetlock, "Political Culture and the Problem of Double Standards: Mass and Elite Attitudes toward Language Rights in the Canadian Chapter of Rights and Freedoms," *Canadian Journal of Political Science* 22 (1989): 259–84.

16. See McGrade, "Rights, Natural Rights," in Kretzmann et al., *Cambridge History*, 746.

17. D. E. Lunscombe, "Natural Morality and Natural Law," in Kretzmann et al., *Cambridge History*, 707.

18. See Brian Tierney, "Public Expediency and Natural Law: A Fourteenth-Century Discussion on the Origins of Government and Property," in Brian Tierney and Peter Linehan, eds., *Authority and Power: Studies in Medieval Law and Government* (Cambridge: Cambridge University Press, 1980), especially 175–77.

19. See Tierney, "Villey, Ockham, and the Birth of Individual Rights," in

Witte and Alexander, *Weightier Matters*, 152; McGrade, "Rights, Natural Rights," in Kretzmann et al., *Cambridge History*, 742; and Tierney, "Public Expediency," in Tierney and Linehan, *Authority and Power*, 175–77.

20. See Tuck, *Natural Rights Theories*, 48–50. For background, see Thomas F. O'Meara, "Spanish Theologians and Native Americans in the Years after Columbus," (paper delivered at the Kellogg Institute, University of Notre Dame, 31 October 1991); and Lewis Hanke, *Aristotle and the American Indians: A Study in Race Prejudice in the Modern World* (Bloomington: Indiana University Press, 1959).

21. Tuck, *Natural Rights Theories*, 3.

22. See Marshall, *Human Rights Theories in Christian Perspective* (Toronto: Institute for Christian Studies, 1983), 13–14. In this sense John Locke is not a rights theorist since he begins not with an assertion of rights but with an assertion of duties. This is why his *Second Treatise* opens with a rejection of suicide: since we are God's property, we cannot damage ourselves and we cannot allow anybody else to damage us.

23. See the comments in L.W. Sumner, *The Moral Foundation of Rights* (Oxford: Clarendon, 1987), 126.

24. See Marshall, "Dooyeweerd's Empirical Theory of Rights," in C. T. McIntire, ed., *The Legacy of Herman Dooyeweerd* (Lanham, Md.: University Press of America, 1985),. 124f.; and "Two Types of Rights."

25. I try to give some examples of this individualism as it relates to ecological concerns in my "Does the Creation Have Rights?" in *Studies in Christian Ethics* 6 (Summer 1993): 31–49; and more generally in my "Justice and Rights: Ideology and Human Rights Theories," in Sander Griffioen and J. P. Verhoogt, eds., *Norm and Context in the Social Sciences* (Lanham, Md: University Press of America, 1990), 129–50.

26. Quoted in Meirlys Owens, "The Notion of Human Rights: A Reconsideration," *American Philosophical Quarterly* 6 (1969): 244.

27. Glendon, *Rights Talk*, x–xi, 14.

28. Glendon, *Rights Talk*, 109–10.

29. George Grant, *Technology and Empire*, (Toronto: Anansi, 1969), 114.

30. See, for example, Kishore Mahbubani, "The United States: 'Go East Young Man,' " *The Washington Quarterly* 17 (Spring 1994): 5–23.

31. MacIntyre, *After Virtue*, 65. See also my "Dooyeweerd's Empirical Theory of Rights," in *The Legacy*, 124–25.

32. Johan van der Vyver, "Constitutional Options for Post-Apartheid South Africa," *Emory Law Journal* 40 (1991): 771.

33. I have tried to explore this theme at greater length in "Human Rights and Religious Toleration," in John Witte and Johan van der Vyver, eds., *Religion and Human Rights* (Leiden: Martinus Nijhoff, forthcoming).

34. Herman Dooyeweerd, *A New Critique of Theoretical Thought*, 4 vols. (Philadelphia: Presbyterian and Reformed, 1969), 3: 685. See also Marshall, "Dooyeweerd's Empirical Theory of Rights."

35. See, for example, Joan Lockwood O'Donovan, "Subsidiarity and Political Authority in Theological Perspective," *Studies in Christian Ethics* 6 (1993): 16–33; and Jonathan Chaplin, "Subsidiarity and Sphere Sovereignty: Catholic and Reformed Conceptions of the Role of the State," in Francis P. McHugh and Samuel M. Natale, eds., *Things Old and New: Catholic Social Teaching Revisited* (Lanham, Md.: University Press of America, 1993), 175–202.

36. I have tried to discuss this point in relation to the welfare state in "The Idea of Welfare Rights," (paper presented at the Conference on Welfare Responsibility, Center for Public Justice, Washington, D.C., May 1994).

37. Maurice Cranston, *What Are Human Rights?* (New York: Basic Books, 1962), 54 and chap. 3. For a summary of these discussions, see Jack Donnelly, *Universal Human Rights in Theory and Practice* (Ithaca: Cornell University Press, 1989), 31ff.

38. Quoted in Raymond Plant, "A Defence of Welfare Rights," in Ralph Beddard and Dilys M. Hill, eds., *Economic, Social and Cultural Rights* (London: MacMillan, 1992), 30. Plant also adds that the necessity to deal with scarcity means that utilitarian and consequentialist arguments must come into play and that this undermines the whole structure of a rights-based discourse; see p. 31.

39. Maurice Cranston, "Human Rights: Real and Supposed," in D. D. Raphael, *Political Theory and the Rights of Man* (London: MacMillan, 1967), 52.

40. Quoted in Sally Morphet, "Economic, Social, and Cultural Rights: The Development of Governments' Views," in Beddard and Hill, 87–88.

41. See, for example, Susan Moller Okin, "Liberty and Welfare: Some Issues in Human Rights Theory," in J. Roland Pennock and John W. Chapman, eds., *Human Rights* (New York: New York University Press, 1981), 230–56.

42. Note that this does not give a universal responsibility to respect the right; responsibility is limited to fellow citizens.

43. It is, of course, possible to make a four-fold division by dividing negative rights into political and economic negative rights. The latter could include, for example, rights not to be interfered with in economic actions, plus what are generally called property rights. The problem is that property is a juridical concept, not an economic one, and is in fact a form of right already (a right of use, or a right of exclusive use); hence, we would run into the complexity of rights to rights. In order to avoid complicating the discussion unduly at this juncture, I work simply with an undifferentiated view of negative rights.

44. The United Nations can investigate states' conduct under the terms of the *International Covenant on Civil and Political Rights*, but the *International Covenant on Economic, Social and Cultural Rights* requires only participating states to report on their own activities. The covenant on political rights was formulated as a *standard* of conduct; the covenant on social and economic rights was formulated as a *goal* of policy. Similarly, in the European system, the *Social Charter* was kept separate from the *European Covenant on Human Rights*. Despite being the most developed international system of economic guarantees, it has what David Forsythe calls "a certain vagueness" in its standards. He adds

that "it is not . . . clear how those standards have affected national public policy." Many national constitutions are also careful to restrict and focus their economic rights. Some expressly specify that their economic guarantees are statements of principle and are not justiciable, others note that their provisions are to be limited by available fiscal resources. See Paul Marshall, "Rights Talk and Welfare Policy," in James W. Skillen and Stanley Carlson-Thies, eds., *Welfare in America: Christian Perspectives on a Policy in Crisis* (Grand Rapids, Mich.: Eerdmans, 1996); and David P. Forsythe, *The Internationalization of Human Rights* (Lexington, Mass.: Lexington, 1991), 69.

45. See Mary Ann Glendon, "Rights in Twentieth Century Constitutions: The Case of Welfare Rights," *Journal of Policy History* 6 (1994): 140–56.

46. I have sought to address some of these questions in *Human Rights Theories in Christian Perspective* and in "Innate Rights and Just Relations," *Koers* 56 (1991): 139–49.

47. Theodor Meron and Allan Rosas give a good example in "A Declaration of Minimum Humanitarian Standards," *American Journal Of International Law* 85 (1991): 375–81.

On the Importance of Natural Rights: A Response to Paul Marshall

Joseph Boyle

The tyrants of our day go to some length to deny the reality of the human rights their regimes regularly trample. This suggests that the affirmation of human rights by international bodies such as the United Nations is vitally important and that these rights must be held to be moral and universal rights, since they are not effectively established within the law and political culture of these tyrannies. Justifying universal, moral rights is, however, problematic, for the very concept of universal human rights seems to be a creation of Western liberal society, rooted in controversial Enlightenment ideas, and increasingly under attack even in the West by communitarian critics of individualism. The attempt to convince Third World societies to accept the Western canon of human rights thus seems like an invitation for them to govern themselves by precisely those norms that make Western societies so devoid of a sense of the common good and that create the social space for so much of what is most squalid in them.

If I understand Paul Marshall's essay, it is these two sets of considerations that situate his inquiry. His main question is: How are we to defend universal human rights independently of the inadequate conceptual framework within which they usually are justified? This is a difficult question, and he makes it more difficult by rejecting standard notions of natural or inherent rights. Marshall's proposed answer is that rights should be justified not by reference to properties of persons, such as autonomy, but by a theory of the state that articulates the inevitable limits of its power over citizens. The result is that only negative rights, that is, rights that provide limits on government power and protect the immunities of citizens, are, or at least are clearly shown to be, justified universal rights. Consequently, economic rights, what Catholics would call the requirements of social justice, are not genuine moral rights but political ideals or desiderata.

I am sympathetic to the concerns that shape Marshall's inquiry, but I think that a certain conception of natural right is of greater social and political utility than Marshall allows. Moreover, there are economic rights, such as the right to health care and the right to education, that are natural and in a sense universal. First, however, I state the grounds for my sympathy with much of Marshall's analysis.

Christian morality, at least as far as its norms are concerned, is based on a fundamental precept: the command to love God above all things and one's neighbor as oneself. The implications of these moral principles are most readily stated as a set of specific obligations or duties. How rights fit into this normative framework is not immediately evident. Surely, at least some of the obligations derivable from the love commandments can also be stated in terms of duties to respect others' rights. The second love command has thus been held to justify the precept forbidding murder. It provides a ground for a duty generally not to kill others, but we are not mislead if we state instead that we should respect others' right to life. What is added by talking about the duty to respect a person's right to life and not simply talking about the obligation not to kill that person? Joseph Raz suggests an answer. He defines rights as follows: " 'X has a right' if and only if, other things being equal, an aspect of X's well-being (his interest) is a sufficient reason for holding some other person(s) to be under a duty."[1] Rights thus exist only when duties are justified by reference to the well-being of persons (which I assume also underlies the second love command). They do not have normative status independently of the moral principles that attribute moral significance to aspects of people's well-being or of the moral reasoning that establishes the sufficiency of a person's interests to generate duties in others.

It is true nevertheless that what neighbor love requires of us cannot be fully specified in terms of respecting others' rights. We can fail to love our neighbors even if we respect all their rights. Of course, we will fail to love our neighbors if we do not respect their morally justified rights, but even if respecting others' rights is necessary for living in accord with the love commandments, it is plainly not sufficient. This suggests that the category of rights is normatively less fundamental and less encompassing than that of obligations or responsibilities, though it is a way of referring to the ground in human well-being for many of the specific duties derived from it. If this is correct, rights cannot be moral "trumps" with a special peremptory force that overrides all other moral considerations but are ordinary moral considerations subject to the same casuistry and criticism as all other moral considerations, just as legally established rights are honed, qualified, and applied by legal reasoning. As Marshall emphasizes, this way of thinking about rights takes us away from a narrow fixation on rights as properties of individuals rooted in their autonomy. It points instead toward broader moral considerations about such things as the nature of human well-being, social obligation, the requirements of the common good, and justice. Rights may not be inherently political, but they are inherently social.

When rights are thus demystified of their independent moral status and special peremptory force, we may wonder whether they are completely dispensable from our moral vocabulary. I suspect that we could say everything true about social morality without ever using this term (though not without justifying many duties by reference to the well-being of those to whom the duties are owed). Still, such language is morally important.

First, it takes a special point of view on interpersonal relations: that of the persons harmed or helped by actions and omissions of others that affect them. That point of view, even if it adds nothing normatively essential, does provide a focus easily missed in moral analysis.[2] In particular, without clearly specifying precisely what those duties are or precisely who has them, that focus does facilitate our noticing that a person's well-being can generate duties. For example, it is important to know that children have a right to education even if one is not clear about who exactly has a duty to provide it.[3]

Second, as Maritain suggested (Marshall, 155), the very fact that rights are intermediate moral conceptions allows for agreement or consensus about them in a way that is much less likely on fundamental matters of moral conviction. An example is the right of a competent patient to refuse medical care. The legal right is well defined and the moral right is widely accepted, but beyond this, when the justifications begin, there is disagreement. A set of universal human rights is now part of the so-called *jus gentium*, the common customs recognized by all humankind as normative. Ideally, these customs reflect the requirements of moral truth, but because of their wide acceptance they have a social significance independent of the deeper moral considerations that can justify them.

If Christian morality must tug at modern conceptions of rights to show how they can fit within a morality defined by its basic precepts, some aspects of these conceptions seem to resist altogether any such effort. When we focus, for example, on a person's making rights claims to ward off the demands of others in the name of personal freedom, the stark opposition between the individualism of modern rights conceptions and Christian morality is unavoidable: how does autonomy, the freedom to do as one pleases, get moral purchase in a view of things that is based on obedience to God and service to others, even to the point of radical self-sacrifice? Standing on one's rights may sometimes be appropriate for someone dedicated to carrying his or her cross, but the tension is obvious. An individualistic society, in which each person's standing on his or her rights is taken as morally decisive, is hardly a society whose members willingly cooperate for the common good, much less lay down their lives for others.

Catholic social teaching, which has emphasized human rights especially since the early 1960s, includes a useful resolution of this tension. This tradition holds to a version of the correlativity of rights and responsibilities to others that I have already sketched, but it also links rights and responsibilities in a further way. Individual rights are seen within this tradition as a way of protecting and facilitating the capacity of people to carry out their responsibilities to God, themselves, and others. In other words, in Catholic social teaching rights are not justified because they allow people to do as they please, but because they create the social conditions for morally good living.[4]

The immunities protected by negative rights, such as the right to practice religion freely, are justified because by blocking inappropriate coercion from authorities and others they create the social space for responsible decision making. Many important decisions cannot be responsibly made except by certain people for whom they are vitally important. For example, the right to refuse medical treatment locates final medical decision-making authority in the patient, not on the assumption that whatever patients want is good but because only they must live with the treatment and its results and fit them into their overall vocation. Similarly, the right to private property is understood as a generally necessary condition for people to carry out their responsibilities, have discretion over their lives, and fulfill the obligation to make good use of that part of nonhuman creation that is at their disposal. Good use is governed by the principle of "the universal destination of goods," so property must be used fairly to serve human needs, but the judgment about how things are best used for this purpose cannot be made responsibly simply by governments and other institutions. Those who use property, whose lives are interwoven with and dependent on it, are often best able to tell how it can best serve human good, hence the recent Catholic emphasis on the importance of widespread ownership of resources and, in particular, the means whereby people make their livelihood.[5]

The rights justified by this approach obviously can be easily abused in the name of autonomy or the freedom to do as one wishes. Catholic social teaching accepts this as a side effect of what it regards as the only way to organize society responsibly. Within limits, authorities of various kinds can act to prevent irresponsible actions by individuals and groups, but they cannot take over the business of living their lives. Even if they could succeed, an essential part of the common good of society is destroyed, namely, the self-perfection of each person through his or her responsible and creative action, so the critique of individualism should be separated from the critique of immunity-protecting rights.

According to Catholic social teaching, it is not only negative rights that facilitate the fulfillment of human responsibilities. Entitlements are also justified in this way. The reality of rights such as the right to education and the right to health care, along with the standard array of modern welfare rights, is affirmed, and these rights are justified at least in part by the fact that they provide people the necessary means for living responsibly. One's first reaction to talk such as this is likely to be that suggested in Marshall's essay: this is just rhetoric, loose talk that articulates ideals but implies no serious responsibility on anyone's part and simply debases the language of rights. I agree that serious talk about positive rights or entitlements requires that we be prepared to get specific about exactly what and exactly how much a right entitles one to and, just as important, who has the duty to provide the object of the entitlement. To answer these questions, one must begin to move toward specifying what the entitlement would amount to if it were legally established. Still, as Raz's conception of rights suggests, there is a moral point in referring to the ground in human well-being for duties that are not completely specified. In affirming a basic right to health care, Pope John XXIII was not trying to create an early draft of President Bill Clinton's health reform program, but he was not just waving at desiderata, either. He was, in effect, saying that there is a serious social obligation grounded in people's interest in getting health care.

I agree, moreover, with Marshall that rights are inherently interpersonal and so cannot be inherent or natural in any sense that denies their interpersonal character. I think, however, that there is an intelligible conception of natural rights. Many rights arise from contracts or promises; they depend on mutual consent and so are not natural but consensual. Similarly, positive rights, those established in law, often include elements of legislative or judicial choice or convention. They too are not natural. Some rights, however—for example, the right to life—designate a relationship between human well-being and certain duties that does not include any decision or convention. These I would call natural rights, and I think that is what Catholic teaching means by the idea: rights created by moral reasoning as distinct from human decision.[6]

I also agree with Marshall that entitlements differ from negative rights or immunities in very important ways. In particular, the costs of refraining from meddling in people's lives are obviously much less significant than those of acting to help people. This implies that the objects of negative rights are much more easily specified than those of positive rights, and this in turn makes it generally easier to see who has the duties that correspond to negative rights. All of that conceded, however, I believe that reasons of the general kind that justify the affirmation of universal negative rights also justify the affirmation of positive political and economic rights. If the negative rights that bind political regimes arise from the fact that the well-being of persons taken individually and in community imposes a duty on those holding political authority to restrain the use of the power they must have to function, then similarly grounded obligations to provide for the necessities of life can generate positive, political and economic, rights.

Let me illustrate this claim by considering the right to health care. Without denying the primacy of the responsibility for their own health that individuals and families have, it seems clear that the Golden Rule requires that we provide neighborly assistance to others whom we can help in this regard. There is therefore a natural obligation to others in the matter of health care. Moreover, when the means exist in modern social organization for people to carry out this obligation more effectively by common action that makes use of public institutions and arrangements, then it would be wrong for them, individually and corporately, not to undertake the common action, provided that doing so did not destroy their discretion to live their lives.[7]

Organized communal action to provide health care efficiently and fairly is thus a moral requirement. This will often involve political regulation and might even require that the political society itself provide services. Societies differ in ways relevant to determining who, besides taxpayers, must support and provide services, and the level of services to be provided as a matter of right and so on are important contingencies that may call for resolution by political choice. These contingencies are not themselves, however, a matter of decision and have no tendency to call into question either the natural obligation or the responsibility to use modern social organization to fulfill it. Since the right to health care designates the derivation of this last duty, there is a right to health care that is as natural and as universal as this duty. To refuse to acknowledge the right is to suggest that the duty is not real, and that can be most harmful, not least because it can leave those of us in wealthy societies secure in our delusion that those we can help, even outside our polities, are not neighbors whom we are commanded to love.

In a word, although there is much of importance and interest in Marshall's rich essay over which I have passed in silence, I have focused on a set of its central concerns that I believe are, from the perspective of Catholic social teaching, sound. I have also suggested, however, that Marshall is too skeptical about the prospects of the Christian affirmation of positive economic rights.

Endnotes

1. Joseph Raz, *The Morality of Freedom* (Oxford: Oxford University Press, 1986), 66.
2. For a discussion of this point, see John Finnis, *Natural Law and Natural Rights* (Oxford: Oxford University Press, 1980), 205–10.
3. See Raz, *Morality*, 184–85.
4. Pope John XXIII, *Peace on Earth (Pacem in terris)* (Washington, D.C., National Catholic Welfare Conference, 1963), paragraphs 28–30.
5. See Germain Grisez, *The Way of the Lord Jesus*, vol. 2: *Living a Christian Life* (Quincy, Ill.: Franciscan Press, 1993), 788–806.
6. Grisez, *The Way of the Lord Jesus*, 329–30.
7. I develop this argument at greater length in "Right to Health Care and Its Limits," in *Scarce Medical Resources and Justice* (Braintree, Mass.: The Pope John Center, 1987), 17–25.

Conclusion

Chapter 7

Idealism Without Illusions: Christian Morality and International Politics in the Post-Cold War Era

George Weigel

If a group of scholars had gathered for a look into the future of international politics from the vantage point of the middle of the last decade of the nineteenth century, it is sobering to think of what they quite probably would *not* have anticipated. In 1894 the British, French, German, Austro-Hungarian, and Russian empires looked reasonably secure, albeit in varying degrees; and if the Ottoman Empire seemed enfeebled, its possible demise would probably not have been regarded as a bellwether of imperial collapse on the grand scale but, rather, as an opportunity for other empires to advance their interests in southeastern Europe and the Levant. A mere twenty years later, though—a historical nanosecond—events were set in train that resulted in an enormous slaughter, the utter collapse of four of those empires, the rise of new states, the emergence of lethal ideologies wedded to high-tech means of mass destruction, and, ultimately, the dislocation of Europe as the center of world culture and political power.

The consequences of the crisis of European civilization that began in July 1914, a crisis almost entirely unanticipated in its scope and its historic impacts, are still being played out in venues as various as Novosibirsk, Sarajevo, Budapest, Kraków, Berlin, Paris, London, Rome, and Belfast. If, in 1894, any mainstream student of international affairs had confidently predicted World War I, the triumph of Bolshevism, the Versailles rearrangement, the rise of fascism, World War II, the Cold

War, the emergence of the European Community, and of NATO, and the collapse of communism, he would almost certainly not have seen his paper published in this volume but might well have been remanded over to what were then still called lunatic asylums.

Viewed from 1894, the emergence of the United States as the lone world superpower would have seemed improbable, and the rise of an enormous engine of economic growth and prosperity in East Asia wholly unlikely. No one in 1894 predicted the rapidity of decolonialization that swept through Africa and Asia from the late 1940s through the mid-1960s. Neither did anyone foresee the depth of catastrophe that would be visited on postcolonial sub-Saharan Africa, which is arguably in worse shape today than in 1487, when Bartolomeu Dias began probing southward along the West African coast.

In addition, who, in 1894, would have dared to suggest that a cruel system of institutionalized mass coercion on a historically unprecedented scale would be brought to an end by a successful nonviolent revolution? Who would have been bold enough to predict that the world's most aggressively secular ideology would find its match (and, in some instances, its conqueror) in a revitalized Christianity? Who would have foreseen the rise of activist Islam, the "Wesleyan third wave" of evangelicals and Pentecostal Protestantism in Latin America, the resurgent papacy, or any number of other indicators that "unsecularization" was a dominant fact of international life at the end of the twentieth century?

Historical prognostication is always fun and sometimes even interesting, which perhaps explains why, despite the spectacular myopia illustrated by the examples I have just cited, there has been no lack of entrants in the international futurist sweepstakes since the end of the Cold War. We have had Francis Fukuyama's boisterously Hegelian claim that the end of history is at hand in the final triumph of liberal democracy and the free market, a claim accepted, in different ways and to different degrees, by Patrick Glynn and Joshua Muravchik.[1] Paul Johnson has proposed a new world order in which a United Nations with greatly expanded powers manages international security, a world free trade zone spreads the fruits of enterprise around the globe, and a new colonialism repairs the botches that the failed states of the Third World have made of their independence.[2]

At the other end of the optimism/pessimism spectrum, Robert Kaplan envisions a twenty-first century in which the developed world is an enclave of stability and prosperity surrounded by an international ghetto of violence, disease, starvation, radical environmental degradation, and general chaos.[3] Samuel Huntington has provocatively suggested that in the twenty-first century, a "clash of civilizations" will replace traditional nation-state and imperial rivalries. At least one polemical battle in Huntington's global culture wars has already been engaged, with the rise of an East Asian school that proposes that individual liberties on the Western model are incompatible with the orderliness necessary for economic takeoff in the developing world.[4] As if all this ferment were not enough, the United States has experienced since the fall of the Berlin Wall a resurgence of isolationist sentiment unparalleled since the mid-1930s.

Back to Basics

Happily, my assignment does not involve adjudicating among the claims and counterclaims advanced by Fukuyama, Johnson, Kaplan, Huntington, and Lee Kuan Yew. On the prognostication front, at least, we may take a lesson from the late, unlamented Mao Zedong and "let a thousand flowers bloom." Given the unsettled character of international public life today, the pace of technological change, the aforementioned fact of unsecularization, and the creakiness of both the post-Westphalian state system and the post-World War II system of international organizations, the more possible new-world-order models in play, the better for the debate. Perhaps we may also hope that in a decade or two the flowers that have bloomed will be arranged into something resembling a more or less orderly garden.

While I shall decline the futurist's crystal ball, I do want to offer a theologian's counsel to the strategist, in these terms: any serious future forecasting about the contours of the post-Cold War world will benefit immensely by grappling with the inescapable moral element in all politics. It is, indeed, precisely because there are, empirically and intellectually, so many balls in the air at the end of the twentieth century that a revisiting of the normative framework for foreign policy analysis and prescription is in order. For while the world changes, some things about the world, and about the human beings who do "world affairs," do not change, at least essentially, and some attention to those hardy perennials may help us avoid vertigo amidst the dizziness occasioned by our daily scanning of the *New York Times*.

I should thus like to do two things in the balance of this chapter: (1) I want to suggest a number of key moral themes, drawn from what I understand to be classic Christian social ethics, whose presence in the new policy debate is essential if that debate is to engage international public life in its fullest dimensions; and (2) I want to identify three new issues that will be of importance to American Christians wishing to refine a normative framework for foreign policy analysis in our new circumstances.

By way of a final prefatory note, let me say that, in thinking through the normative dimension of U.S. foreign policy, it is important for Christians to remind themselves that they are engaging in something of a second-order exercise. As Christians, we know that the end of history has already been revealed in the resurrection of Jesus Christ and his ascent to the right hand of the Father in glory. That puts us in a rather distinctive position vis-à-vis the world: a position aptly described by the anonymous author of the second-century "Letter to Diognetus" in these terms:

> . . . though they are residents at home in their own countries, their behavior is more like that of transients; they take their full part as citizens, but they also submit to anything and everything as if they were aliens. For them, any foreign country is a homeland, and any homeland a foreign country.[5]

Christians, then, are "resident aliens." Christians are people who know with confidence that history will be fulfilled in the time-beyond-time, so they can tackle their mundane tasks as analysts and citizens without kicking against the goads in a desperate or frenzied attempt to force God's kingdom into history here and now. Knowing that the Son, the first-born of many brethren (Rom. 8:29), has been raised to glory and knowing that he, not we, will build the City of God, we can relax a bit about politics, even international politics: not to the point of indifference, insouciance, or irresponsibility, but in the firm conviction that, even in the extremities of the world's agony, Jesus remains Lord (Phil. 2:11).

It is indeed precisely the conviction that the lordship of Christ is the ultimate truth of history that puts us in a position to work well at the tasks of history, which include, but are not reducible to, the tasks of politics. The great Swiss theologian Hans Urs von Balthasar described the source and distinctive character of Christian hope, which is the font of Christian action in the world, in these terms:

> Only Christianity has the courage to affirm the present, because God has affirmed it. He became a man like ourselves. He lived in our alienation and died in our God-forsakenness. He imparted the "fullness of grace and truth" (John 1:17) to our here and now. He filled our present with his presence. But since the divine presence embraces all "past" and all "future"

in itself, he has opened up to us all the dimensions of time. The Word that became flesh is the "Word in the beginning"; in him we have been "chosen before the foundation of the world." It is also the "final word," in which everything in heaven and on earth shall be caught up together: Alpha and Omega. . . . [Thus] it is not possession, but a being possessed, that lends wings to Christian hope. It vibrates with the thought that the earth should reply to heaven in the way that heaven addressed earth. It is not in his own strength that the Christian wants to change the earth, but with the power of grace of him who—transforming all things—committed his whole self for him.[6]

Within that fundamental horizon of theological affirmation there are any number of ways in which credal Christians can describe the second-order principles by which, in their considered judgment, foreign policy ought to be ordered. For the past ten years or so, I have been refining a set of propositions that attempt to establish a basic moral framework for foreign policy analysis in which the realists' "norming norm" of the national interest is given due consideration but without accepting the notion of the amorality of international politics that got attached to that notion through the work of Hans Morgenthau and his disciples. My propositions are influenced by a natural law approach to moral reasoning, by my understanding of what is perennial in history and what is distinctive to our era, and by modern Catholic social doctrine. The propositions have been developed in a deliberate attempt to transcend the sterile realist/idealist logjam that has driven the theorists into an intellectual cul-de-sac, blinded policymakers to some of the most dynamic currents at work in international affairs in the late twentieth century, and deepened the native skepticism of the American people about "foreign entanglements."[7]

The National Interest and the National Purpose: Ten Theses

There Is No Escape from Moral Reasoning in Politics

Politics, even international politics, is an irreducibly moral enterprise, because politics is a human activity and human beings are distinguished from other animals precisely by their capacity to reflect and to choose. Human beings are human beings because they are acting persons, or moral agents. Politics (as Aristotle affirmed and Hans Morgenthau denied) is thus an extension of ethics. To attempt to subtract the moral element from politics is to debase public life and to disfigure public policy.

History Can Be Bent to Our Wills

Those who deny the possibility of purposefulness in this kind of world, for reasons of complexity or because of the impersonal forces of history, have not reflected very deeply on recent history. The twentieth century is replete with examples of men and women whose purposeful policies bent events to their wills. V. I. Lenin, Adolf Hitler, Mao, Winston Churchill, and the founders of the state of Israel are among the obvious examples. In the more morally admirable of these cases as well as in the more odious, concepts of purpose were informed and tempered by concepts of interest. Interest and purpose seem, empirically, to be linked, and the linkage has the appearance of a dialectic in which interest and purpose reciprocally interact and are thus mutually refined.

Moralism Is of No Use in Statecraft

There is a traditional form of American moral thinking, which one can call "cultural Protestantism," that identifies political morality with the injunctions of the Sermon on the Mount. It is a morality of intentions, deeply suspicious of the very concept of interest, uncomfortable with the exercise of power, and tending toward literalism in its appropriation of the Bible. This species of moral*ism* is inadequate to the tasks of moral reasoning and practical action required of statesmen.

Realism's Critique of Moralism Remains Essential to Wise Statecraft Today

The older American morality (or moralism) was the object of the critique of the realist school in the foreign policy debates of the 1930s and 1940s. The realist critique, particularly as articulated by Reinhold Niebuhr, remains a necessary corrective to the many flaws of this cultural Protestantism and its secular heirs.

To put the matter more positively: understanding the inevitable irony, pathos, and tragedy of history, being alert to the problem of unintended consequences, maintaining a robust skepticism about all schemes of human perfection (especially those in which politics is the instrument of salvation), cherishing democracy without worshiping it—all these elements of Niebuhr's moral sensibility are essential intellectual furnishings for anyone who would think wisely about interest and purpose in U.S. foreign policy. Realism today is thus less a comprehensive framework for thinking about foreign policy than a crucial set of cautions essential to the exercise of practical reasoning about America's role in the world.

Realism Must Be Completed by a Concept of Human Creativity in History

Realism, and especially Christian realism, must guard against premature closure in its thinking about the possibilities of human action in this world. As Niebuhr put it, we must never forget "the important residual creative factor in human rationality." Things can change—things can be made to change—for the better, sometimes.

Social Ethics Is a Distinctive Moral Discipline

As America ponders its responsibilities and duties in the world, the moral reasoning we need will reflect the morally distinctive nature of political action. It will not confuse politics with interpersonal relationships; thus "social ethics"—moral reasoning about common public action through politics—should be understood as a discipline with its own canons and its own methods of assessment. These are related to, but not identical with, the moral reasoning appropriate to answering the question, "But what should I do?" The moral reasoning we need will demonstrate to the policymaker that his choice is not between an immoral or amoral Realpolitik, on the one hand, and naïveté (dealing with international outlaws as if they were refractory children or difficult relatives), on the other.

National Interest Includes Bringing Some Order to International Public Life

The irreducible core of the national interest is composed of those basic security concerns to which any responsible democratic statesman must attend, but those security concerns are not unrelated to a larger sense of national purpose: we defend America because America is worth defending, on its own terms and because of what it means for the world. Those security concerns that make up the core of the national interest should thus be understood as the necessary inner dynamic of the pursuit of the national purpose.

In addition, the larger American purpose in world affairs is to contribute, as best we can, to the long, hard, never to be finally accomplished domestication of international public life, to the quest for ordered liberty in an evolving structure of international public life capable of advancing the classic goals of politics: justice, freedom, order, the general welfare, and peace. Empirically and morally, the United States cannot adequately defend its national interest without concurrently seeking to advance these goals in the world. Empirically and morally, those goals will not be advanced when they are pursued in ways that gravely threaten the basic security of the United States.

National Purpose Is Not National Messianism

The national purpose should be seen as a horizon toward which our policy (and our polity) should strive. That horizon of purpose helps us measure the gap between where we are and where we ought to be, but it is not something that we shall achieve in any final sense. Understanding the national purpose this way is a barrier against the dangers of a simpler, and more dangerous, notion of national "mission," which implies a far shorter time line.

Casuistry, Informed by the Virtue of Prudence, Is the Moral Art Appropriate to International Statecraft

The practical relationship between national interest and national purpose is defined, for both the moral analyst and the policymaker, through casuistry—the moral art of applying principles to world politics by means of the mediating virtue of prudence. Prudence does not necessarily guarantee wise policy; it does reduce the danger of stupid policy based on moralistic or Realpolitik confusions.

The Argument over the Relationship Between "Interest" and "Purpose" in Foreign Policy Is Perennial but Not Necessarily Circular

The dialectic of national interest and national purpose will remain unresolved. Pursuing a narrow concept of interest without reference to purpose risks crackpot realism. Pursuing grand and noble purposes without regard for the responsibilities of safeguarding the national interest risks utopianism. The temptation toward crackpot realism or utopianism may be unavoidable, the world being what it is, but succumbing to those temptations is not unavoidable, given a clear understanding of both the inherently moral nature of politics and the distinctive canons and methods of social ethics.

The debate over the right relationship between the national interest and the national purpose thus will continue, given the nature of politics and the historical character of the American people and their democratic experiment. If it is informed by a proper understanding of the distinctive character of social ethics, however, the argument will not be circular and may yield a measure of wisdom from time to time.

Three Issues

With those propositions, or theses, in place as a possible normative framework for analysis, let me raise three pressing issues for those who would think about America and the world as Christian realists, which is to say, as idealists without illusions.

The Extension of Just-War Theory: Preemption

The Gulf War caused a flurry of commentary on the *in bello* issues of proportionality and discrimination raised by the air/land battle tactics that the United States and its allies had employed. While those arguments are sure to continue (and rightly so), we must also devote increasingly serious attention to the *ad bellum* side of the just-war ledger, with an eye to not merely refining but actually extending the tradition in order to provide guidance to policymakers and military personnel in the new technological, political, and ideological circumstances in which we find ourselves.[8]

The *ad bellum* issue that is now unavoidable, given the realities, is just cause. We began to see some modest exploration of a possible extension of the just-cause criterion during the debate immediately after Saddam Hussein's invasion of Kuwait, as several rationales for the justice of the allied cause were examined: reversing an aggression; rescuing the beleaguered people of Kuwait; stabilizing a volatile region of the globe; nuclear nonproliferation; and defending oil resources (and, a posteriori, the world economy, which was so heavily dependent on those resources). The United Nations Security Council resolutions authorizing the use of force by the allies specified the *casus belli* as the violation of Kuwait's sovereignty by Iraq's invasion and occupation. Whatever the international legal rationale, however, to suggest that the plight of Kuwait was the only motivation for the allied coalition's action would be naïve.

Over the past several generations, and under the shadow of nuclear and other weapons of mass destruction, just-war thinking has tended to constrict the components of just cause. Traditionally, three kinds of action satisfied the just-cause criterion: defense against aggression; the recovery of something wrongfully taken; and the punishment of evil. Recently, though, the first of these—defense against aggression—has been taken to be the primary, and perhaps even the only, component of just cause. That, for example, is the definition of just cause that informs Articles 2 and 51 of the United Nations Charter.

Developments in both international politics and weapons technology have conspired to suggest that it is time to reopen the debate over just cause. Take, for example, the preemptive Israeli attack on Iraq's Osirak nuclear reactor in 1981. According to the most recent understandings of just cause, that action was unjustified. Yet who could deny today that the Israeli attack was a rather straightforward example of precisely what the just-war tradition is supposed to facilitate: the use of proportionate and discriminate armed force in the service of peace and security?

The question of preemptive action also arises because of the phenomenon of terrorism, a form of political violence that by definition does not conform itself to any recognizable moral standards. It is the problem of nuclear proliferation, however, that has sharpened the debate on the boundaries of just cause, for we now face a situation in which several rogue states, including North Korea, Iraq, Libya, and Iran, are working overtime and in violation of the nonproliferation treaty to build nuclear weapons. Each of these states could also develop, without too much ado, an intermediate-range ballistic missile capability. The world will thus likely have to confront the reality of a nuclear-armed state whose patterns of international behavior are not altogether reassuring.

J. Bryan Hehir has warned against using the nonproliferation issue as the occasion for extending the boundaries of just cause in these terms:

> I am prepared to argue that only the resistance-to-aggression rationale should be accepted . . . as a *casus belli*. In a world where threats to proliferation are likely to increase . . . the moral arguments should strictly limit what constitutes *cause for war*. Proliferation, for example, is a deadly serious threat to international order but there are a range of methods to address the question which are short of war. Establishing a precedent that resort to force is an appropriate method to restrain proliferation erodes the case which should be made about other means to address proliferation, and it increases the likelihood that force will be used.[9]

Something important seems to be missing here: I would call it the regime factor. I would indeed argue that a careful extension of the just-cause criterion requires us to make the regime factor a crucial part of our moral analysis. No one would seriously suggest a preemptive strike against the British nuclear submarine force or the French *force de frappe*, either of which could do a lot more damage than the Iraqis or the North Koreans are likely to be able to do in the near future, yet there may be a morally compelling case for preemptive military action against the modest nuclear capability of an Iraq or a North Korea. Why? Because of the nature of the regimes in Baghdad and Pyongyang, which intensifies the threat of proliferation drastically.

The Iraqi and North Korean nuclear programs do not exist in a historical vacuum. Rather, they are the real-world expression of evil political intentions, the character of which has been made plain over many years. Precisely for the same reason that we do not contemplate preemptive action against Britain or France, I believe we can, without collapsing into the moral vulgarities of Realpolitik, contemplate the possibility of proportionate and discriminate preemptive action against Iraq, North Korea, and similar rogue regimes in the service not simply of nonproliferation in the abstract but of war prevention in the concrete.

Such action ought to strengthen rather than weaken the case against the premature resort to force. Nonproliferation efforts will look increasingly incredible to rogue regimes unless it is made clear that, should nonmilitary means fail, other forms of nonproliferation enforcement are available and will be used in these limited circumstances where the weapons threat is amplified dramatically by the regime factor. Successful preemptive military action could thus strengthen nonmilitary nonproliferation efforts vis-à-vis rogue regimes in the future, for those efforts will be seen to have teeth. By discouraging proliferation fevers among more rational states, preemptive, discrete military action in the limited case of the rogues also could further decrease the likelihood that force will be used in the future.

Given the regime factor, it may even be possible to make the case for preemption within the traditional understanding of the components of just cause. The regime factor, properly weighed, may allow us to consider the possession of nuclear (or chemical, or biological) weapons and the means to deliver them over long distances by certain types of regimes or terrorist organizations to constitute in itself "imminent aggression," in the face of which proportionate and discriminate military action would be morally justifiable. Cross-border aggression will remain the most obvious justification for the resort to armed force in the defense of peace and security, but it cannot be the only cause for war; otherwise, we end up holding the untenable position that a *casus belli* exists when Burkina Faso invades Mali but not when Iraq or North Korea or Iran imminently threatens to do immense damage with weapons of mass destruction.[10]

Refining the Terms of Statecraft: Sovereignty and Self-Determination

Christian social theorists from Reinhold Niebuhr through Pope John Paul II have been generally chary of nationalism, seeing in it a temptation to idolatry that, if succumbed to, can have the most horrific consequences. No one who has read a newspaper in the last six months can doubt that those concerns are well founded. The quest for self-determination, however, remains one of the most powerful dynamics in world politics today, and sovereignty remains the formal norm by which the international system is organized. Indeed, the kinds of mayhem and human degradation described vividly by Robert Kaplan and other chaos theorists certainly suggests that considerable areas of the world desperately need the security and order provided by functioning, sovereign states. On the other hand, the economic and technological realities of postindustrial society suggest that the state, the political embodiment of sovereignty and the political expression of self-determination, may well be on the wane as a powerful actor in the twenty-first century.

I do not pretend to know how this curious bifurcation of reality will play itself out empirically, but from a Christian normative point of view, I think there are some things that we can say with reasonable confidence about the limits of both sovereignty and self-determination as moral claims in international public life.[11] State sovereignty, and the consequent immunity of states from interference in their internal affairs, is not an exceptionless norm. As a matter of historical fact, states voluntarily limit their claims to noninterference by acceding to international human rights agreements and by joining regional political-economic entities like the European Community. Moral reasoning itself also leads us to conclude that the principle of state sovereignty cannot be considered exceptionless. If Nazi Germany had forsworn aggression after recovering the Rhineland and Sudetenland and had proceeded to implement the Final Solution to the Jewish Question within its own internationally recognized borders, would the principle of state sovereignty have meant that other states were forbidden to interfere in this internal German affair?

Most reasonable people today would regard that suggestion as morally absurd. But suppose an Indian government, led by militant Hindu nationalists and capable of deploying nuclear weapons, decided to settle the "Pakistan problem" and redress what it considered the fundamentally unjust division of the subcontinent in 1947, using its claims to Kashmir as the opening wedge for military action. Suppose the government of Turkey decided to rid itself of the Kurds in the same manner as it once decided to rid itself of the Armenians. Would such affairs be no one else's business under the principle of state sovereignty?

Put like that, the question seems to answer itself: whatever else it may mean, the sovereignty principle cannot mean that states are free to engage in the indiscriminate slaughter of religious, racial, or ethnic minorities within their borders. When such a thing is taking place, others can justifiably intervene to stop the killing. The hard question that Sudan and Rwanda and Bosnia put before us is whether other states—or that oft-invoked phantom, the international community—have a *duty* to intervene. Some powerful religious leaders and moral analysts, not least Pope John Paul II, have suggested that the answer to that question is "Yes".[12] But the establishment of such a moral duty in the abstract does not tell us much about any possible American responsibility to see to the fulfillment of that duty in concrete circumstances in which American interests are not discernibly engaged, at least insofar as our political culture understands our interests today. Here is an area where serious debate and a clarification of our normative understanding of the American role in the world is urgently needed.

As for self-determination, the ghost of Woodrow Wilson will, I trust, forgive me if I assert flatly that the "right of self-determination" cannot trump all other claims. The reason is that claims to be exercising a right to self-determination do not exist in a historical vacuum. They inevitably rub up against other claims, some of which may be prior claims. They take place within a state system whose stability has moral and political value. They are made in a world where economic autarky is impossible and in which claims to self-determination inevitably involve lives beyond the claimant's boundaries. If the right to self-determination was the trump that Wilson sometimes seemed to assume, then the result would surely by a Hobbesian war of all against all.

The blunt fact of the matter is that this is and seems likely to remain a world in which some nations cannot be states, yet some nations have claims to self-determination and the exercise of state sovereignty that cannot be reasonably denied. How can we distinguish between the two? History can help sort these things out. When, as in the case of the Baltic states, independent statehood has been snuffed out by a brutal process of invasion and subjugation within the living memory of many persons, the claim to a reconstruction of national sovereignty and self-determination carries a great weight of moral force (which, to be sure, raises another question: Is there a statute of limitations on national grievances?). Considerations of regional and internal stability will also figure in these determinations. To take the Baltic states again, recovery of their independence did not seem likely to result in an unraveling of public order, nor did they seem likely to start making irredentist claims on their neighbors. Questions of economic viability also need to be raised in addressing claims to self-determination. If it is true that no nation-state today can be an economic island, it is also true that economic development, stability, and growth seem far likelier for some regions and nations if they are part of a larger political unit.

Self-determination cannot, then, trump all other claims. In some cases the claim ought to be accepted and a new nation-state recognized, but in other situations, because of historical, economic, and regional-security factors, nationhood cannot lead to statehood. What then? Can cultural independence and autonomy be protected within, say, a loose federal system? If by "federal" we mean not a replication of the American system but a mode of political association in which some limited powers are granted to a national political authority while other powers are reserved to local, regional, or, conceivably, ethnic authorities, then various federal or confederal schemes may be the intermediate arrangement down which passions for autonomy and independence can be channeled.

The issue thus need not be conceived as sovereignty or subjugation. There are surely ways to allow a plentiful expression of ethnic, religious, and national identity without the full trappings of sovereign statehood. Those intermediate arrangements will likely loom larger in importance as the world becomes at once more internationalized and more localized and ought to be of particular interest to Christian thinkers who recognize both the value of cultural integrity and the dangers posed by nationalism as an ideology.

Living in an "Unsecularized" World

The "unsecularization" of the world to which I referred at the outset and which Samuel Huntington, alone among the prominent future-forecasters, seems to take seriously, raises two issues of particular interest to American Christians thinking about post-Cold War international politics. The first of these has to do with the relationship between Islam and the West; the second has to do with the social and political impacts of the "Wesleyan third wave" in Latin America and Africa.[13]

That the interaction between Islam and the West will be a major determinant of the history of the twenty-first century is conceded by virtually all serious commentators. Unhappily, Western, and specifically American, understandings of Islam, its variant forms, and the many roles it plays in vastly different Islamic societies are not highly developed. The tendency has thus been to reduce the widespread Islamic revival that is affecting societies as disparate as Libya and Indonesia to a question of militant and indeed violent "fundamentalism," a description that, in this instance, obscures far more than it illuminates. That we have to get beyond this caricature for the sake of serious analysis and policy planning is obvious; some of the interreligious scholarship that has recently explored just-war thinking in Christianity and Islam is a step in the right direction.[14]

Even as we strive to get beyond the media caricature of "Islamic fundamentalism," however, there are also some hard truths to be faced. The Islamic revival's critique of secularism will be congenial to many Westerners concerned about the moral decay in their societies, but the fact remains that Islam has yet to provide the religious and moral underpinnings for a sustained democratic experiment anywhere in the world. We can admire the religious fervor of many Muslims, but there are legitimate concerns about the capacity of Islam, in its present state of theological and legal development, to legitimate a theory of religious freedom.

Then there is Islamic supersessionism, perhaps the most fundamental issue of all in the encounter between Islam and the West. The core Islamic belief that the revelation to Muhammad finally and definitively supersedes the revelations to Abraham, Moses, and Jesus cannot be understood on the analogy of the relationship between Christianity and Judaism. No orthodox Christian can claim, in the light of Romans 9–11, a supersessory relationship to Judaism similar to that which Islam claims vis-à-vis both Christianity and Judaism. Whatever else they believe about the finality of God's revelation in Christ, Christians believe that the covenants with Abraham and Moses are abiding covenants: God does not break his covenantal promises. Christian understandings of the definitive and unsurpassable character of God's self-revelation in Jesus of Nazareth, moreover, leave no room for a further divine revelation to Muhammad that would add anything to what has already been revealed in Christ.

The Christian understanding of the history of salvation thus also puts Christians in a different theological relationship to Judaism than to Islam. Christians accept that the covenants with Abraham and Moses are an integral part of salvation history; Christians cannot say the same about

Muhammad's claims to a supersessory revelation, for to do so would be to contradict the Christian understanding of the finality of God's revelation in Christ. Put another way, Christians and Jews believe their communities to be divinely entangled in a singular way that Christians cannot say is replicated in their relationship to Islam, nor does Islam, for its part, have any understanding of a divinely ordered and enduring relationship between itself and living Christianity or living Judaism.

These theological questions come into political focus in terms of Islamic monism, the claim that the rightly ordered society is an Islamic society. There are no parallels to Matthew 22:21 ("Render unto Caesar what is Caesar's, and to God what is God's") in the Koran, nor has Islamic theology or legal theory ever developed a widely accepted distinction between the *potestas* of the political community and the *auctoritas* of the religious community. This has led, among many other things, to the *dhimmi* ("head tax") system in Islamic society and the second-class citizenship of non-Muslims in societies governed by Islamic law.

Some Western commentators have suggested that what Islam needs is the kind of demythologization of its sacred texts that Jews and Christians have attempted since the rise of higher criticism in the eighteenth century. The far more urgent question, it seems to me, is whether Islam will give birth to an Augustine: a major theological figure who, writing from within the classic Islamic tradition, will desacralize politics and open the social space for a genuine pluralism in Islamic societies. Absent such a figure, the encounter between Islam and the West, at the level of world politics, is almost certain to remain strained, and the strain will not be relieved by Western religious leaders and scholars who exhibit toward Islam today the client status that was too often exhibited toward communist regimes in Central and Eastern Europe during the last decade of the Cold War. The encounter between Islam and the West need not lead to that kind of intense, worldwide, geopolitical conflict, but one does not lessen the chances of such a conflict emerging by failing to face facts, political facts and theological facts.

Much more briefly, the international politics of the twenty-first century will almost certainly be tested by the rapid spread of evangelical and fundamentalist, typically Pentecostalist, Protestantism in Latin America and Africa. As demonstrated by David Martin and Amy Sherman, many of the public impacts of this "third Wesleyan revolution" are admirable indeed—as individual lives are transformed, considerable social and economic progress seems to follow[15]—but so, in the Latin American case, does social conflict, as the evangelical insurgency abuts cultures and polities that have been at least nominally Catholic for centuries. The recent North American joint statement, "Evangelicals and Catholics Together: The Christian Mission in the Third Millennium," was intended in part as an opening probe toward the establishment of mutually agreed rules of engagement for evangelicals and Catholics in situations of potential conflict.[16] It would be an enormous tragedy if the evangelical/ Catholic encounter should result in public scandal and a consequent weakening of the mission of the church or in the destabilization of societies on the cusp of consolidating their transition to democracy and the free economy. Here, too, theology, in terms of both Catholic and evangelical self-understanding, seems likely to have a pronounced effect, for good or ill, on the politics of nations, and North American religious communities will be players in the international political arena in wholly different ways than those to which they have become accustomed in the past fifty years or so.

A Call to Responsibility

The confusions of the post–Cold War world, and the consequent difficulties for strategists and policymakers, should not be minimized, but neither should they be exaggerated. In retrospect, it can seem self-evidently clear that containment was the only reasonable policy option in the late 1940s. At the time, as Dean Acheson's memoirs make plain, there was no such self-evident clarity.[17] The policy-making process in the late 1940s was not distinguished by relatively easy choices; it was distinguished by policymakers of wisdom and great personal courage. If we find ourselves dissatisfied, perhaps even dismayed, by the erratic course of American foreign policy since the Gulf War, we need not blame the world and its complex follies; we should, rather, look to ourselves and to our leaders.

The final question here is an irreducibly moral one: whether the United States will be the responsible superpower. There is much talk today, from both liberals and conservatives, about the national interest. What must always be remembered, though, is that defining the "national interest" is never an amoral exercise in political algebra. On the contrary, it is always an exercise in public moral reasoning. As the late Charles Frankel once put it, "the heart of the decision-making process . . . is not the finding of the best means to serve a national interest already perfectly known and understood. It is the determining of that interest: the reassess-

ment of the nation's resources, needs, commitments, traditions, and
political and cultural horizons—in short, its calendar of values."[18]

Those of us who work on the normative aspects of the foreign policy
debate are often regarded in the scholarly guilds and within the policy
community as the odd cousins at the picnic. No doubt we bring a
distinctive angle of vision to the debate over the formulation of grand
strategy, but the fact remains that the questions with which we wrestle
are, as Frankel says, "at the heart of the decision-making process." We
have nothing to apologize for in being Christian realists, or idealists
without illusions. If we were more confident of that, perhaps our interests
and our insights would have a more discernible effect on the way in
which our country exercises its leadership in the world.

Endnotes

1. See Francis Fukuyama, "The End of History?" *The National Interest* 16
(Summer 1989): 3–18; and Fukuyama, *The End of History and the Last Man*
(New York: Free Press, 1992). See also Patrick Glynn, "Is Nationalism the Wave
of the Future?" *Commentary* (August 1994): 42–45; and Joshua Muravchik,
Exporting Democracy: Fulfilling America's Destiny (Washington, D.C.: AEI
Press, 1991).

2. See Paul Johnson, "Wanted: A New Imperialism," *National Review* (14
December 1992): 28–34.

3. See Robert D. Kaplan, "The Coming Anarchy," *Atlantic Monthly* (February 1994): 44–76.

4. See Samuel Huntington, "The Clash of Civilization?" *Foreign Affairs*
72:3 (Summer 1993): 22–49; and responses to Huntington from Fouad Ajami,
Robert L. Bartley, Liu Binyan, Jeane J. Kirkpatrick, and Kishore Mahbubani in
Foreign Affairs 72:4 (September/October 1993): 2–26. See also Kishore Mahbubani, "The United States: 'Go East, Young Man,' " *The Washington Quarterly*
17:2 (Spring 1994): 5–13.

5. *The Apostolic Fathers*, 2d. ed., trans. J. B. Lightfoot and J. R. Hammer, ed.
and rev. Michael W. Holmes (Grand Rapids, Mich.: Baker, 1989), paragraph 6.1.

6. Hans Urs von Balthasar, "The Three Forms of Hope," in *Truth Is
Symphonic: Aspects of Christians Pluralism* (San Francisco: Ignatius Press, 1987),
190–92.

7. An earlier version of these propositions may be found in George Weigel
and John P. Langan, eds., *The American Search for Peace: Moral Reasoning,
Religious Hope, and National Security.* (Washington, D.C.: Georgetown University Press, 1991). The form in which the propositions appear below is adapted
from my book *Idealism Without Illusions: U.S. Foreign Policy in the 1990s* (Grand
Rapids, Mich.: Eerdmans, 1994).

8. The discussion that follows is adapted from my essay, "Just War After the Gulf War," in *Idealism Without Illusions*, 143–59.

9. J. Bryan Hehir, "Worldwatch," *Commonweal* (28 February 1992): 8–9.

10. The lethal equation of rogue states plus weapons of mass destruction plus ballistic missile capability also suggests the urgency of developing and rapidly deploying effective systems of missile defense. Whatever the relative merits of the moral and strategic arguments in the Strategic Defense Initiative controversies of the 1980s, our circumstances have dramatically changed, and in these new circumstances it seems to me utterly irresponsible—which is to say, gravely immoral—not to proceed to develop and deploy, for ourselves and for other threatened states, systems of missile defense that could blunt the threat of nuclear, chemical, or biological weapons terrorism on a mass scale. For such deployments to be resisted by those who also resist the notion of preemption is doubly irresponsible.

11. The discussion that follows is adapted from my essay, "Beyond Moralism and Realpolitik," in *Idealism Without Illusions*, 97–103.

12. See, for example, "Discourse of His Holiness Pope John Paul II at the General Audience of Wednesday, 12 January 1994," in *Giornata Mondiale di Preghiera per la Pace nei Balcani: La Pace È Possibile!* (Rome: Pontifical Council for Justice and Peace, 1994).

13. The discussion of Islam that follows is greatly condensed from my essay, "Waiting for Augustine," in *Idealism Without Illusions*, 177–93.

14. See, for example, James Turner Johnson and John Kelsay, eds., *Cross, Crescent, and Sword* (Westport: Greenwood, 1990).

15. See David Martin, *Tongues of Fire: The Explosion of Protestantism in Latin America* (Oxford: Basil Blackwell, 1990); and Amy L. Sherman, "And Be Ye Transformed: Christian Orthodoxy and Socio-Economic Transformation in Guatemala" (Ph.D. diss., University of Virginia, 1994).

16. The statement is printed in full in *First Things* 43 (May 1994): 15–22.

17. See Dean Acheson, *Present at the Creation: My Life in the State Department* (New York: W. W. Norton, 1969).

18. Charles Frankel, *Morality and U.S. Foreign Policy* (New York: Foreign Policy Association, 1975), 52.

Index

210

Index

military, 145–51; and natural law, 50, 51, 54, 55, 56, 58, 60n16, 67; opposition to, 88; and rights, 49, 87; and state sovereignty, x, xii, xiv, 43, 44, 45, 52, 66, 198–99
Huntington, Samuel, 25n22, 31, 57, 188–89, 200

idealism; and intervention, 86, 87, 88, 147; without illusions, 191; liberal, 123; and realism, xii, 4, 72, 79
ideology, 14, 45, 150, 155, 187
Ignatieff, Michael, 113–15
imminent aggression. *See* aggression, imminent
imperialism, 4, 33, 68, 107, 122
impossibility theorem, 95
individualism, 173n25, 180; critique of, 177, 181; ontological, 12; Western secular, xiv, 156, 162–63, 171
Innocent X (Pope), 42; *Zel domus*, 42
interdependence; world of, xii, 9, 14, 18, 65, 68–69, 92n34
international authority (political); appropriately limited, 19, 20, 21, 22, 23; and the nation-state, xi; new forms of, 4, 6, 8, 12, 18, 30
international law, ix, xiii; contemporary, 130, 131, 133, 134, 135, 138, 142, 147, 158; defined, 43, 56; and Grotius, 52; and independence movements, 109; and the pacific union, 94, 98, 101
Iraq, 60n16, 197
Ishkhanian, Rafael, 125; "The Law of Excluding the Third Force," 125
Islam, 155, 201–2; and monism, 202; and supersessionism, 201–2
isolationism, 189

John Paul II (Pope), 110, 112, 198, 199
John XXIII (Pope), 106, 181, 183n4; *Pacem in terris*, 106, 107
Johnson, James Turner, xiv, 47, 62n44, 127–43, 208

Johnson, Paul, 188
Judaism, 82, 83, 87, 201–2
jus gentium, 50
just-war theory; and ethics, 57, 127–42, 145–51; expansion of the, 54; and Islam, 201; and preemption, 195–98; tradition of, xiv, 47
justice, international; effective system of, 17, 21, 22; and Kant, 99; and nation-state sovereignty, xii, 4, 11, 12, 15, 30; and natural law, 54, 68, 69; social, 178; vindicative, 128, 129, 130, 131–32, 133, 134, 135, 136, 137, 139, 149; and world order, xi, 31, 33, 34

Kant, Immanuel, xii, 4, 9, 15, 16, 71–90, 93–101; Christian doctrine in, 75–77; *Groundwork of the Metaphysic of Morals*, 75; *Religion within the Limits of Reason Alone*, 75, 77
Kaplan, Robert, 188, 198
Keane, John, 107
Kennan, George, 86
Kennedy, (President) John F., 134
Keohane, Robert, 3, 5
Kierkegaard, Søren, 162
Kingdom of God, 77, 190
Krasner, Stephen, 59n9
Kuyper, Abraham, 18

Lake, Anthony, 71
Langan, John, 149
Languet, Hubert, 49, 57, 69
League of Nations, 16, 37
legal rights. *See* rights, legal
Leighton, Alexander, 47
Lenin, V. I., 4, 192
"Letter to Diognetus" (anonymous), 190
"levels of analysis," 94
Licht, Robert S., *Old Rights and New*, 156
Locke, John, 173n22

About the Contributors

Joseph Boyle (Ph.D., Georgetown University) is Professor of Philosophy and Principal of St. Michael's College, University of Toronto. He is the coauthor of *Nuclear Deterrence, Morality, and Realism* (Oxford University Press, 1987) and "Natural Law and International Affairs," in *Traditions of International Law* (Cambridge University Press, 1992).

Alberto Coll (J.D. and Ph.D., University of Virginia) is Professor of Strategy and Policy at the United States Naval War College. He served as Principal Deputy Assistant Secretary of Defense from 1990 to 1993. He is the author of *The Wisdom of Statecraft: Sir Herbert Butterfield and the Philosophy of International Politics* (Duke University Press, 1985).

Justin Cooper (Ph.D., University of Toronto) teaches Political Science at Redeemer College in Ontario. He has served in various administrative capacities, including as Academic Dean and Vice President for Academic Affairs, and was recently named President of Redeemer College. He is a contributor to *International Conflict and Conflict-Management* (Prentice-Hall, 1988) and *Political Theory and Christian Vision* (University Press of America, 1993).

Jean Bethke Elshtain (Ph.D., Brandeis) is the Laura Spelman Rockefeller Professor of Ethics at the University of Chicago. She is the author of many books, including *Women and War* (Basic Books, 1987), *Just War Theory* (New York University Press, 1992), and *But Was It Just? Reflections on the Morality of the Persian Gulf War*, with David DeCosse (Doubleday, 1992).

Vigen Guroian (Ph.D., Drew University) is Associate Professor of Theology at Loyola College in Maryland, Adjunct Professor at St. Mary's Seminary, and Lecturer at St. Nersess Armenian Seminary.

Among his many writings are *Incarnate Love: Essays in Orthodox Ethics* (University of Notre Dame Press, 1987) and *Ethics after Christendom: Toward an Ecclesial Christian Ethic* (Eerdmans, 1994).

John Hare (Ph.D., Princeton University) is Professor of Philosophy at Calvin College. He has served as a Congressional Fellow and as Staff Associate of the House Foreign Affairs Committee. His publications include *Ethics and International Affairs*, with Carey Joynt (MacMillan, 1982) and *The Moral Gap: Kant, Human Limits, and God's Assistance* (Oxford University Press, 1995).

James Turner Johnson (Ph.D., Princeton University) is Professor of Religion, Associate in the Graduate Department of Political Science, and University Director of International Programs at Rutgers University. Included in his many publications are *Just War Tradition and the Restraint of War* (Princeton University Press, 1981), *Can Modern War Be Just?* (Yale University Press, 1984), *Cross, Crescent and Sword: The Justification and Limitation of War in Western and Islamic Tradition*, with John Kelsay (Greenwood, 1990), and *Just War and the Gulf War*, with George Weigel (Ethics and Public Policy Center, 1991).

Luis E. Lugo (Ph.D., University of Chicago) is Professor of Political Science at Calvin College and Associate Director of the Center for Public Justice in Washington, D.C. He is the editor of *Religion, Public Life, and the American Polity* (University of Tennessee Press, 1994).

David Lumsdaine (Ph.D., Stanford University) teaches in the Political Science Department at Yale University. He is the author of *Moral Vision in International Politics: The Foreign Aid Regime, 1949–1989* (Princeton University Press, 1993).

Paul Marshall (Ph.D., York University) is Senior Fellow in Political Theory at the Institute for Christian Studies in Toronto and Adjunct Professor in the Department of Philosophy at the Free University of Amsterdam. He has written extensively on the subject of human rights and is the author of *Human Rights Theories in Christian Perspective* (ICS, 1983) and *Politics and Christian Vision*, with Jonathan Chaplin (University Press of America, 1994).

Daniel Philpott (Ph.D., Harvard University) is Visiting Research Fellow at the Center of International Studies, Princeton University. His recently completed dissertation is entitled "Revolutions in Sovereignty: A Study of Ideas in International Relations." He is the author of "In Defense of Self-Determination," *Ethics* (January 1995).

James Skillen (Ph.D., Duke University) is Executive Director of the Center for Public Justice in Washington, D.C. His many publications include *International Politics and the Demand for Global Justice* (G. R. Welch, 1981), *Political Order and the Plural Structure of Society* (Scholars Press, 1991), and *Recharging the American Experiment: Principled Pluralism for Genuine Civic Community* (Baker, 1994).

Alexander Webster (M.T.S., Harvard; Ph.D., University of Pittsburgh) is a parish priest in the Orthodox Church and Adjunct Professor of Religious Studies at George Mason University and of Moral Theology at St. Sophia Ukrainian Orthodox Theological Seminary. He is the author of *The Price of Prophecy: Orthodox Churches on Peace, Freedom, and Security* (Eerdmans, 1994).

George Weigel (M.A., University of St. Michael's College, Toronto) is President of the Ethics and Public Policy Center in Washington, D.C. He is the author of several books, including *Tranquillitas Ordinis: The Present Failure and Future Promise of American Catholic Thought on War and Peace* (Oxford University Press, 1987), *American Interests, American Purpose: Moral Reasoning and U.S. Foreign Policy* (Praeger, 1989), *Just War and the Gulf War*, with James Turner Johnson (Ethics and Public Policy Center, 1991), and *Idealism Without Illusions: U.S. Foreign Policy in the 1990s* (Eerdmans, 1994).